TOMB OF THE PANZERWAFFE

The Defeat of the 6th SS Panzer Army in Hungary 1945

Aleksei Isaev & Maksim Kolomiets

Translated and edited by Stuart Britton

Helion & Company

Helion & Company Limited
26 Willow Road
Solihull
West Midlands
B91 1UE
England
Tel. 0121 705 3393
Fax 0121 711 4075
Email: info@helion.co.uk
Website: www.helion.co.uk
Twitter: @helionbooks
Visit our blog http://blog.helion.co.uk/

Published by Helion & Company 2014
Designed and typeset by Bookcraft Limited, Stroud, Gloucestershire
Cover designed by Paul Hewitt, Battlefield Design (www.battlefield-design.co.uk)
Printed by Gutenberg Press Limited, Tarxien, Malta

Text © Aleksei Isaev & Maksim Kolomiets 2009. English edition translated and edited by
Stuart Britton, © Helion & Company Limited 2013.

Maps © Helion & Company Limited 2014.
For © of photographs see credits within the book.

Originally published as *Razgrom 6-I tankovoi armii SS. Mogila Pantservaffe* (Moscow: Iauza, 2009).

ISBN 978 1 909982 16 1

British Library Cataloguing-in-Publication Data.
A catalogue record for this book is available from the British Library.

Front cover: A King Tiger from the 509th Heavy Panzer Battalion that has been destroyed by an internal explosion. Rear cover: A German Flakpanzer IV abandoned on a Budapest street. In the background, a German glider that has crashed into the wall of a building is visible. These gliders were used to bring in supplies to the city's garrison.

For details of other military history titles published by Helion & Company Limited contact the above address, or visit our website: http://www.helion.co.uk.

We always welcome receiving book proposals from prospective authors.

Contents

List of photographs   iv
List of maps   x
List of tables   xi

Part I
Gille and Balck Hurry to the Relief of the Budapest Garrison   13

1   Introduction   15
2   *Konrad I*: A Hasty Surprise   22
3   *Konrad II*: A Double Blow   35
4   Operation *Paula* Becomes *Konrad III*   42
5   The Front is Restored   62
6   The Storming of Budapest   74
7   Results and Conclusions   91

Part II
The Final German Offensive of the Second World War   99

8   Plans of the German Command   101
9   German Panzer Forces   106
10   Plans of the Soviet Command   116
11   Defensive Preparations   119
12   Anti-tank Defenses   130
13   The Armored Units of the 3rd Ukrainian Front   136
14   Operation *Frühlingserwachen* (Spring Awakening)   142
15   Combat Operations in the Sector of the 57th Army   159
16   Fighting on the Drava River   164
17   The Use of the Front's Tank Forces   167
18   Conclusions   172

Notes   176
Literature and sources   177
Index   178

List of Photographs

A Soviet T-34/85 tank with tank riders aboard it, preparing for an attack. Hungary, end of 1944. 17

A Pz.Kpfw.IV tank knocked out by a shell hit in the rear of the hull. (TsAMO) 17

A destroyed Wespe self-propelled artillery vehicle. The fractures in the sides of the armored fighting compartment were most likely caused by penetrations from large-caliber artillery shells. 18

Commander of *Armeegruppe Balck, General der Panzertruppen* Hermann Balck. (Bundesarchiv, Bild 101I-732-0118-03, photo: Bauer) 18

Obergruppenführer und General der Waffen-SS Herbert Gille, commander of IV SS Panzer Corps. (Bundesarchiv, Bild 101I-090-3916-14, photo: Etzhold) 19

Commander of the 5th Guards Cavalry Corps Major General S.I. Gorshkov. 26

Commander of the 4th Guards Army General of the Army G.F. Zakharov. 26

Commander of the 1st Guards Mechanized Corps Lieutenant General of Tank Forces I.N. Russianov. 26

Commander of the 3rd Ukrainian Front Marshal F.I. Tolbukhin. 26

An M4 Sherman tank, obtained through the Lend-Lease program, of one of the Soviet tank units. The 1st Guards Mechanized Corps was equipped with Shermans. 27

A knocked-out StuH 42 self-propelled howitzer. 27

A knocked-out Pz.IV Ausf.H tank with carefully applied winter camouflage. 28

A StuG 40 self-propelled gun that has become immobilized in the mud and was abandoned by its crew. The number "136" was left there by the Soviet inspection team. Note the waffle-pattern Zimmerit. 28

A Pz. V Ausf.A Panther, bogged down in the mud and abandoned by its crew. This tank probably belonged to the 6th Panzer Division. 29

Another King Tiger of the 509th Heavy Panzer Battalion, abandoned on a street in a Hungarian town. 29

The crew of an SU-76 self-propelled gun receives an order; Hungary, 1945. 37

An 88mm anti-aircraft gun abandoned in its firing position on the approaches to Budapest. (TsAMO) 37

A knocked-out Tiger tank of the SS Panzer Division *Totenkopf*. (TsAMO) 38

A close-up view of *Totenkopf*'s knocked-out Tiger tank. The shell hole in the front armor plate is clearly visible. (TsAMO) 38

An abandoned Bergepanzer III repair-recovery tank. The number "25" was applied by the Soviet inspection team. 39

A StuG 40 self-propelled gun abandoned on the battlefield. The machine is fitted with a Saukopf gun mantlet and bears the tactical number "712". 39

Commander of the 18th Tank Corps Major General of Tank Forces P.D. Govorunenko. 46

A knocked-out German Panther tank. The penetrating shell hole is clearly visible in the upper forward armor. 46

A burned-out German Panther Ausf. G tank. The tank has plainly "settled" as a result of the collapse of the torsion bars due to the fire. (TsAMO) 47

A Hummel self-propelled artillery vehicle destroyed by artillery fire. The number "5" has been painted on by the Soviet inspection team. 47

A knocked-out King Tiger of the 509th Heavy Panzer Battalion. The tank was struck by a shell in the flank in the vicinity of its engine compartment. 52

One more knocked-out King Tiger. Its tactical marking, the letter "G", is visible on the tank's front armor. 52

A disabled Panther Ausf. A in Hungary, January 1945. (TsAMO) 53

A close-up view of the flank of the tank in the preceding photograph. Plainly, it has been literally riddled with anti-tank rounds. Note the roller wheels that have been shot through by armor-piercing shells. 53

A bogged down and abandoned Tiger of the *Totenkopf* Division. 57

Commander of the 26th Army Lieutenant General N.A. Gagen. 67

A T-34/85 tank with tank riders aboard. In view of the almost complete absence of armored personnel carriers in the Red Army, tanks were often used to transport infantry. 67

A German 75mm PAK-40 anti-tank gun left behind in its position in the Budapest area. (TsAMO) 68

A StuG III self-propelled gun with its gun removed. Most likely, this machine was abandoned and cannibalized for its useful parts in order to repair other StuG IIIs. 68

A knocked-out Panzerjäger 38(t) Ausf.M (Marder III) 75mm self-propelled anti-tank gun. 69

A knocked-out Panther, Hungary, January 1945. Shell holes are clearly visible in the side armor of the turret. (TsAMO) 69

An StuG 40 abandoned on the street of a Hungarian villages. 70

Commander of the 2nd Ukrainian Front Marshal R.Ia. Malinovsky. 78

Commander of the 3rd Ukrainian Front F.I. Tolbukhin at work in his headquarters. 78

A Wespe self-propelled artillery vehicle abandoned by its crew. The machine presumably belonged to the 13th Panzer Division. 78

A knocked-out Panther. The blotches on the turret are most likely the results of the fire. 79

A flame-throwing Flammpanzer III tank, abandoned by its crew during the fighting in Budapest. 79

A knocked-out and burned-out Panther Ausf.G; Budapest area, January 1945. 80

A view of a Budapest street after the storming of the city – burned-out vehicles and building walls riddled by shells and bullets. (TsAMO) 80

The wreckage of a German 88mm anti-aircraft gun on a Budapest street. 81

An armored wagon on a Budapest street. The recognition symbol of the Hungarian Army is clearly visible on the side of the wagon. (TsAMO) 81

An SdKfz.250 of one of the German motorized units abandoned on a Budapest street. (TsAMO) 82

Hummel self-propelled howitzers, left abandoned on a Budapest street. (TsAMO) 82

An 88mm gun mounted on the chassis of a Bussing Nag on a Budapest Street. Note
    the white rings around the barrel of the gun, denoting the number of knocked-out
    tanks.   82
Soviet tankers examining the abandoned Hummels shown in the photograph on the
    previous page. (TsAMO)   83
The same self-propelled howitzers pictured from above. (TsAMO)   83
A Hungarian Nimrod self-propelled anti-aircraft gun on a Budapest street, February
    1945. (TsAMO)   84
The wreckage of a German self-propelled anti-aircraft gun in front of the Calvinist
    Church in Budapest. (TsAMO)   84
A German Flakpanzer IV abandoned on a Budapest street. In the background, a
    German glider that has crashed into the wall of a building is visible. These gliders
    were used to bring in supplies to the city's garrison.   85
A graveyard of German equipment in Budapest. In the foreground are two
    disassembled RSO (Raupenschlepper Ost) fully tracked prime movers. (TsAMO)   85
A Hungarian-manufactured Turan I tank abandoned in a Budapest suburb.   86
A snow-covered 88mm anti-aircraft gun in one of Budapest's parks. (TsAMO)   86
Obergruppenführer der Waffen-SS Karl von Pfeffer-Wildenbruch, commander of the
    Budapest garrison. (Bundesarchiv, Bild 101III-Ege-237-06A, photo: Hermann Ege)   87
Generalmajor Gerhard Schmidhuber, commander of 13th Panzer Division.
    (Bundesarchiv, Bild 101I-088-3743-15A, photo: Fischer)   87
A German 150mm sFH 18 howitzer abandoned on the approaches to Budapest.
    (TsAMO)   94
A Panzerjäger IV abandoned by its crew. A shell is embedded in the barrel of the gun. 94
Searchlights and sound detection equipment aboard platform cars seized by Soviet
    troops. Hungary, end of 1944.   95
An abandoned Hummel self-propelled artillery vehicle. The gun's barrel is fixed in its
    travelling position.   95
An anti-aircraft Flakpanzer IV Mobelwagen with the 37mm Flak 43 cannon,
    February 1945, Budapest area.   96
A captured Hungarian-manufactured Turan I tank on a railroad platform.   96
Soviet soldiers and officers inspecting a Panther, knocked-out on a Budapest street. 97
An abandoned Munitionsträger (ammunition carrier) Hummel in Budapest.
    (TsAMO)   97
Amphibious Volkswagen Schwimmwagen abandoned in Budapest. (TsAMO)   98
An abandoned Wespe self-propelled howitzer. The tracks have been removed, most
    likely as a matter of convenience for towing.   103
German armored vehicles seized by Soviet troops: A Hummel self-propelled howitzer
    and a Pz. IV tank. Note the arcs welded onto the Hummel's fighting compartment
    to provide for a tarpaulin covering.   104
A StuG 40 self-propelled gun, which has become the booty of Soviet troops. A shield
    for a machine gun is visible on the roof.   104
A deeply mired Panther, abandoned by its crew. Spare track sections have been
    mounted on the tank's turret as supplementary protection.   105

Commander of Sixth SS Panzer Army, *Oberstgruppenführer und Generaloberst der Waffen-SS* Josef "Sepp" Dietrich (left). (Bundesarchiv, Bild 183-J28625, photo: Roeder) — 105

A knocked-out Panzerjäger IV tank destroyer. Note the Zimmerit coating covering the armor. — 109

A disabled Pz.IV Ausf.H. The camouflage is clearly visible, as are the spare track sections installed on the tank's frontal armor. — 109

A Panther tank, prepared for the repair of its drive train and abandoned during a retreat. — 110

A King Tiger from the 509th Heavy Panzer Battalion that has been destroyed by an internal explosion. — 110

A knocked-out King Tiger of the 509th Heavy Panzer Battalion. The number "52" was applied by the Soviet inspection team. — 111

An abandoned Bergepanther repair-recovery tank; Hungary, January 1945. — 111

An abandoned Panther of the 23rd Panzer Division. The divisional insignia is visible on the front armor, as is the number applied by the Soviet inspection team – "62". — 112

A scout commander reviewing an order. In the background is an M3 Scout Car, obtained through Lend-Lease. These armored cars equipped the reconnaissance units of the Soviet tank and mechanized corps. — 118

A collecting station for disabled equipment which has been seized by attacking Soviet troops. In the foreground is a Panther Ausf.G; in the background a Tiger Ausf.E heavy tank and several more machines are visible. — 118

A divisional M-30 Model 1938 122mm howitzer in action. By 1945, these guns made up the bulk of the artillery in the Red Army's rifle divisions. — 122

Cavalrymen occupying a defensive position. The crew of a 45mm anti-tank gun is manhandling the gun into a firing position. Note the characteristic fur caps worn by Soviet cavalrymen. — 122

Lieutenant G. Kuzmin's company attacks with the support of a 45mm anti-tank gun. By 1945, these guns were already virtually useless against the latest German tanks, but nevertheless were still in use in the Red Army. — 123

The on-board ammunition within this Panther Ausf.G has clearly exploded. The tactical marking "AJ9" is visible on the turret. Presumably, this tank belonged to the 2nd SS Panzer Division *Das Reich*. — 123

An SU-76 self-propelled gun in combat in a village. These self-propelled guns were second in prevalence only to the T-34 tank in the Red Army. — 133

Soviet artillery caught in a traffic jam on one of the roads at the front. Studebaker trucks acquired from the United States were used to tow the 76mm divisional cannons. — 133

A Soviet anti-tank artillery regiment, equipped with 57mm ZiS-2 anti-tank guns, on the march. — 134

A Soviet anti-tank regiment, equipped with captured 75mm PAK-40 guns, on the march. A Studebaker truck obtained through Lend-Lease is being used as a tow vehicle. — 134

Soviet soldiers training to use a captured PAK-40 75mm anti-tank gun. — 135

A disabled and burned-out King Tiger of the 509th Heavy Panzer Battalion, vicinity of Lake Balaton, March 1945. — 135

An SU-85 on the move. These self-propelled guns were used as tank destroyers, but
with the widespread introduction of the T-34/85 tank they lost their significance,
since they were no longer better armed than the T-34 and lacked turrets.   140

A T-34/85 tank, camouflaged with branches, waits in ambush.   140

ISU-122 self-propelled guns. Despite its slow rate of fire, the 122mm cannons of these
self-propelled guns were used with success in combat with German panzers.   141

A column of T-34/85 tanks. This scene was typical for the Red Army – infantry riding
on the tank's hull, with cases of ammunition mounted on the sides.   147

An abandoned StuG 40 self-propelled gun in the area of Lake Balaton, February 1945. 147

A Jagdpanzer IV/70(A) tank destroyer, knocked out in the area of Lake Balaton. The
machine has Drahtgeflecht [wire mesh] Schürzen side skirts and is wearing the
remnants of winter camouflage.   148

A Wespe self-propelled howitzer destroyed by artillery fire; Lake Balaton area,
February 1945.   148

Yet another knocked-out Wespe self-propelled howitzer. These self-propelled guns,
possessing armor protection against shell fragments and firing from covered
positions, were a hard nut to crack, and only a direct hit could knock them out.   149

A PzKpfw. VI Ausf.B King Tiger of the 509th Heavy Panzer Battalion. Its tactical
designation "213" is visible on the turret.   149

A completely burned-out Pz.IV Ausf.J in the area of Lake Balaton, March 1945.   150

A Jagdpanther tank destroyer left burned-out on a street of a Hungarian village in the
area of Lake Balaton, March 1945.   150

A Marder III self-propelled gun, abandoned by its crew. The abandoned tank destroyer
is being used as a road sign; it bears a marker indicating the direction of Glatz. 151

An abandoned Jagdpanther on a road. The machine has no visible damage, so it may
have broken down or run out of fuel. Vicinity of Lake Balaton, March 1945.   151

A broken-down Panther Ausf.G, abandoned by its crew. Lake Balaton area, March
1945.   152

ISU-152 self-propelled guns on the march. The ISU-152 was equipped with the
powerful 152mm gun and was an irreplaceable means of struggle against enemy
fortifications and stone buildings in 1945.   162

A German Panther Ausf.G with the number "134", given to it by the Soviet inspection
team. The tank has no visible damage. Probably it was abandoned by the crew after
experiencing mechanical problems.   162

A Panther Ausf.G tank, stuck in the mud and disabled.   163

A German Pz.IV Ausf.H tank, knocked out by Soviet artillery. It offers a good look at
its camouflage.   163

A SU-100 self-propelled gun. These self-propelled guns became the Red Army's serious
counter to the German "beasts" – the Tiger and Panther tanks – at Lake Balaton.   165

A knocked-out Panther; most likely, this tank became the victim of anti-tank fire from
both flanks – the gun is pivoted to the left, and a shell hole is plainly visible in the
right side of the hull.   165

The same machine as in the previous photograph, seen from a different angle. It is
clearly visible that the tank is lacking a Zimmerit coating.   166

A Panther Ausf.A, left abandoned by its crew.   166

A bogged-down and abandoned Panther Ausf.G. Judging from the attached tow cable, the Germans had unsuccessfully attempted to free the tank from the mud.   169

An ISU-152 on the move. In the background, Hungary's characteristic hilly terrain is visible.   170

A Flakpanzer IV Wirbelwind self-propelled anti-aircraft vehicle, destroyed by the direct hit of a large caliber shell. The gaping hole in the side of the hull is clearly visible.   170

Soviet officers examining a Pz.IV tank, abandoned on a street of a Hungarian town. Note the tank's Schürzen armored skirting, designed to protect the tank against anti-tank rifle rounds and hollow-charge shells.   171

This bogged down StuG 40 assault gun is fitted with a Saukopf gun mantlet and has a Zimmerit coating.   174

A Marder III self-propelled gun, destroyed by Soviet artillery fire.   175

In a literal sense, the German spring offensive became mired in mud: A Pz.IV Ausf.J tank, bogged down in a cornfield. Two more Pz.IV tanks are visible in the distance.   175

List of Maps

In colour section

Map 1   Repulse of the German Counteroffensives *Konrad I* and *II*, 1-11 January 1945
Map 2   Repulse of the Third German Counteroffensive (*Konrad III*) 18-27 January 1945
Map 3   The General Course of Combat Operations between 6 and 15 March 1945
Map 4   Repulse of the 6th SS Panzer Army's Offensive, 6-15 March 1945

List of Tables

1. Condition of the Divisions of the IV SS Panzer Corps on 1 January 1945   22
2. Condition of the Tank Park of the 1st, 3rd, 3rd SS and 5th SS Panzer Divisions on
    15 January 1945   44
3. Condition of the Divisions of the IV SS Panzer Corps on 1 February 1945   71
4. Number of Combat Sorties and Hours of Flight per 1 Combat Loss   92
5. The Number of Tanks and Self-propelled Guns in the Divisions of Army Group
    South as of the Evening of 5 March 1945   114
6. Status of the Armor Complement of the Sixth SS Panzer Army's Divisions as of
    13 March 1945   115
7. Artillery and Mortars in the Units of the 3rd Ukrainian Front on 6 March 1945
    (Excluding the Bulgarian First Army and the Yugoslav Corps)   131
8. Available Armor in the Armored Forces of the 3rd Ukrainian Front as of
    24.00 5 March 1945   139
9. German Armor Losses as Reported by the 3rd Ukrainian Front's Armies over
    6-15 March 1945   173

Part I

Gille and Balck Hurry to the Relief of the Budapest Garrison

1

Introduction

"Whoever has visited Lake Balaton will never forget it even once. Like an enormous pallet, it has been splashed with all the colors of the rainbow. The blue mirror of the water strikingly reflects the emerald green of the banks and the ornate buildings beneath orange tile roofs. It is no coincidence that songs are sung and legends written about Balaton."[1]

With this poetic introduction, one of the combat veterans of the fighting in Hungary begins his tale. Soviet soldiers and officers fought in Hungary at a time most unsuitable for admiring the local scenery: January – March 1945. However, they were looking at the Hungarian landscape with different eyes, the eyes of conquerors. They were slogging through mud on the outskirts of the capitals of hostile countries, and the end of the war was now close. Thus the vineyards and forests covered with dirty gray snow and the buildings with their empty window frames appeared completely differently to the fighters of the Red Army than they would have to a side observer. However, one could not say that the quiet landscape back then was safe even behind the front lines. The situation in Hungary was rather hostile, and flowers weren't being tossed onto the passing vehicles of the Red Army's advancing armor columns. Hungary was an ally of Nazi Germany. When the fortunes of war turned against the Red Army for a spell, the Hungarians who had been sourly smiling at the Soviet soldiers and officers just the day before were now firing at them from the attics of the "buildings beneath orange tile roofs."

On the whole, the fighting at Lake Balaton is not a "forgotten battle". The last major offensive of the German Army in the Second World War was a widely known event. Even people who were only quite superficially interested in military history knew of the existence of Lake Balaton and the Hungarian town with the elaborate name of Székesfehérvár.

To a certain extent, Hungary's notable role in the events of the final months of the war was the result of a combination of circumstances. At a time when a calm before the storm was prevailing in the autumn of 1944 on other battlefronts stretching from the Baltic to Silesia, the Soviet offensives that had been launched on the southern flank of the Soviet-German front back in the summer were still in motion. By the end of 1944, the Soviet 2nd and 3rd Ukrainian Fronts had entered the territory of Hungary, reached the approaches to Budapest from the east, and had also forced a crossing of the Danube River to the south of the capital. The next phase of the Soviet offensive out of the bridgehead on the western bank of the Danube resulted in a breakthrough of the so-called Margarethe Line and to the encirclement of Budapest together with its German and Hungarian garrison.

Hitler's impulsive decision to launch a relief attack followed on 24 December 1944, a day before the ring closed around Budapest. It is impossible to say that this was a simple whim. From a political point of view, Hungary remained the final ally of the Third Reich in its agonies. From an economic standpoint, almost the final sources of oil that remained under Germany's control were in Hungary. The country also lay on the path to Austria, where significant productive capacities of the German military industry were concentrated. From the military point of view, the loss of such an important defensive line as the Danube River, as well as the threat of losing the communications hub of Budapest, meant a loss of resilience on the southern wing of the Eastern Front. It would be possible to hold Budapest only for a very limited amount of time via the Germans' typical scenario of supplying the fortress by air. After this, the road hub would pass to the complete control of the Soviet forces. Given that the fronts in Poland, East Prussia and Kurland (Courland) were relatively quiet, Hitler's temptation to throw reserves into the fighting in Hungary and to reverse the events at Budapest in Germany's favor was at least explicable.

Several days later, the wheels of the German war machine began to turn, and tens of thousands of German troops were put into motion. The German armies standing on the Vistula River received a terrible blow from their own high command – the IV SS Panzer Corps was withdrawn from their ranks and sent to Hungary. In December 1944, it had been positioned north of Warsaw, ready to repel the next attempt by the Red Army to storm the Polish capital.

The reputation of the commander of the IV SS Panzer Corps, *Obergruppenführer* and General of SS Troops Herbert Gille, was far from an insignificant factor in the *Führer*'s choice. It was he who had broken through to the German units encircled in the Korsun-Shevchenkovsky pocket and had held open the escape route for them. At the time, he had been commanding the 5th SS Panzer Division *Wiking*. Just the radio message alone that Gille was coming to their relief raised the morale of the German units encircled in Budapest, and gave them hope of rescue.

Naturally, certain objective factors also played a role in Hitler's decision. The divisions of Gille's panzer corps had much more personnel than the divisions of General Walther Nehring's XXIV Panzer Corps. The SS *Wiking* Panzer Division had two extra battalions – I Battalion of both the *Norge* and *Danmark* Panzer Grenadier Regiments, which had been destroyed in the Baltics. These two battalions had been reconstituted, but it was thought to be senseless to return them to isolated Kurland. Thus they were attached to the SS 5th Panzer Division *Wiking*'s roster, and continued to fight as part of it until May 1945.

If there was also the factor of the *Führer*'s great trust in Himmler's organization, it didn't outweigh arguments of reason. The German 96th and 711th Infantry Divisions were also sent to the Budapest axis to reinforce the infantry component of Gille's IV SS Panzer Corps.

Back in August 1944, the arrival of the two SS panzer divisions in Poland had sealed the fate of the Warsaw Uprising and had stopped the seemingly irresistible Soviet advance toward the Polish capital. In the event of the start of a new Soviet offensive near Warsaw, the IV SS Panzer Corps doubtlessly would have had a real influence on the course of events. However, this powerful and dangerous panzer formation was sent to Hungary literally just two weeks before the launching of the Soviet Vistula-Oder operation. This decision to a great degree determined Germany's strategy in the 1945 campaign. In February 1945, almost half of the German panzer divisions on the Eastern Front were operating in Hungary.

However, unlike the many other German relief attempts, the intention of which had been to evacuate the encircled groupings, IV SS Panzer Corps was to fight its way into Budapest in order to strengthen the defense of the Hungarian capital and to re-establish the front along the Margarethe Line. In a word, Gille's IV SS Panzer Corps was supposed to restore the situation to the point where it had existed prior to the launching of the Soviet offensive, which had led to Budapest's encirclement. Having accomplished this, the SS divisions might return again to Poland.

After the *Führer* had earmarked the use of the IV SS Panzer Corps for use at Budapest, it was necessary to select the axis of the attack. An attack out of the area of Székesfehérvár, bypassing Lake Velence from the south (the so-called Operation *Paula*) promised success in view of the terrain, which was suitable for panzer operations. However, in this case, an additional 900 cubic meters of fuel would be required, as well as five additional days to assemble the forces. The second option was an offensive across the shortest distance to Budapest, practically parallel to the course of the Danube north of Lake Velence. This option received the code name "*Konrad*". Its main shortcoming was the need to attack across hilly, wooded terrain, but its main advantage was the element of surprise. Each day and hour of delay was working to the benefit of the Soviet troops, who were busily strengthening the defenses of the outer ring of Budapest's encirclement. The more

A Soviet T-34/85 tank with tank riders aboard it, preparing for an attack. Hungary, end of 1944.

A Pz.Kpfw.IV tank knocked out by a shell hit in the rear of the hull. (TsAMO)

A destroyed Wespe self-propelled artillery vehicle. The fractures in the sides of the armored fighting compartment were most likely caused by penetrations from large-caliber artillery shells.

Commander of *Armeegruppe Balck, General der Panzertruppen* Hermann Balck. (Bundesarchiv, Bild 101I-732-0118-03, photo: Bauer)

Obergruppenführer und General der Waffen-SS Herbert Gille, commander of IV SS Panzer Corps. (Bundesarchiv, Bild 101I-090-3916-14, photo: Etzhold)

quickly the attack was launched, the greater the prospects for crushing a still not fully prepared defense. Guderian himself was an advocate of Operation *Paula*, but his protégé General Walther Wenck and the command of Army Group South supported Operation *Konrad*.

In the end, the German High Command opted for *Konrad*. The then chief of staff of the IV SS Panzer Corps *Obersturmbannführer* Schönfelder later talked about this choice:

1. Time played a major role;
2. The strength of the defending troops in Budapest was almost exhausted and unable to resist;
3. The shortest distance to the operation's objective was the determining factor.

The season of the year and the terrain made the attack of panzers more difficult, but this was accepted as part of the bargain.[1]

Gille, his headquarters and his men were effectively temporary guests in Hungary. They wanted to finish the job quickly and return to Warsaw.

The operation's top leaders were new in their posts, as well as in the given theater of combat operations. This includes Gille, who had just arrived from Poland – he was going to have to go into battle straight from the trains. However, the situation was only a little better with those above him in rank and post. Only General of Infantry Otto Wöhler, the commander of Army Group Center, was to some extent familiar with the theater of combat operations – he had previously commanded the Eighth Army in Hungary. However, he was new to his role as commander of an army group. At the onset of the operation to break the Soviet ring around Budapest, he had been in his new post for just eight days. General of Panzer Forces Balck was commanding forces in Hungary for the first time, and only recently had accepted command of the Sixth Army. He was one of the most decorated and well-known German panzer commanders of the Second World War. By January

1945, he held the Knight's Cross with Swords, Oak Leaves and Diamonds, whereas his superior Wöhler had only the Knight's Cross with Oak Leaves. But if for Gille the assignment to break through to Budapest was a nod to his past services, for Balck the new assignment was a reduction in post. Prior to this he had been commanding Army Group "G" in the West. The bestowing of the designation "army group" to the Sixth Army only somewhat offset the bitter pill of removal from command of an army group for Balck. Having served the greater part of the war in the East, Balck's career in the West simply never took off. He himself later characterized his relationship with the Commander in Chief in the West von Rundstedt as "strained". The return to the Eastern Front was a chance for Balck to restore his reputation as a military commander.

The terrain would play a major role in subsequent events. Both Operation *Konrad* in January and the Operation *Frühlingserwachen* [Spring Awakening] in March were conducted by the Germans in one and the same area. Therefore it makes sense to stop and dwell in more detail in the description of the upcoming area of combat operations. By its topography, the area can be precisely divided into two portions, a northern and a southern.

The northern portion of the area from the line Csákvár – Mór to the banks of the Danube River east of Komárno is covered by the forested Vérteshegység Mountains, or more simply, the Vértes Hills. These hills, part of the Transdanubian Mountains, stretch along a slanting axis from south to north. Their rounded peaks rise approximately 300 meters above the surrounding terrain, reaching an elevation of 630 meters above sea level. The slopes of these hills are cut by deep and narrow ravines, which are overgrown with trees. There are very few roads or even passages through the hills here. The movement of all types of troops was possible only along a single railroad, two paved roads and one dirt road. In those places where the roads cut through the ridges and rocks, defiles ranging from 10 to 40 meters in width are created. There are no pedestrian or vehicular bypasses around these terrain bottlenecks.

There are relatively few populated points in the Vértes Hills; in the majority they are located in the foothills and valleys. They are primarily mining settlements found in areas where there are bauxite deposits. Numerous paths lead from the villages into the hills, which typically come to an abrupt halt at cliffs and ravines. These footpaths are accessible only for the movement of infantry.

West of the Vértes Hills in the expanse stretching from Komárno to the Kisbér – Környe railroad lies rolling, open terrain with elevations of 100 to 230 meters. This area has a well-developed network of paved and dirt roads, the majority of which come together in the area of Tata, thereby making that town a major road hub. After the ring closed around Budapest, the Red Army fought to gain access to this area.

North of the Vértes Hills, the Danube River follows a west to east course, before turning to the south and proceeding to Budapest. The right bank of this river in this sector rises well above the left bank, which permits a view of the lower terrain out to 10-12 kilometers. A highway and railroad main line run along a narrow corridor of level ground that is 1.5 to 2 kilometers wide and parallels the right bank of the Danube between Komárno and Budapest. It was only in this corridor that all types of troops could operate.

To the east, closer to Budapest, the hills gradually diminish and descend into a rolling plain with an altitude of 190 to 300 meters above sea level. The road network in this area is better-developed than in the hills. Most of the roads run from the west toward Budapest, and from Bicske to the south.

From this description of the terrain, the dilemma confronting the German command becomes clear. There was not enough fuel for Operation *Paula*, while *Konrad* would force them to break through forests and mountain defiles. According to the topography and the development of the road network, the northern portion of the area, in which the January combat operations unfolded, presented substantial difficulties for an offensive, especially one employing tank and mechanized formations. The plan relied upon the element of surprise and the strength of the attack, which would permit the attackers to pass quickly through the Vértes Hills and to emerge on the plain on the approaches to Budapest.

The southern portion of the area for conducting a January offensive to break the ring around Budapest was considerably more suitable for tank operations. It consists of open ground (with elevations of 100 to 200 meters), which gradually descends from the southern spurs of the Vértes Hills to the east, southeast and south. This region possesses a well-developed network of railroads, paved roads and dirt roads. Here, the city of Székesfehérvár is located, which is the second largest road hub in Hungary. Six railroads and more than ten paved and dirt roads come together in the area of Székesfehérvár, four of which approach the city from the west, two from the north, two from the south, and two from the direction of Budapest. The entire territory of the southern region contains a large number of settlements, which are connected by dirt and paved roads. Their homes and building are primarily stone, with a large quantity of cellars, underground wine vaults, attics and gardens. There are a lot of vineyards in this area, with detached stone buildings, and a large number of country estates, manor farms and farmsteads.

The presence of a multitude of small rivers and canals somewhat casts a pall over the favorable picture of the southern sector. The most significant of them are the Sárviz, Sió, Málom and Kapos Canals, and the Vali Laszlo River. They all flow from the northwest to the southeast and enter the Danube south of Budapest. These rivers and canals are not fordable; however, their narrow width makes it possible to cross them with the assistance of improvised means.

2

Konrad I: A Hasty Surprise

The early start date of the offensive was prompted by the Germans' selection of a risky plan for the operation, but it forced the launching of the operation before the forces for it had fully assembled. By the start of the offensive, only 32% (28 of 87 trains) of the 5th SS Panzer Division *Wiking* had arrived; 66% (51 of 77 trains) of the 3rd SS Panzer Division *Totenkopf*; and 40% (20 of 46 trains) of the 96th Infantry Division. The 711th Infantry Division hadn't even started unloading in the designated area. The assembly of all these divisions wasn't completed until 8 January 1945.

Going over to the offensive before completing the assembly of forces worsened the already less than lustrous condition of the SS formations. Despite the exertions of the Third Reich's military industry that was tottering on the edge of collapse, *Wiking* and *Totenkopf* were experiencing a shortage of the most necessary combat equipment. There was a problem even with machine guns: Of the 1,191 light machine guns according to TO&E [table of organization and equipment], *Totenkopf* had only 536. Of the authorized 1,011 tracked vehicles, *Wiking* had 442, and only 658 of the 921 ordinary trucks. This made the panzer grenadier regiments of the divisions more like motorized regiments. According to the system of assessing mobility in the *Wehrmacht*, as expressed in percentages, *Wiking* had a relatively low indicator of less than 50%. On its part, *Totenkopf* had extremely few armored halftracks – much fewer than it had possessed at Kursk. The general condition of the divisions of Gille's IV SS Panzer Corps can be seen in Table 1.

Table 1 Condition of the Divisions of the IV SS Panzer Corps on 1 January 1945

	3rd SS Panzer Division Totenkopf	5th SS Panzer Division Wiking
Manpower	17,425	17,425
Pz. III	1	–
Pz. IV	30 (4)	10
Pz. V	20 (7)	22 (2)
Pz. VI	11*	–
StuGs	27 (5)	4 (1)
JgPz IV	19 (1)	–
SdKfz Half Tracks	69 (11)	162 (13)
Guns	52 (6)	56
Mobility	80%	46%

The numbers within the parentheses indicate the number of vehicles under short-term repair.
* Pz VI Ausf. E Tigers

The preparation of Operation *Konrad* within a compressed period of time led to the fact that the German panzer forces already present in Hungary were only minimally involved in the first relief attack. In addition to the freshly arriving units of the IV SS Panzer Corps, only *Kampfgruppe von Pape*, which had been defending in the area within the bend in the Danube, went on the attack.

At that moment, its roster included the bulk of the 271st Volksgrenadier Division, the elements of Panzerkorps *Feldherrnhalle* that remained outside of the Budapest pocket, the 208th Panzer Battalion (31 Pz. IV and 17 JgPz IV/70(A)), which had been sent from the Supreme Command Reserve, and two of the three *kampfgruppen* (from the 6th and 8th Panzer Divisions) that were available in December. The German *kampfgruppen* consisted of a panzer battalion, a motorized infantry battalion equipped with halftracks, and the self-propelled howitzers (the Hummel 150mm and Wespe 105mm) of the artillery regiment. They were less vulnerable against artillery blocking fire than soft-skinned vehicles or dismounted infantry, and as a result of this were able to penetrate deeply into the enemy's defenses.

The bulk of the German panzer divisions already in Hungary had become widely scattered on both sides of the Danube River and were thus unable to be used quickly as a unified force for the relief attack. The main forces of the 3rd and 6th Panzer Divisions were still on the north side of the Danube River, while the 1st and 23rd Panzer Divisions were defending at Székesfehérvár and at Mór.

The haste in putting together the counteroffensive was not simply an idle whim of the German high command, since every hour was working to the favor of the Soviet defenders of the outer ring of encirclement. On the eve of the New Year of 1945, feverish preparations for the next round of battle were being made by both sides. The defensive battle at Balaton was fundamentally different from that at Kursk in the summer of 1943. The Soviet troops literally had only several days for improving their positions on the outer ring of Budapest's encirclement.

At 19.00 on 30 December 1944, the commander of the Soviet 4th Guards Army G.F. Zakharov gave his subordinate troops both defensive and offensive tasks. A German-held salient had formed in the center of the 4th Guards Army's front lines at Mór, out of which the Germans might be able to develop an offensive into the rear of the defending Soviet units north and south of that town. General Zakharov issued an order for an attack in the first days of 1945 to pinch off this salient at its base. However, the primary assignment of the Army's rifle corps was defensive. Before 1 January 1945, the 4th Guards Army went on the defensive on a sector of 160 kilometers (including the bank of Lake Balaton). The 31st Guards Rifle Corps was given a sector of 48 kilometers, the 68th Rifle Corps – 18 kilometers, the 20th Guards Rifle Corps – 24 kilometers, the 135th Rifle Corps – 16 kilometers, and the 21st Guards Rifle Corps – 20 kilometers, as well as approximately 35 kilometers of the southern shoreline of Lake Balaton. The average numerical strength of a rifle division of the 4th Guards Army was 5,386 men. Of the 4th Guards Army's 14 rifle divisions, 11 had a numerical strength of between 5,000 and 6,000 men, which was barely half of their table strength. Such a situation was typical for the Red Army in 1945. The struggle against the remnants of the defeated German and Hungarian units in the forests of the Vértes Hills was absorbing additional troops and equipment. The Axis remnants were attacking Soviet rear echelon units and even headquarters. This also made the situation in Hungary substantially different from that at Kursk in 1943.

However, the January fighting at Balaton also unquestionably had aspects that made it similar to other Soviet defensive battles of the war. An inability to surmise the enemy's plans was common for many Soviet defensive operations. The January fighting in Hungary was no exception. The 4th Guards Army was deployed with a greater density of force closer to its left flank, in the area of Székesfehérvár. It was here that the reserve 41st Guards Rifle Division and 7th Mechanized Corps (77 tanks and 25 self-propelled guns) were deployed, together with other reinforcements. The 4th Guards Army's headquarters was also in Székesfehérvár. Given the terrain, this is unsurprising – a German counterattack in the area of Székesfehérvár appeared more logical. The 31st Guards Rifle Corps was defending on the right flank of the 4th Guards Army. As a consequence of the fact that the forces of the neighboring 2nd Ukrainian Front on the right were somewhat lagging behind the 3rd Ukrainian Front, part of this rifle corps had to be detached in order to defend the banks of the Danube. A regiment of the 4th Guards Rifle Division was positioned here with its front oriented to the north. The 34th and 80th Guards Rifle Divisions were holding the rest of the Corps' sector with their fronts facing the west. The 80th Guards Rifle Division, which was positioned on the axis of the IV SS Panzer Corps' main attack, had gone over to the defensive only at 20.00 30 December 1944. The division's units were unable to dig even one continuous trench line in the rocky soil.

The objective factors, related to the weakness of the Soviet defenders' positions, were made worse by subjective factors. Afterward, in Order No. 11 of 14 January 1945, the commander of the 4th Guards Army pointed to serious shortcomings in the preparation of the 80th Guards Rifle Division's defensive set-up: "The Tavares – Agostyán highway, which was thought to have been mined, was in fact not mined; the mines were lying non-emplaced on the roadside, and subsequently they were found and disarmed by the enemy without difficulty."[1] Most likely, the lack of defensive preparations was simply due to the fact that no one believed the enemy would attack and everyone looked upon defensive measures with indifference. Moreover, the Vértes Hills gave natural benefits to any defender.

The presence of the 18th Tank Corps, which had been pulled back into the reserve and which was directly subordinate to Front headquarters, somewhat offset the dangerous situation on the right flank of the 4th Guards Army. This Corps had suffered relatively light losses in the course of the December offensive and had retained its strike capabilities. On 31 December 1944 it numbered 110 T-34 tanks, as well as 18 ISU-122 and 15 SU-85 self-propelled guns. The 18th Tank Corps was in readiness to counter both attempts by the Budapest garrison to break out and any possible German counterattack against the outer encirclement ring. One of its brigades (the 170th Tank Brigade) was still at the front near Dunaalmási at the start of Operation *Konrad*. It had been left there with the aim of supporting the infantry in the storming of that town.

The 18th Tank Corps was not the only mobile formation at the call of the 3rd Ukrainian Front's command. General I.N. Russianov's 1st Guards Mechanized Corps had been sent to Hungary from the *Stavka* Reserve. This corps started its history as the 100th Rifle Division, which had distinguished itself in the first days of the war in the combat for Minsk and for this reason became the 1st Guards Rifle Division. In 1942 it was re-formed into a mechanized corps. In 1943, the 1st Guards Mechanized Corps took part in the battles for the Donbass, Zaporozh'e and Kirovograd. After this it was withdrawn to Poltava into the *Stavka* Reserve, where it spent the next 13 months refitting. On 8 December 1944, at a directive from the Red Army's General Staff the corps began loading aboard trains, which departed for the front one after another. Situated in reserve, the 1st Guards Mechanized Corps was fully staffed with officers and men. By December 1944, this mechanized corps could have been boldly called "Siberian" – 70% of its personnel were Siberians, who had managed to receive excellent tactical training as infantry. In contrast, its tanks had arrived not long before the departure to the front, and there hadn't been time to conduct joint training with them. The tanks that reached Russianov's formation were not standard-issue – the corps was equipped with American Sherman tanks that had been received through Lend-Lease. This at first caused certain problems for the 1st Guards Mechanized Corps' repair teams, which had been trained on T-34 tanks. Russianov's corps also had three self-propelled artillery regiments equipped with the latest SU-100 tank destroyers. The 1st Guards Mechanized Corps began unloading from the trains on 24 December 1944, the very same day that Hitler ordered the IV SS Panzer Corps to be sent to Budapest. The arrival of the 1st Guards Mechanized Corps and the three SU-100 regiments can be considered as a reaction of the Soviet high command to the German commitment of several panzer divisions into the fighting in Hungary in November – December 1944.

The 46th Army became one more actor in the pending drama, though it was still lurking offstage. The main forces of General Shlemin's army were besieging Buda; however, a number of its formations had been pulled out of the front line and in the process they effectively became a reserve for the defense of the outer ring of encirclement. Its 86th Guards Rifle Division was in a defensive posture south of Esztergom [called Gran by the Germans] with its front facing the east. In the event of a breakout by the Germans and Hungarians from Budapest, it was to block their path. In addition, the 46th Army's 2nd Guards Mechanized Corps (31 tanks and 13 self-propelled guns) was also now in reserve. It had also received the assignment to block any breakout from Budapest, if such an event took place. Finally, the 49th Guards Rifle Division was engaged in mopping up the forests lying to the west of the encircled Hungarian capital. These three formations hadn't been drawn into the assault on Budapest, which meant it wasn't necessary to lose time to disengage them from combat.

By the second half of the war, a so-called "air army", which included fighters, ground attack aircraft, reconnaissance aircraft, artillery observation airplanes and bombers that operated in support of one or another *front*, had become standard in the Red Army. Accordingly, in addition to the all-arms armies, an air army was subordinate to each *front*'s headquarters, but its precise composition varied according to the importance and nature of the tasks facing the ground troops. The composition of the 3rd Ukrainian Front's 17th Air Army as of 1 January 1945 was characterized by the following numbers (the figure to the left of the slash shows operational aircraft, while the number to the right of it shows aircraft under repair at the time):

La-5 fighters: 79/15
Iak-3 and Iak-9 fighters: 202/13
Il-2 ground attack aircraft: 345/27
B-3 (A-20 Boston) bombers: 98/13
Po-2 night bombers: 94/3
Pe-2 reconnaissance aircraft: 12/2
Iak-9 reconnaissance aircraft: 2/6
Il-2 artillery spotters: 17/4
Iak-9 artillery spotters: 12/0

Thus, the 17th Air Army as of 1 January 1945 had a total of 861 operational aircraft.

According to both its numbers and composition, the 17th Air Army could be characterized as an air army designated for operations on a secondary axis. Air armies on key directions had two or three times the number of aircraft. In addition, the 17th Air Army had no Pe-2 dive bombers at all, not to mention any of the powerful Tu-2 twin-engine bombers, which were comparable to the German Ju-88. Domestically-produced bombers were partially replaced by Lend-Lease Bostons. These weren't bad aircraft, but they were unable to dive bomb.

The comparatively small 17th Air Army becomes even more lackluster when compared to the enemy's air force. Despite the attention that Hitler had focused on Hungary, the German *Luftflotte* [Air Fleet] 4 that was operational on the German southern flank was not the largest. On 10 January 1945, of the four *Luftwaffe* air fleets in the east (1, 4, 5 and 6), the numerically largest was *Luftflotte* 6, which was operating in Poland and East Prussia. It numbered 822 combat aircraft. However, according to the data for 10 January 1945, *Luftflotte* 4 in Hungary stood in a respectable second place with 588 combat aircraft (78 single-engine fighters, 56 bombers, 199 ground attack aircraft, 101 night attack aircraft, 38 long-range reconnaissance aircraft, 67 short-range reconnaissance aircraft, and 49 transport aircraft). In addition to the 3rd Ukrainian Front's 17th Air Army, *Luftflotte* 4 also faced the 2nd Ukrainian Front's 5th Air Army, which had 642 operational combat aircraft on 1 January 1945, also with A-20 Bostons in place of Pe-2s. However, all the same the correlation of forces in the air here was worse for the Soviet side than on other directions of advance in this period.

Commander of the 5th Guards Cavalry
Corps Major General S.I. Gorshkov.

Commander of the 4th Guards Army
General of the Army G.F. Zakharov.

Commander of the 1st Guards Mechanized
Corps Lieutenant General of Tank Forces
I.N. Russianov.

Commander of the 3rd Ukrainian Front
Marshal F.I. Tolbukhin.

An M4 Sherman tank, obtained through the Lend-Lease program, of one of the Soviet tank units. The 1st Guards Mechanized Corps was equipped with Shermans.

A knocked-out StuH 42 self-propelled howitzer.

A knocked-out Pz.IV Ausf.H tank with carefully applied winter camouflage.

A StuG 40 self-propelled gun that has become immobilized in the mud and was abandoned by its crew. The number "136" was left there by the Soviet inspection team. Note the waffle-pattern Zimmerit.

A Pz. V Ausf.A Panther, bogged down in the mud and abandoned by its crew. This tank probably belonged to the 6th Panzer Division.

A King Tiger of the 509th Heavy Panzer Battalion, abandoned on a street in a Hungarian town.

In view of the swift regrouping of Gille's IV SS Panzer Corps from the Warsaw area to Hungary, Soviet intelligence didn't manage to acquire reliable evidence of the arrival of fresh enemy formations before the start of *Konrad*. In its intelligence summary produced at 22.00 1 January 1945, that is, just several hours before the launching of the enemy offensive, the headquarters of the 4th Guards Army came to the following conclusion: "The enemy is striving to hold its present positions with all its forces; on separate sectors of the front, the adversary is undertaking attacks for reconnaissance purposes and with the aim of improving local positions." At that moment, it had relatively solid intelligence about the arrival of *Wiking* at the front from prisoners. Yet it simply had no information at all about *Totenkopf*. It isn't surprising, given such attitudes, that the anti-tank mines had been stacked on the side of the roads instead of being emplaced.

Soviet forces were the first to go on the attack in the new 1945 year. At 11.00 1 January, five rifle divisions in the center of the 4th Guards Army went on the offensive with the aim of seizing Mór. The attackers were met by heavy fire and had no success. Heavy snow began falling that afternoon. Despite the exceptionally poor flying weather, the German *Luftwaffe* became active. In groups of several aircraft, they bombed targets close behind the Soviet front line in the sector targeted by Operation *Konrad*. These small groups of 3 to 10 aircraft each became the harbingers of the German offensive. But times had changed, and instead of large swarms of Stukas, now the Germans were operating in small groups of fighter-bombers.

At 22.00 1 January 1945, small groups of German tanks and infantry began to probe the Soviet defenses, but at 2.30 2 January, the main forces of the IV SS Panzer Corps entered the fighting. The defensive positions of the 80th Guards Rifle Division were broken by a powerful blow on a narrow front, and the Germans emerged in the rear of the defending regiments and attacked the division's headquarters in Agostyán. Command and control over the division's units became disrupted. Simultaneously, in the time period between 1.00 and 5.00 2 January, a landing party from the 96th Infantry Division crossed the Danube and managed to drive the units of the 4th Guards Rifle Division out of a number of villages on the Danube's right bank. Soon, the infantry of the river crossing linked up with panzers that were attacking from the west. Part of the 80th Guards Rifle Division and the 18th Tank Corps' 170th Tank Brigade (27 tanks) became encircled. From the very start of the operation, two directions of enemy attack became clear: along the Danube and through Agostyán. On the former axis of advance, the IV SS Panzer Corps was operating, while *Kampfgruppe von Pape* was attacking on the latter axis. For a certain amount of time, General Gorba managed to keep the Germans out of Agostyán by holding a narrow pass in the hills. However, the blocking force in the pass, which had held up all day against German tank attacks on 2 January, was outflanked by enemy infantry on the following morning.

The 31st Guards Rifle Corps' defensive front was swiftly crumbling, and in essence it was necessary to create a new one. The 41st Guards Rifle Division, which was located in Zakharov's reserve, was 60 kilometers away from the point of the German breakthrough, and it would require no less than a day and a half or even two days before it could move out. In addition, at the start of the German offensive, it still wasn't clear whether the German attack toward Agostyán was the main attack or just a pinning attack. The 3rd Ukrainian Front commander F.I. Tolbukhin decided to split up the attack grouping that was targeting Mór. The 93rd Rifle Division, which had been attacking on a narrow front, was pulled out of the front line and received an order to make a forced march to Tarján. This would require the division to conduct a march of approximately 45 kilometers. At Tarján, it would block the path of the German advance out of the wooded, hilly area through Bicske onto the plain.

The dismantling of the 4th Guards Army's attack grouping didn't stop with the removal of the 93rd Rifle Division. Tolbukhin also pulled the 40th and 62nd Rifle Divisions out of the front line and into the reserve. In addition, General Gorshkov's 5th Guards Cavalry Corps was taken out of the fighting near Mór. On the evening of 1 January, it had joined the attack on that town, but it had also had no success. Already on the morning of 2 January, it received a fresh order to march to a new area of assembly.

However, it was no longer possible to resurrect a line of defense and extend its right flank to the Danube River with just the forces of the 4th Guards Army alone. This could only be accomplished with additional forces of the 3rd Ukrainian Front. Front commander Tolbukhin decided to create a new line of defense 16-20 kilometers behind the 4th Guards Army's already ruptured positions as quickly as possible, while delaying the German advance with screening forces. The German axis of advance along the bank of the Danube had been identified as the most dangerous one at the time. Soviet mobile divisions could reach the new line of defense most quickly, so the 18th Tank Corps (minus its 170th Tank Brigade) received an order to move to a blocking position in the path of the German penetration. The 86th Guards Rifle Division and the 46th Army's 2nd Guards Mechanized Corps moved out toward the same place. Just like the Russian fairy tale, the rifle division and mechanized corps pivoted, with their backside now to the forest (Budapest) and their front facing Ivan Tsarevich (the IV SS Panzer Corps). The orientation of the front of the two formations had flipped 180 degrees, blocking the enemy's path to Budapest along the bank of the Danube.

Tolbukhin was an artilleryman, and this left a definite imprint on his style of conducting a defensive operation. He ordered Zakharov to move up *Katiusha* rocket launchers, artillery (including anti-aircraft and anti-tank artillery) and mortars, which had passed to his control from the roster of the 18th Tank Corps and the 5th Guards Cavalry Corps, to the new line of defense. It should be noted that the Germans also used this tactic. In the course of defensive battles, they would create combat groups of anti-tank guns and artillery, which had greater mobility than did the infantry, and deploy them on the axis of the enemy advance.

On 3 January, the firmness of the new line of defense was tested by attacks by German panzer formations. The reserves that had moved up at Tolbukhin's and Zakharov's orders entered the fighting. Units of the IV SS Panzer Corps that were attacking along the right bank of the Danube collided with the defenses of the 86th Guards Rifle Division and the 18th Tank Corps, which had been reinforced with anti-tank artillery. Fierce tank battles developed for control of the Bajna road hub. Hours literally decided everything. The 110th Tank Brigade and the 363rd Self-propelled Artillery Regiment equipped with ISU-122s entered Bajna at 5.30 on 3 January and immediately ran into the leading units of the 3rd SS Panzer Division *Totenkopf*. They managed to drive back the Germans and keep possession of this important road junction. That afternoon, the SS troops launched furious but unsuccessful attacks on Bajna from the north, and then from the west and east. The outflanking maneuvers of the Germans were anticipated and parried.

The activity of the *Luftwaffe*, according to the standards of 1945, was rather high on the day of 3 January. Altogether, the Germans conducted approximately 350 individual combat sorties. Groups of 15-20 fighter-bombers almost continuously hung in the air above the combat positions of elements of the 18th Tank Corps in Bajna. In the course of the day, 6 T-34 tanks and 2 ISU-122 self-propelled guns of the 110th Tank Brigade were left burned out after their attacks. The 181st Tank Brigade lost 5 more T-34 tanks and had an additional 3 rendered immobile.

The actions of the Soviet reserves that had hurried up to confront *Kampfgruppe von Pape* and the 5th SS Panzer Division *Wiking* were less successful. The successful advance of the attackers created a salient in the Soviet line, the perimeter of which was longer than the initial front of the defense, thereby requiring additional Soviet units to hold it. In the process, the attacker had the possibility to choose the next axis of attack with the creation of a local superiority of force at the selected point of the attack.

On the second day of the operation, the German units that had been moving through Agostyán from the west to the east altered their axis of attack. Now their path of advance ran almost directly from north to south through Tarján toward Bicske, toward an exit from the hilly, wooded terrain.

Forward units of the 93rd Rifle Division managed to reach Tarján on 3 January, but lacked the time to build a continuous line of defense. In the middle of the day, they were enveloped from both flanks and compelled to retreat.

Both sides made changes in their plans due to the results of the fighting on 3 January. The strong blocking force across the road to Budapest, created by the units of the 46th Army and the 18th Tank Corps that had been moved from that city, forced the Germans to search for reserves in order to strengthen the attack grouping. For this purpose, the main forces of the 6th Panzer Division returned from the northern bank of the Danube. Now it was to rejoin its armored grouping (that was part of *Kampfgruppe von Pape*).

On its part the Soviet command, recognizing the shakiness of the newly created line of defense, strove to reinforce it as much as possible. The 7th Mechanized Corps was still sitting in reserve in Székesfehérvár. However, an unusual combat group under the leadership of the deputy commander of the 4th Guards Army Major General Filippovsky was detached from it and sent to repel the enemy attack. It consisted of the 16th Mechanized Brigade, the 78th Guards Heavy Tank Regiment, and the 1289th Self-propelled Artillery Regiment (a total of 16 T-34, 12 IS-2, 4 SU-85, 7 SU-76, 8 armored halftracks, and 20 85mm guns). Filippovsky was also given control of the 41st Guards Rifle Division and the 152nd Howitzer, the 222nd and 127th Cannon Artillery Regiments, as well as the 205th Mortar Regiment. In addition to Group Filippovsky, a significant amount of rocket artillery was moved up to the approaches to Bicske. Already by the morning of 4 January, 13 M-13 rocket artillery battalions and 1 M-31 battalion were positioned here – which represented a large portion of the 3rd Ukrainian Front's *Katiusha* rocket launchers. The so-called "Guards mortars" mounted on trucks were always one of the Soviet command's most maneuverable reserves. The *Katiusha* rocket launchers could be assembled on a selected axis much more quickly than regular artillery, especially heavy artillery.

The German counteroffensive also compelled an urgent crossing of the freshly arrived 1st Guards Mechanized Corps to the western bank of the Danube. According to plan, it was to cross using a 60-ton pontoon bridge. However, the bridge had been swept away by drifting ice (a large amount of floating ice was moving down the Danube at the time), and as a result the crossing was organized by two ferry boats towing armored launches. Naturally, this significantly slowed the pace of the river crossing. By 6.00 4 January, only the combat elements, without their rear services and a majority of the vehicles, had crossed the Danube. The motorized riflemen moved up to the front line on foot. A group of 59 SU-100 from three self-propelled artillery regiments under the command of the deputy artillery commander of the 1st Guards Mechanized Corps Colonel Sveshnikov had been moved out in advance of the infantry. By 8.00 4 January, it had already assembled in the Bicske area.

The events of 4 January demonstrated the correctness of the decisions that had been made by Tolbukhin and Zakharov. It was Group Filippovsky, which had been created at their order that prevented the Germans from reaching operational space on this day. Having bypassed the 93rd Rifle Division in Tarján and driven the 12th Guards Cavalry Division from its positions, *Wiking*'s tanks had lunged on to the south toward Bicske, and penetrated to the village of Mány, which lay just 4.5 kilometers to the north of Bicske. From there, it would take only one more bound in order to break out of the hilly and wooded area onto the plain west of Budapest. However, on the afternoon of 4 January, the mobile units of Group Filippovsky that had come hurrying up struck the southward attacking German units in the flank. Threatened with encirclement, the German units that had been advancing at a heady pace that morning were compelled to recoil in retreat. By evening, Group Filippovsky's rifle units had moved into position, and the defenses on the approaches to Bicske became sufficiently solid to withstand an enemy panzer attack.

In the northern sector of the offensive on 4 January, the Germans again used the method of crossing the Danube, which allowed them to outflank the 86th Guards Rifle Division and shove it back to the east. Here, the two infantry divisions of Gille's IV SS Panzer Corps were continuing the offensive along the course of the Danube River. However, the Soviet defenses had in the interim been bolstered by the 2nd Guards Mechanized Corps, which stopped the enemy advance.

In the meantime, *Totenkopf* was stubbornly assaulting Bajna. On the night of 3 January, the village had been attacked by German panzer grenadiers equipped with panzerfausts. Bajna increasingly took on the semblance of a mousetrap, as *Wiking*'s advance had pushed far beyond the defenders' left flank. On the morning of 4 January, the 110th Tank Brigade and the regiment of ISU-122s were pulled out of Bajna to the south of the village, where they took up concealed positions on hilltops behind a stream. However, here the Soviet tanks and self-propelled guns that were deployed in ambush were pounced upon by German fighter-bombers. According to the list of the 18th Tank Corps' irrecoverable losses for the day 4 January, 5 (!!!) heavy ISU-122 self-propelled guns were knocked out or destroyed by German bombs in the vicinity of the village of Bajna. In addition to these losses, on 3-4 January 15 T-34 tanks had been destroyed by German artillery fire in the Bajna area. However, the outcome of the fighting for Bajna was decided by *Wiking*'s attack west of Bajna, which penetrated to the village of Mány. Although this breakthrough couldn't be exploited by the Germans, the units of the 18th Tank Corps in the Bajna area were now in danger of being encircled. By the morning of 5 January, they had been withdrawn to the line Mány – Zsámbék, where they tied in with the defenses of Bicske. By this time, the 110th Tank Brigade and the 363rd Self-propelled Artillery Regiment had been reduced to 15 T-34 tanks and 8 ISU-122 self-propelled guns (of the 37 T-34 and 19 ISU-122 they had possessed on 1 January).

Since the defensive battle was being prolonged, it no longer made sense to leave the "breakwaters" of encircled units in the enemy rear. On the night of 3 January, the 80th Guards Rifle Division and the 170th Tank Brigade at the order of the commander of the 4th Guards Army broke out of their encirclement along the hilly, forested roads. Approximately 100 vehicles, as well as 11 T-34s and 11 SU-85s managed to return to friendly lines. The tankers even managed to bring out their wounded.

While the divisions that had received the initial enemy attack were bringing themselves back to order, the newly constructed defensive line was subjected to the next series of panzer attacks by *Kampfgruppe von Pape* and *Wiking*. However, with the arrival of the 40th and 41st Guards Rifle Divisions on the approaches to Bicske, the defensive front stiffened to the necessary degree. Even the main forces of the 6th Panzer Division which were added to the German attack grouping on 6 January didn't alter the situation. All of the German attacks on Bicske were repulsed. For the role he played in the several days of defensive fighting, Colonel M.F. Malyshev, the commander of the 16th Mechanized Brigade that had most distinguished itself in the combat, was awarded the Order of the Red Banner.

Having pulled alongside the 5th SS Panzer Division *Wiking,* the 3rd SS Panzer Division *Totenkopf* was also unable to overcome the 18th Tank Corps' defenses on the approaches to Zsámbék. The Soviet tank corps' combat ranks had been fleshed out with the arrival of the 49th Guards Rifle Division from Budapest. This axis was also reinforced with the three self-propelled SU-100 artillery regiments from the 1st Guards Mechanized Corps. They had been shifted from the Bicske area and placed under the operational control of the commander of the 18th Tank Corps. Since it wasn't clear where the Germans would strike next, the group of three SU-100 regiments had to extend their front significantly. It was at Számbék where the latest Soviet self-propelled tank destroyers had their first baptism by fire.

On the morning of 7 January, the Germans went on the attack toward Számbék. Blocking their path was the 382nd Guards Self-propelled Artillery Regiment of SU-100s. Under the enemy onslaught, the infantry of the 49th Guards Rifle Division fell back and left the SU-100 tank destroyers alone to face the attacking German units. The Germans threw infantry against the self-propelled guns. In the course of it they employed anti-tank grenades and Molotov cocktails, while the crews of the self-propelled guns, which lacked machine guns, fought back with whatever infantry weapons they had at hand. Over the day of combat the regiment lost half of its strength – 9 self-propelled guns were left burning, and 2 were knocked out. However, there was no German breakthrough on this axis. By 8 January 1945, the first German offensive with the aim of freeing Budapest, now known as Operation *Konrad I*, had been stopped.

3

Konrad II: A Double Blow

In the course of the stubborn fighting for Bicske, the troops of the 3rd Ukrainian Front succeeded in preventing a breakthrough by the IV SS Panzer Corps to the much more favorable ground for tank operations east of the Vértes Hills. Thus the SS troops had been forced to fight in the hilly, wooded terrain west of Budapest which was much less favorable for tank operations. Before the plan of Operation *Paula* was revived anew, the IV SS Panzer Corps made another attempt to breakthrough to Budapest. For this attempt, forces were regrouped to the SS Panzer Corps' left flank, to the sector adjacent to the Danube. This next operation received the code name "*Konrad II*". In Soviet descriptions of the events, the second breakthrough attempt is usually connected with the attack in the area of Zámoly, although from the German point of view, this attack was part of *Konrad I*. However, in view of the fact that chronologically the counterattack at Zámoly overlaps with *Konrad II*, it makes sense to discuss these events in one section.

Because it was difficult not to notice the arrival at Bicske of the Soviet divisions that had been removed from the front between Lake Balaton and the Danube the German command decided to pin down the enemy with an attack in the area of Székesfehérvár. Moreover, the shifting of the divisions away from the central sector of the Soviet defenses on the outer ring of Budapest's encirclement meant the weakening of that sector. This promised some success to *General der Panzertruppen* Hermann Breith's III Panzer Corps that was operating here. Simultaneously, the IV SS Panzer Corps was to resume its attacks in the direction of Budapest down the road paralleling the Danube River.

Despite the crisis on the 4th Guards Army's right flank, the main forces of the 7th Mechanized Corps had remained in the Székesfehérvár area. This trump card concealed in Tolbukhin's sleeve proved to be very fortuitous. On the axis of the German III Panzer Corps' (which was also known as *Korpsgruppe Breith*) advance, the 4th Guards Army's 20th Guards Rifle Corps was defending, holding a sector that was 28 kilometers wide. All three of its divisions were in the front line. The 20th Guards Rifle Corps' commander had only one destroyer anti-tank artillery regiment in his anti-tank reserve. The corps was reinforced with an army-level artillery group consisting of the 123rd Cannon Artillery Brigade (with 34 152mm howitzers) and the 188th Cannon Artillery Regiment (with 12 122mm guns). A large part of the corps' strength and means was concentrated in the sector of the 5th Guards Airborne Division, since the enemy's main attack was expected in its sector. The division was defending a sector with a width of 9 kilometers. According to the manpower of the Soviet divisions that was typical for 1945, the 5th Guards Airborne Division's sector could be assessed as rather broad and vulnerable. However, it had the entire 7th Mechanized Corps standing behind it, as well as the anti-tank reserve of the commander of the 20th Guards Rifle Corps, and the army-level artillery group was in its firing positions.

Korpsgruppe Breith's offensive began on the morning of 7 January. The shock grouping was unified under the command of the I Cavalry Corps, and consisted of the 3rd and 23rd Panzer Divisions and the 4th Cavalry Brigade. By 13.00, enemy tanks had managed to break through the combat positions of the infantry of the first echelon. The 23rd Panzer Division reached Hill 225 in the area of Borbály, where it encountered the 251st Destroyer Anti-tank Artillery Battalion in its firing positions; the Soviet anti-tank gunners repulsed this attack. The Germans responded by bringing artillery fire down on the battalion's positions, and knocked out 11 of the guns. After this, the enemy tanks with a renewed attack managed to take Hill 225.

After the direction of the enemy attack had become apparent, the 20th Guards Rifle Corps began to regroup its artillery reserve. At 18.00 7 January, it was reinforced with the 262nd and 438th Destroyer Anti-tank Regiments, the 212th, 221st and 230th Howitzer Artillery Regiments, the 1232nd Cannon Artillery Regiment and the 200th Mortar Regiment from the 68th and 135th Rifle Corps and the army reserve. Altogether on the first day of the enemy offensive, 43 76mm anti-tank guns, 63 122mm howitzers, 10 152mm howitzer cannons and 16 120mm mortars arrived to help repel the Germans.

In addition, the 7th Mechanized Corps, which was backstopping the 20th Guards Rifle Corps, entered the fighting in the very first hours of the enemy offensive and operated jointly with the rifle units. On the evening of 6 January, it had numbered 63 T-34 and 15 IS-2 tanks, as well as 10 SU-85 and 10 SU-76 self-propelled guns, and thus represented a serious counter to German panzer attacks.

If previously Tolbukhin had preferred to use tank units and formations in order to gird his defenses, with the start of the German offensive toward Zámoly, he decided to launch a counter-attack. This change in strategy didn't happen right away. With his first order to the 1st Guards Mechanized Corps, the 3rd Ukrainian Front commander foresaw moving up the 1st Guards Mechanized Brigade into the second echelon of the defending rifle units on the axis of the German offensive. This order was issued at 20.00 on 7 January. The next morning, though, at 10.00 8 January, Tolbukhin changed his mind and re-directed the 1st Guards Mechanized Brigade and the 9th Guards Tank Brigade to counterattack the enemy's shock grouping in the flank. Already by 16.00 8 January, the brigades were nearly poised to go on the attack. However, the counterattack force still hadn't fully assembled by the designated time, and Russianov appealed to the Front commander with a request to postpone the start of the counterattack to the following day. Tolbukhin had no opposition to this, so the counterattack was set for the morning of 9 January. If the counterattack had been designated for this later time from the very outset, the units of Russianov's corps might have been able to reach the jumping-off area at night. However, the enemy detected the movement during the day of 8 January, so the counterattack lost the element of surprise.

The weather became the next blow to Tolbukhin's attempt to use the mechanized units for a counterattack. The commander of the 1st Guards Mechanized Corps recalled:

> That night, as the Guardsmen were moving into their jumping-off lines, snow began to fall, and by morning it was snowing so heavily that nothing was visible beyond 50 meters. The heavy, wet flakes covered up the tanks' vision slits and gun sights, obscuring all vision. However, at 9.30 our artillery struck the fascists' positions, and the tanks and motorized infantry moved out. Extreme attentiveness, care and precise teamwork were required in order not to drift off course and jumble the combat formations, and not to mistake our own units for enemy troops.[1]

The heavy snowfall continued until the middle of the day on 9 January.

Like many other counterattacks staged during defensive operations throughout the war, the counterstroke by the two brigades of the 1st Guards Mechanized Corps near Zámoly was prepared in great haste. The artillery of the 20th Guards Rifle Corps, which was supposed to support them, was located in positions that were suitable for defense, 3 to 5 kilometers behind the front line. At the same time, the cannon brigade had just 225 shells for 20 guns, while the howitzer regiment had 1,000 shells. Thus the artillery preparation was extremely brief, just 3 minutes long. The enemy's anti-tank defenses could not be suppressed by such light activity, and the Sherman tanks were met by heavy anti-tank artillery fire.

The crew of an SU-76 self-propelled gun receives an order; Hungary, 1945.

An 88mm anti-aircraft gun abandoned in its firing position on the approaches to Budapest. (TsAMO)

A knocked-out Tiger tank of the SS Panzer Division *Totenkopf*. (TsAMO)

A close-up view of *Totenkopf*'s knocked-out Tiger tank. The shell hole in the front armor plate is clearly visible. (TsAMO)

An abandoned Bergepanzer III repair-recovery tank. The number "25" was applied by the Soviet inspection team.

A StuG 40 self-propelled gun abandoned on the battlefield. The machine is fitted with a Saukopf gun mantlet and bears the tactical number "712".

Russianov recalled:

> The combat on 9 January was hard and prolonged. The discharges of heavy guns, the explosions of shells, mines and grenades, and the chatter of long machine-gun bursts continued until nightfall on the snow-covered rolling plains south and west of the Hungarian villages of Zámoly, Csala and Pátka. Around noon, the enemy launched strong tank counterattacks out of the area of Gyula. The fascist and Soviet armor vehicles became intermingled at almost pointblank range. The victor was the one who managed to get off the first shot.[2]

By 16.00 9 January both brigades, having suffered heavy losses, were forced to fall back to their jumping-off positions. The 1st Guards Mechanized Brigade lost 19 tanks and had 123 men killed, 210 wounded and 303 missing in action. The 9th Guards Tank Brigade lost 27 tanks, and had 33 men killed, 48 wounded and 4 missing in action. With such results of the day, at 22.00 Russianov received a verbal instruction from Tolbukhin to halt the attacks. It was confirmed by a written order the following morning at 5.00, which gave the two brigades a new assignment to take up lines of defense on the approaches to Zámoly. The 382nd Regiment of SU-100 tank destroyers was moved up to the same place. The firmness of the 1st Guards Mechanized Corps' positions was tested on 11 January, when as a result of 13 attacks, the Germans managed to seize Zámoly. However, they were unable to advance further.

On the night of 8 January 1945, the reinforced SS Panzer Grenadier Regiment *Westland* of the 5th SS Panzer Division *Wiking* was relieved by units of the 6th Panzer Division. The concealment of the relief was facilitated by the mist and heavy snowfall. After a march along the snow-covered roads to the north, the SS troops had re-assembled in the area south of Esztergom [Gran] by the evening of 9 January. Their new assignment was to attack together with units of the 96th and 711th Infantry Divisions in the direction of Budapest. In view of the fact that the march had required almost the entire day, the situation was relatively quiet in the sector of the pending offensive. The divisions of the 46th Army spent the day improving both their front that faced the east on the approaches to Budapest, as well as their front that faced the west.

Soon, *Wiking's* second panzer grenadier regiment *Germania* was also relieved and the entire division assembled on the new axis of attack. In addition to the regrouping of his IV SS Panzer Corps' units, Gille at the initiative of Balck organized the so-called *Gruppe Phillip*, which was to launch a "cavalry charge" along the south riverbank road to Budapest. It was composed, to be sure, not of dashing cavalrymen, but of a reinforced battalion of the *Feldherrnhalle* Division, the bulk of which was encircled in Budapest; for its armored component, Major Phillip's *kampfgruppe* had 5 tanks and 6 armored halftracks. In view of the fact that Soviet troops were holding the opposite bank of the Danube, the very idea of such a breakthrough attempt reeked of adventurism. However, Balck placed great hopes upon it. Approximately 200 tons of various supplies had even been stockpiled in Esztergom [Gran], which were supposed to be delivered to the besieged Hungarian capital in the wake of *Gruppe Phillip's* advance.

Gille's plan was more realistic. He intended to breakthrough to Budapest along the road through the Pilis Mountains, which lie northeast of the Vértes Hills in the bend of the Danube River. However, having barely gotten underway, *Konrad II* was thrown into doubt. On the evening of 9 January, Guderian informed the command of Army Group South about the latest *Führer* order. It was intended to regroup the IV SS Panzer Group further to the south for an outflanking maneuver. However, such a regrouping would have required no less than five days. Army Group South commander General Wöhler persuaded Guderian to give him one more chance to break through to Budapest over the shortest route. At 1.00 10 January, the Chief of the Command Group for the Army General Staff General Wenck reported to Wöhler that his request had been granted, and the operation could continue. Meanwhile, on the night of 9/10 January, the advancing Germans took Szomor.

However, due to some still unknown reasons, the offensive was temporarily suspended. The order to resume the attack followed only close to the evening of 10 January, and the resumption achieved no noticeable successes. As was to be expected, the "cavalry charge" by *Gruppe Phillip* also went nowhere – it was stopped by fire from the northern bank of the Danube. In the conditions when the German high command had already made a choice in favor of regrouping and attacking in the south, bypassing Lake Velence, modest successes meant the cancellation of the operation. Guderian and Wenck gave Wöhler several hours to achieve any sort of notable success. If he failed to achieve it, *Konrad II* would be cancelled and the regrouping would begin.

The use of the entire 5th SS Panzer Division *Wiking* on the left flank of the IV SS Panzer Corps somewhat invigorated its offensive. Pilisszentkereszt, just 20 kilometers from Budapest, was taken by the assault group of SS Panzer Grenadier Regiment *Westland*, and the units of the 46th Army's 99th Rifle Division that were defending it were pushed back to the southeast of the village. It seemed that Budapest was now only a stone's throw away. However, the German high command didn't think so. Guderian informed Wöhler that the *Führer* considered an offensive in the Pilis Mountains to have no prospects. The SS troops were to be immediately pulled out of the fighting on this axis and sent to the new assembly area.

Corps commander Gille attempted to save the situation and made a direct appeal to Himmler. He believed that Himmler had more influence over the *Führer* than Guderian. However, independent of the degree of influence over Hitler, the weightiest argument would be success on the battlefield. Yet the IV SS Panzer Corps still couldn't boast of any. Attempts by Gille's men to seize the village of Dorog on the night of 11/12 January failed. The 86th Guards Rifle Division, reinforced by the 37th Guards Mechanized Brigade of the 2nd Guards Mechanized Corps, withstood the German attacks.

Still, forward elements of the IV SS Panzer Corps were now just 17 kilometers away from Budapest. The attackers could even see the glow above the city and hear the rumble of the cannonade in support of the Soviet assault within the city. However, the question was whether it was possible to cover these remaining kilometers. The German Supreme Command didn't think so.

It is interesting that *Wiking*'s attack wasn't assessed by the Soviet side as a serious threat. The measures taken by the Soviet command speaks most eloquently of the threat it perceived *Wiking*'s attack presented. In view of the sharpening situation in the sector of the 99th Rifle Division in the area of Pilisszentkereszt on 12 January, the commander of the 2nd Guards Mechanized Corps directed just 3 T-34 tanks to that place. At that moment, the 2nd Guards Mechanized Corps had 36 T-34 tanks, and 10 SU-85 and 19 SU-76 self-propelled guns. Thus the departure of the aforementioned T-34s isn't even worth mentioning. The 17th Air Army was inactive due to the poor weather conditions. Therefore the conclusion can be drawn that only minimal efforts were made in order to halt Gille's offensive. The offensive of the IV SS Panzer Corps' left flank was stopped by the forces of Soviet rifle divisions, only insignificantly reinforced with tanks. One can only guess what might have been achieved by the left flank divisions of Gille's IV SS Panzer Corps, had they been reinforced. However, at that moment the decision of the German high command regarding the withdrawal of the SS divisions to a new assembly area was at the very least well-founded.

4

Operation *Paula* Becomes *Konrad III*

By the middle of January 1945, it began to seem that the threat that had unexpectedly taken shape over the 3rd Ukrainian Front was receding. At 2.35 on 17 January, the commander of the 4th Guards Army issued a combat order to the corps commanders:

1. According to information from prisoners and deserters, the enemy is withdrawing SS units from the Budapest axis to the west.
    The possible withdrawal of tank units, which had been operating in the area of Zámoly and Sárkeresztúr is being noted by observers as well.
    Army commanders have been ordered: 1. Strengthen reconnaissance and observation, particularly by officers. Ensure the taking of prisoners in every sector.
2. By the active operations of reconnaissance troops and pursuit detachments, prevent possible enemy attempts in separate sectors to break contact with the aim of taking up more advantageous lines.

As we see, an enemy retreat was seen as a possible scenario. This view virtually discounted the possibility of a new offensive. In fact, at this same time in Poland, three Soviet *fronts* had gone into motion as part of an offensive that went down in history as the Vistula-Oder operation. The German front on the axis leading to Berlin began quickly to fall apart. It was logical to assume that the German panzer divisions, which had been concentrated in Hungary in a period of relative calm on other directions, would return once again to Poland and East Prussia. Hungary, of course, was of definite economic significance for Germany, but defense of the German capital plainly outweighed it.

Intelligence, it seemed, was confirming these logical conclusions. At first, several alarm bells were ringing on the left flank of the 4th Guards Army. Prisoners and deserters from the Hungarian 20th Infantry Division, who had been captured or had crossed the frontline on 13-14 January, were reporting about rumors that were circulating among the soldiers regarding a joint offensive with the Germans. However, there was little trust in the Hungarians. Not long before this, on 10 January, deserters from the Hungarian 8th Infantry Division gave news of the approach of German battalions with the aim of going on the offensive on 11 January. However, no German attacks took place on that date. Other Hungarian deserters on 16 January, on the contrary, gave information on the movement of vehicles belonging to the *Totenkopf* and *Wiking* Divisions from Tata to Komárno, that is, away from the front. Aerial reconnaissance observed German road traffic in various directions, but without any clearly intensified movement in any single direction.

However, all this information proved to be pieces of a picture that was completely different from the one the intelligence officers of the 3rd Ukrainian Front were drawing. Despite problems with fuel supplies, the German command had no intention to use the shortest path in order to switch the IV SS Panzer Corps from the left flank to the right. The divisions of the IV SS Panzer Corps were in fact withdrawn through Komárno to the city of Györ not only for the purpose of returning to their previous sector of the front. Having suffered failure in the offensive over the shortest distance to Budapest, the Germans had decided to change their strategy radically. Now the attack was to come across the favorable tank terrain to the north of Lake Balaton. In documents of the IV SS Panzer Corps, the operation unfolded under the code name *Kräutergarten* ("Herb Garden"), but at the headquarters of *Armeegruppe Balck,* it was called "*Konrad III*". The attacking divisions moved into their jumping-off positions for the offensive literally just several hours before the start of the operation. In these circumstances, there was little hope for the opportune seizure of prisoners by Red Army scouts. The possibilities of aerial reconnaissance were also limited. The Germans conducted the march to the front during the nights with careful concealment from aerial observation during the daylight hours. As a result, Soviet aerial reconnaissance didn't detect the enemy's concentration of forces on the new German offensive axis.

To be just, it must also be said that German intelligence committed a similar miscalculation. In the section "Assessment of the enemy" in the order for the new offensive, signed by the commander of the IV SS Panzer Corps General Gille, it is stated: "The enemy is defending in front of the Corps with the forces of one Guards fortified district, two Guards rifle divisions, and one regular rifle division." This assessment didn't correspond to the real situation on 18 January 1945. The two Guards rifle divisions had already been removed from this front and sent to repel the preceding German offensive in the north. On the axis chosen by the German command only S.I. Nikitin's 1st Guards Fortified District and the 252nd Rifle Division were positioned. To be more precise, the main German attack fell upon the left-flank regiment of the 252nd Division (a front of 5 kilometers) and the entire sector of the 1st Guards Fortified District (a front of 13 kilometers). After *Konrad I* and *Konrad II*, Zakharov's 4th Guards Army had practically exhausted its own reserves. Reserves in the form of the 63rd Mechanized Brigade and a self-propelled artillery regiment, which had been designated at the order of the commander of the 135th Rifle Corps P.V. Gnedin, were distributed equally behind the 135th Rifle Corps' front.

The SS Panzer Divisions *Totenkopf* and *Wiking* were to be the main assault group for *Konrad III*. They were respectively given as attachments the 509th Heavy Panzer Battalion of King Tigers, and the 303rd Assault Gun Brigade. The inadequate amount of forces given the large area for the proposed operation forced the Germans to look for unusual solutions. The assault group of the German 3rd Panzer Division that was operating on the southern flank received the reconnaissance battalions of the 1st and 23rd Panzer Divisions as reinforcements. Its assignment was to make a rapid crossing of the Sió Canal and to hold the line of that canal in order to guard the flank of the main grouping as it was advancing toward Budapest. This canal exits Lake Balaton and flows southeast to the Danube, and thus was a suitable line for repelling Soviet attacks from the south. The 1st Panzer Division was to cover the northern flank – the Germans were anticipating counterattacks from the direction of Székesfehérvár. See Table 2 for the types and amounts of armor of the divisions involved in the operation.

As we see, the number of combat-ready tanks was much smaller than their total number. The losses suffered in the preceding offensives noticeably reduced the shock strength of the four German panzer divisions. Reinforcement of the *Schwerpunkt* was a necessary precondition for the success of Operation *Konrad III*. The fresh 509th Heavy Panzer Battalion (45 King Tigers and 3 self-propelled anti-aircraft guns) was a fine addition, with the help of which it might be possible to batter down the Soviet defenses. The 303rd Assault Gun Brigade entered the battle fully equipped with StuG III (75mm guns) and StuH (105mm guns) self-propelled guns – a total of 45 vehicles. The addition of I Battalion of the 24th Panzer Regiment (which initially belonged to the 24th Panzer Division and numbered 60 Panthers, of which 45 were combat-ready on 19 January 1945) to the 1st Panzer Division's roster was an equally useful reinforcement.

Table 2 Condition of the Tank Park of the 1st, 3rd, 3rd SS and 5th SS Panzer Divisions on 15 January 1945

	1st Panzer	3rd Panzer	3rd SS Panzer *Totenkopf*	5th SS Panzer *Wiking*
Pz. IV	16 (9)	19 (15)	20 (9)	10 (3)
Pz. V Panther	34 (11)	42 (10)	19 (4)	16 (4)
Pz. VI	–	–	? (9)	–
Jg.Pz. IV	–	–	15 (6)	13 (2)
StuGs	2 (1)	11 (9)	31 (15)	5 (0)
Pz.IV(70)	–	12 (9)	–	–

Note: The number to the left of the parentheses gives the total number of tanks and assault guns including those under short-term repair, while the number within the parentheses indicates the number that were serviceable.

Artillery support for the offensive was to be provided by the 403rd Volks Artillery Corps and the 17th Volks Mortar Brigade (equipped with launchers for rocket shells with a caliber from 150mm to 300mm). The Volks Artillery Corps had mixed battalions of 105mm light field howitzers and up to 210mm mortars, as well as 170mm cannons, including captured Soviet 122mm guns. In view of the shortage of aviation fuel, the long-range 170mm cannon were given assignments that were typical for the *Luftwaffe* – to block the approach of Soviet reserves.

In essence, the new plan of the German command was a reincarnation of Operation *Paula*, which had previously been rejected due to the lack of fuel. Problems with attacking through forests and hilly defiles forced a second look at an offensive across the plain. The land between Lake Balaton and Székesfehérvár was almost ideally suitable for tank operations. This was a slightly rolling plain with isolated forests and patches of woods. The snowpack was shallow; in the woods, gullies and wine vineyards, the fresh snow cover reached 20 centimeters, but on the open plains it was only 5 to 10 centimeters deep and offered no hindrance to the maneuver of armor.

Although the terrain between Balaton and Székesfehérvár was more advantageous for the use of armor than the Vértes and Pilis Hills, there was the problem of overcoming canals. In Gille's order it is stated: "After suppressing the initial enemy resistance, the 5th SS Panzer Division, 3rd SS Panzer Division and 1st Panzer Division, paying no attention to a threat to their flanks, will advance to the line of the [Sárviz] canal and seize a bridgehead in order to prevent the enemy from consolidating along the canal, and will secure a crossing of our forces to the opposite bank with the aim of continuing the offensive."

In the situation that the units and formations of the 4th Guards Army were in at the beginning of January 1945, a rapid breakthrough to the Sárviz Canal and the seizure of a crossing over it had been for all practical purposes unrealistic. However, by the morning of 18 January, the defense in this sector had been significantly weakened. The army and Front reserves were positioned behind the center (near Székesfehérvár) and right flank of the 4th Guards Army. The 3rd Ukrainian Front had been given the 133rd Rifle Corps (the 21st, 104th and 122nd Rifle Divisions) from the *Stavka* Reserve, but by 18 January its assembly on the western bank of the Danube hadn't been completed. The only advantage the defense owned was the time that had been spent fortifying the positions between 30/31 December 1944 and 17 January 1945.

The 3rd Ukrainian Front's aviation grouping by the start of the third German offensive had gone through changes in its composition. The combat roster of the 17th Air Army on 17 January 1945 is given in the following numbers (operational/under repair):

La-5 fighters – 148/40;
Iak-3 and Iak-9 fighters – 154/30;
Il-2 ground attack aircraft – 265/33;
B-3 (A-20 Boston bombers) – 97/10;
Po-2 night bombers – 94/2;
Pe-2 reconnaissance aircraft – 18/2;
Iak-9 reconnaissance aircraft – 8/1;
Il-2 artillery spotters – 15/1;
Iak-9 artillery spotters – 9/3.
The total number of operational aircraft was 808.

As we see, the number of Il-2s, in comparison with what the 17th Air Army had at the beginning of January, was significantly reduced. In contrast, the number of fighters grew. Moreover, the composition of the fighter complement had changed – there were more La-5 fighters in the air over Hungary.

The final "signal light" to the Soviet command was the lull in the fighting that was observed on 15 and 16 January 1945 in the sector of defense of the 1st Guards Fortified District. An unusual, unsettling calm settled over the front; the enemy artillery and mortars fell virtually silent. There was also not a single deserter from the Hungarian units. Prior to this, 205 Hungarians had come across the lines by 15 January 1945, an average of more than 10 a day. On 16 January, however, the flow of deserters suddenly ceased. The lack of deserters suggested that the Germans had taken over this sector of the front from the Hungarians. On the night of 17/18 January, the silence was disturbed by the rumbling of motors, the sound of carts, and even human voices that were being carried by the wind. At the same time, the Germans were tightly sealing their front lines; Soviet scouting parties and reconnaissance probes were unable to penetrate the front line.

At 6.30 on 18 January, after a short artillery preparation, four German panzer divisions went on the offensive. Faithful to their tactics, the Germans attacked several sectors and concentrated their forces on narrow fronts. In the section in his attack orders regarding the Soviet defenses, Gille stated: "The combat capability of a fortified district on the defensive should be rated as high." However, in the given case the Germans were overrating the capabilities of the 1st Guards Fortified District. A fortified district was fine for covering passive sectors of the front. Despite the fact that it had 90% of its table strength, Major General Nikitin's 1st Guards Fortified District numbered just 3,122 men, 38 76mm guns, 31 45mm guns, 7 120mm mortars, 32 82mm mortars, 129 heavy machine guns and 124 light machine guns. Nikitin had four battalions in his front line and one in reserve. Only the sectors of the front that were covering routes vulnerable to tanks or roads were mined.

The artillery battalions of the Fortified District met the attacking German tanks with fire from their 45mm anti-tank guns, but their shells ricocheted harmlessly off the armor. The guns were shot up at pointblank range or were crushed beneath tank treads. The fire of the 76mm anti-tank guns was somewhat more effective, but there were few of them. Unfortunately, there were no SU-100 tank destroyer elements on the path of the King Tigers of the 509th Heavy Panzer Battalion. They had all shifted to the 4th Guards Army's right flank. The anti-tank reserve of the 135th Rifle Corps commander was the 1202nd Self-propelled Artillery Regiment, which was equipped with 20 SU-76. This regiment had only just received the brand new SU-76 self-propelled guns straight from the factory and had taken its place within the 4th Guards Army shortly before the described events. On 18 January it found itself in the path of *Totenkopf*, which had been reinforced with King Tigers. The lightly armored SU-76 could offer no serious resistance to the heavy tanks, although they tried to open fire at the King Tigers at a pointblank range from 100 to 150 meters with armor-piercing discarding-sabot shells. Over the day, 12 SU-76 were left burned out,

Commander of the 18th Tank Corps Major General of Tank Forces P.D. Govorunenko.

A knocked-out German Panther tank. The penetrating shell hole is clearly visible in the upper forward armor.

A burned-out German Panther Ausf. G tank. The tank has plainly "settled" as a result of the collapse of the torsion bars due to the fire. (TsAMO)

A Hummel self-propelled artillery vehicle destroyed by artillery fire. The number "5" has been painted on by the Soviet inspection team.

6 more were disabled, and one became bogged down and was blown up by its crew. Having lost practically all its vehicles, the once again "horseless" regiment retreated to the east. If the anti-tank defenses of the 1st Guards Fortified District proved to be weak, its electrified barbed wire entanglements showed themselves to be highly effective – according to Soviet data, the remains of up to 200 German soldiers were found on them.

The rupturing of the 1st Guards Fortified District's front enabled the 1st Panzer Division to envelop the left flank of the 252nd Rifle Division defending to the north and to emerge in its rear. Its left-flank 928th Rifle Regiment was encircled and its men were attempting to break out in small groups. The 932nd Rifle Regiment defending on the right of it was compelled to fall back to the line of a canal flowing south of Székesfehérvár, where it took up a new line of defense. Having penetrated the forward units of the 135th Rifle Corps, the attacking German tanks quickly advanced to Úrhida, where the headquarters of the 135th Rifle Corps was located. Command and control over the corps was lost.

The quick collapse of the 135th Rifle Corps' defenses led to the fact that the anti-tank reserves that were moving up to the front went into action from the march, having no time to prepare positions. The 1249th Destroyer Anti-tank Regiment of the 49th Destroyer Anti-tank Brigade already at 8.30 18 January was taken from its current positions and sent to block the path of advance of the German tanks. The regiment moved out toward Lepsény on the southern flank of the German offensive, which was 10 kilometers behind the starting front lines. The 1249th Destroyer Anti-tank Regiment was equipped with captured German 75mm anti-tank guns. However, it simply had no time to prepare positions. Already en route to the designated area, at 13.00 18 January the anti-tank regiment came under fire from German tanks, which were from the forward units of the 3rd Panzer Division that was advancing toward the Sió Canal. The regiment was forced to deploy hastily and to accept battle from the march. The attacking panzers quickly enveloped the unprepared positions and overran the guns. The regiment quickly lost all 19 of its anti-tank guns. The same fate befell the 438th Destroyer Anti-tank Regiment on the northern flank of the German offensive. It also went into battle from the march, deployed under fire, and quickly lost all 21 of the guns it had.

One of the first mechanized formations that rushed to meet the new German offensive was the 7th Mechanized Corps. It was positioned in the vicinity of Székesfehérvár, from which point it could move quickly to the south into the sector of the neighboring 135th Rifle Corps. Tolbukhin quickly gave the 7th Mechanized Corps the assignment to take up a front behind the crumbling positions of the 1st Guards Fortified District. However, attacked by the freshly arrived Panthers and King Tigers, the defense of the Fortified District's artillery battalions collapsed too quickly, before the mechanized brigades could move up to support them. Units of the 7th Mechanized Corps bumped into the enemy while on the march, without a compact front, and wound up enveloped as the enemy tanks exploited the gaps between their rolling columns. As a result they were forced to fall back to the Sárviz Canal. However, it should be noted that for the heavy tanks of the 509th Heavy Panzer Battalion, the first day of the offensive was not a holiday stroll. Over the day, 11 King Tigers were lost, 7 of them irrecoverably. The battalion's advance came to a halt in front of the demolished bridges across the Sárviz Canal.

The 93rd Rifle Division and elements of the 252nd Rifle Division reached the Sárviz Canal. However, the blown-up bridges managed to check only the left-flank grouping of IV SS Panzer Corps. Further to the south, the canal's bank was totally undefended, and the two SS panzer divisions were able to push on to the east against no resistance. The half-measure in the form of frontline courses of junior lieutenants and the battalions of reserve regiments that were thrown into battle were unable to hold the German attackers for very long.

The 18th Tank Corps could become the lifeline in this situation. It had already played an important role in the defensive battles in the first days of January. By the start of Operation *Konrad III*, it had retained its combat effectiveness – on 17 January the 18th Tank Corps numbered 66 T-34, 8 ISU-122 and 5 SU-85 in service. Govorunenko's corps had again become subordinate to Front command and was positioned in an area southwest of Budapest. Reports had come in from deserters and prisoners about a prepared breakout attempt by the encircled garrison to the west, and the 18th Tank Corps was supposed to prevent it. The position on the path of a possible breakout from Budapest was not particularly satisfactory for use of the corps on the left flank of the 4th Guards Army. The tankers and motorized riflemen would have to show miraculous speed. But already at 17.00 on 18 January, the brigades of the 18th Tank Corps were moving out in order to take up a defense along the line of the Sárviz Canal. The new defensive positions had to be occupied by 8.00 19 January.

However, in view of the rapid advance of the German divisions that had broken into operational space, the idea of creating a new front along the line of the Sárviz Canal proved to be stillborn and could not be realized. By the end of day 18 January, there were no Soviet forces whatsoever on the line of the canal in the area of the town of Sárkeresztúr. As a consequence of this, the attacking SS units were able to create a bridgehead across the canal unhindered, put down bridges across it, and continue their further advance to the east that night. Accordingly, the brigades of the 18th Tank Corps entered combat on the morning of 19 January short of the canal, deprived of any good defensive terrain.

The arrival of the divisions of Gille's IV SS Panzer Corps at the Sárviz Canal cut the path of retreat for the artillery units of the 135th Rifle Corps. Fighting in encirclement, they quickly expended their available ammunition and lost a number of guns and mortars to enemy tank and artillery fire, as well as to overrunning enemy tanks. In this situation, the artillerymen disabled their remaining guns and attempted to break out on foot.

The situation increasingly began to bring back to mind episodes of the summer of 1941. For even greater similarity, the situation in the air changed for a period of time. The *Luftwaffe* managed to seize the initiative. The 4th Guards Army's journal of combat operations has an eloquent entry about the *Luftwaffe*'s activities for 19 January: "The skies cleared, and the enemy air force reigned supreme in the air, meeting no resistance on the part of our air force." Similar words can be found as well in the 252nd Rifle Division's journal of combat operations:

> The enemy air force conducted active operations with Me-109 aircraft, which strafed and bombed our baggage trains, vehicles loaded with ammunition, and approaching reserves of infantry and artillery, thereby creating traffic jams at crossroads and canal crossings, as a result of which the regular supply of ammunition, food and fuel was disrupted, as well as the reinforcement of our units operating at the front with personnel and equipment.

Soviet units in Hungary in January 1945 for a short spell were experiencing the same thing as those who had heard the melancholy howl of the Stuka dive sirens in the summers of 1941 and 1942.

For the sake of justice, it needs to be said that the similarity was mostly superficial. The Messerschmitts loaded with 50kg and 250kg bombs were, of course, less dangerous as strike aircraft than the Stukas loaded with 500kg bombs that were precisely delivered out of dives. Moreover, the dozens of sorties of fighter-bombers in no way compared with the 800-1,000 individual bomber sorties on the axes of the main attacks of the German forces in the most terrible days for the Red Army. In addition, the activity of the 17th Air Army on 18 January, despite the poor weather, was rather high – 718 individual sorties, the majority of which were ground attack missions (547 individual combat sorties by fighters and Il-2s). Soviet pilots engaged in 48 aerial combats, in which they claimed downing 19 Me-109s and 18 FW-190s. In comparison, over the entire month of January 1945, there were 327 aerial combats, which meant the single day of 18 January comprised 15% of all the month's air battles.

The emergence of the Germans into operational space allowed them to strike out simultaneously in several directions, thereby increasing the perimeter of the wedge they had driven into the 3rd Ukrainian Front's sector. It was no longer possible to seal off this penetration with the introduction of reserves and formations taken from quiet sectors. The 18th Tank Corps and units of the 133rd Rifle Corps that were moving toward the Sárviz Canal wound up enveloped from the north and south. Isolated from the Front's main forces, they in fact fell into encirclement. The pocket around them was still not continuous; the encirclement was mostly perceptible in the cutting of main lines of supply, and not complete encirclement by enemy tanks and infantry in solid lines in all directions.

After enveloping and encircling the tank and rifle corps from the Front reserve, the units of Gille's IV SS Panzer Corps no longer faced any obstacles for a further advance to the east. On the afternoon of 19 January, the IV SS Panzer Corps reached the Danube River and the 3rd Panzer Division took Dunapentele [present-day Dunaújváros, which grew up around the former village]. The situation had deteriorated to the point where the 3rd Ukrainian Front command was given the right to determine for itself whether it should continue to hold the bridgehead on the western bank of the Danube or to abandon it. Marshal F.I. Tolbukhin, in a later assessment of the actions of our troops in the area of Lake Balaton in January 1945 stated:

> After the enemy breakthrough to the Danube, the situation for the troops of the 3rd Ukrainian Front became difficult for the first time. The southern flank of the breakthrough was open, and this threatened the 57th Army, 1st Bulgarian Army and 12th Yugoslav Corps, which were occupying positions southeast of Lake Balaton and along the Drava River to its mouth, with encirclement. The pontoon crossings on the Danube were swept away on one night by a storm. The Front headquarters was in the town of Paks, and enemy panzer reconnaissance units were approaching. … Frankly speaking, the situation was dangerous, and we were given the opportunity to decide the question regarding the further usefulness of holding the bridgehead west of the Danube. It was distasteful to fall back behind the Danube: Vienna would become distant, and in the near future there was no hope for a second forced crossing of the Danube, given the enemy's organized defense of it.[1]

As we see, the Soviet command initially viewed the German offensive as an attempt to eliminate the bridgehead held by the 3rd Ukrainian Front on the western bank of the Danube. In reality, the prospect of an attack around the eastern end of Lake Balaton into the rear of the 57th Army also looked threatening. The uncertainty about the enemy plans at first forced the 3rd Ukrainian Front command to allocate its reserves cautiously. The 2nd Ukrainian Front's 30th Rifle Corps, which had been freed up as a result of the successful storming of Budapest before being transferred to Tolbukhin's operational control, was sent to cover the area between Lake Balaton and the Danube River. However, without cooperation among *Armeegruppe Balck*, the 2nd Panzer Army and the main *Südöst* command in the Balkans, such an operation was unrealizable. It should be said that the German command did plan an offensive by the 2nd Panzer Army on this axis. It received the code name *Eisbrecher* ["Icebreaker"]. A start date of 25 January 1945 had even been set for the offensive, but on 24 January an order arrived from the OKH (*Oberkommando des Heeres*, or Supreme Command of the Army) that indefinitely postponed "Icebreaker". In a word, the German command didn't use even the possibility of confusing the enemy regarding the real objective of the new offensive.

Incidentally, even without a clear idea of the enemy's plans regarding the bridgehead as a whole, the situation was threatening. The enemy's rapid advance to the Danube led to the total expenditure of the reserves located in the depth of the 4th Guards Army's dispositions. Despite the diversion of part of the attacking force in order to encircle the 18th Tank Corps and 133rd Rifle Corps, the

Soviet troops were unable to block the enemy's further advance in all directions. The catastrophes of 1941 and 1942 had unfolded according to just the same scenario. If the Danube River hadn't been backstopping the collapsed front, but instead the Front's rear services, the Germans might have made a deep penetration just as they did in Operations *Blau* and *Barbarossa*. Tolbukhin's task was simpler than that of restoring a broken front. The Germans' task was to break through to Budapest, the path to which lay through the gap between Lake Velence and the Danube. The width of this gap was just 17 kilometers, and it was much easier to organize a strong defense based on this narrow neck of land than to rebuild an enormous, shattered front.

However, the commander of the 4th Guards Army no longer had the reserves even for manning a line across a 17-kilometer front. In connection with this, G.F. Zakharov was given control of the 5th Guards Cavalry Corps, the 1st Guards Mechanized Brigade of the 1st Guards Mechanized Corps, the 145th Regiment of SU-100 tank destroyers and a number of artillery units, all from the Front reserve. General Gorshkov's cavalry corps was used to defend the corridor of ground between Lake Velence and the Danube, through which the Germans might break through to Budapest.

In general, a Red Army cavalry division or corps was substantially weaker than its infantry counterpart. However, in the realities of 1945, given the fact that the rifle divisions on average had been reduced by casualties and the lack of replacements to 4,000 – 5,000 men, the cavalry division now looked quite different in comparison. The Red Army's mobile formations, which were its most valuable asset, were better maintained. According to data for 20 January 1945, the 5th Guards Cavalry Corps numbered 17,801 officers and men, 86 45mm and 76mm anti-tank guns, 7 SU-76 self-propelled guns and 26 tanks, which together with its mobility made it an important trump card in the hands of the 3rd Ukrainian Front command.

The cavalrymen received the order to move out to a new line of defense on 19 January from its current area of assembly to the west of Budapest. Now it faced a 95-kilometer march to take up a defense between Lake Velence and the Danube River. The three cavalry divisions began feverishly to construct their defensive positions only around midnight 19 January. Given only several hours of work, the defensive line could hardly have withstood an attack by the IV SS Panzer Corps' main forces. However, the expected mortal blow against the cavalrymen's hastily-prepared positions didn't come at dawn the following morning. Up until 14.00 20 January, the Germans didn't show any activity at all on this key axis for them. At that point, they limited themselves to probes of the defenses in small groups of tanks and infantry. The reason was simply a matter of supply. According to the testimony of prisoners that were seized by the Cossacks, the panzers of Gille's corps on this sector were immobilized by the lack of fuel for the entire day.

The prisoner testimony is confirmed by enemy documents. The German assault grouping, which had made a deep penetration, was actually experiencing supply difficulties. The fact that Soviet troops retained possession of Székesfehérvár, which was a major road hub, seriously complicated the work of the IV SS Panzer Corps' supply units. The weather conditions complicated their work even further. At 2.00 20 January, as the Soviet cavalrymen were feverishly readying a defense, the German Sixth Army's *Oberquartiermeister* [Chief quartermaster] was reporting to *Armeegruppe Balck's* chief of staff: "As a result of the snowfall and strong winds, extremely deep snowdrifts have formed, which are causing lengthy delays in the movement of columns. The delivery of items of supply is being badly delayed."[2]

The 18th Tank Corps and 133rd Rifle Corps, encircled in the Aba – Sárkeresztúr area, played a prominent role in tying down Gille's panzer corps. Even in encirclement, they created a threat to the lines of communication of the SS *Wiking* and 3rd Panzer Divisions that had reached the Danube. At this moment, Govorunenko's tank corps numbered a total of 64 armored vehicles that were still operational, including 51 T-34, 8 ISU-122 and 5 SU-76. In addition, rifle units had fallen into encirclement together with the tankers. This presented a threat to the German lines of communication which the Germans could not ignore, so they could not tarry with the elimination

A knocked-out King Tiger of the 509th Heavy Panzer Battalion. The tank was struck by a shell in the flank in the vicinity of its engine compartment.

One more knocked-out King Tiger. Its tactical marking, the letter "G", is visible on the tank's front armor.

A disabled Panther Ausf. A in Hungary, January 1945. (TsAMO)

A close-up view of the flank of the tank in the preceding photograph. Plainly, it has been literally riddled with anti-tank rounds. Note the roller wheels that have been shot through by armor-piercing shells.

of the pocket. In the blitzkrieg period of 1939-1941, the destruction of encircled enemy units would likely have been handed over to infantry following in the panzers' wake. In January 1945, no longer were there columns of infantry marching behind the panzer spearheads. Thus, the IV SS Panzer Corps had to deal with the encircled Soviet units itself. A strong detachment with tanks was formed from *Wiking* and sent back to the west. This detachment stumbled across the 18th Tank Corps headquarters and subjected it to shelling.

Together with the seizure of Seregélyes by *Totenkopf* on 20 January, the situation around the two encircled Soviet corps became dire. Tolbukhin ordered the corps commanders to break out to the south. The choice of an axis for breakout, strictly speaking, was limited. To the east lay the Danube, which might have been crossed and would have allowed a link-up with friendly forces on its eastern bank, but in the best case this would have come at a heavy cost in combat and auxiliary equipment. This was totally unacceptable, even setting aside the complexities of making a river crossing by the encircled units. To the north were Lake Velence and the 17-kilometer-wide corridor between it and the Danube River. Here, the presence of main enemy forces would have complicated the passage of the front lines. The columns of the encircled troops would have been simply destroyed on their approach to join back up with friendly forces. Only one path remained – to the south.

For the breakout from encirclement, the units and formations of the two corps were split into two separate columns. The right-hand (western) column included the 181st Tank Brigade, the 21st Rifle Division, and a portion of the 122nd Rifle Division. The left-hand (eastern) column consisted of the 110th and 170th Tank Brigades, the 32nd Motorized Rifle Brigade, and the 104th Rifle Division. The headquarters of the two corps were moving in this same column. A collateral effect of the 18th Tank Corps' and 133rd Rifle Corps' breakout from encirclement became the loss of the 4th Guards Army's main supply base at Sárosd Station. The supplies of the troops defending on the entire front from the Danube to Lake Balaton flowed through it. The swiftly unfolding German offensive forced extreme measures to be taken to evacuate the supply stockpiles. On the night of 19/20 January, 37 train cars had been loaded with supplies and sent out. However, naturally there was no time to evacuate the stockpiles completely. For a certain time, the stockpiles remained in an area still controlled by the two encircled corps. However, this couldn't sustain their existence for very long. On the night of 21/22 January, as the Germans approached the station, the remaining stockpiles were torched or blown up. For a long time, the breakout attempt by the encircled Soviet units was accompanied by a fireworks display in the night sky from the 60 burning train cars of ammunition.

The breakout began at 12.00 20 January. The scenarios for both columns were approximately identical: they moved out to the south, toward evening bumped into German blocking forces, and attempted to fight their way through them. The right-hand column met stubborn enemy resistance in the area of the Heinrich Estate. Gathering the tank brigade into a fist, at 19.00 they launched a second attack and successfully broke through. Here the 181st Tank Brigade lost 9 tanks. Having broken through and with enemy pursuers snapping at their heels, the Soviet tankers and infantrymen spent all night fighting their way to the south, and came out of the encirclement on the morning of 21 January. By this time, the 181st Tank Brigade had just 4 tanks left. The losses of the 181st Tank Brigade amounted to 17 T-34 tanks and 2 M-17 halftracks. In addition, its commander Lieutenant Colonel Kublanov was wounded.

The second column came out of the encirclement and reached the area of Herczegfalva with fewer losses – its trump card and battering ram was the regiment of ISU-122 self-propelled guns. The retained combat potential became quickly necessary, because on the following day Herczegfalva was attacked by the German 3rd Panzer Division. In the course of the day of 22 January, the 110th Tank Brigade was involved in heavy fighting for possession of that town. Its losses amounted to 16 T-34 and 2 SU-85. The 18th Tank Corps was kept afloat through replacements – it received 18 T-34 tanks and 20 SU-76 offloaded from trains.

The situation of Govorunenko's tank corps at that moment was of a dual nature. On the one hand, by coming out of encirclement, the units of the two corps relieved the German command of the thorns left embedded in rear of the advancing units. On the other hand, the southern flank of the German offensive was now more vulnerable. The emergence of the Soviet tank corps here created the prerequisites for an effective counterstroke. Finally, the stubborn defense of Herczegfalva, which continued for several days, tied up the German 3rd Panzer Division. In effect, the forces of the four mobile divisions of Gille's panzer corps were now dispersed across a broad front and were attacking in various directions.

The absence of one or two infantry corps, advancing in the wake of the tanks, substantially complicated not only the struggle with the two encircled Soviet corps, but also made the defense of the flanks more difficult. The southern flank of the German assault grouping was in essence being covered by a sparse screen of reconnaissance battalions, one panzer division, and one Hungarian infantry division. The fact that a panzer division and panzer reconnaissance battalions were being forced to screen the offensive greatly diluted the strength of the German assault grouping. Formally, these forces were subordinate to the 3rd Hungarian Army.

The lack of infantry was telling not only on the southern flank, but also on the northern flank in the area of Székesfehérvár. At the beginning of January, the penetration in the direction of Zámoly had extended beyond this city to the north. As a result of the new German offensive, Székesfehérvár was bypassed and enveloped from the south. The 69th Guards Rifle Division of the 21st Guards Rifle Corps, which had been positioned with its front to the west, was regrouped to this axis. It had been forced to extend its front greatly in connection with the collapse of the 135th Rifle Corps' defense and the retreat of Soviet forces to the east. As a result the defending lines around this important road hub were substantially thinned in order to meet this new German threat. Moreover, the city was now virtually semi-encircled. The reliable bulwark of the infantry in the preceding fighting – the 7th Mechanized Corps – was withdrawn from combat by 22 January. It left behind only the composite 16th Brigade, which numbered a total of 4 T-34, 1 SU-85, 3 IS-2 and 2 SU-76. This brigade was sent to defend the northern shoreline of Lake Velence and it was no longer involved in the fighting for Székesfehérvár. However, the defenders of the city were still left with tank units – the 9th Guards Tank Brigade and the 382nd Regiment of SU-100 tank destroyers, which had been transferred from the 1st Guards Mechanized Corps, were operationally subordinate to the 21st Guards Rifle Corps. In these days they were continually being shuffled from place to place around Székesfehérvár's defensive perimeter, because there was no advance knowledge of where the main German assault would be delivered.

Attacks on Székesfehérvár with the united flanks of Breith's and Gille's panzer corps had started already on 20 January. The 23rd Panzer Division was attacking the city from the northwest, while the 1st Panzer Division, reinforced by a fresh Panther battalion (I/24 Panzer Regiment), attacked from the south and southeast. *Kampfgruppe Phillip*, known to us from Operation *Konrad II*, was operating on this same axis. SS Regiment *Ney*, composed of Hungarian volunteers (approximately 2,000 men) was providing the link between the two panzer corps. By the way, this regiment was not named after Napoleon Bonaparte's marshal, but for the name of its Hungarian commander, Karole Nei.

The attack's main assault group was the 1st Panzer Division; the rest of the German and Hungarian units were pinning down the Soviet units elsewhere around the perimeter defending the city. Sooner or later, the Germans would have to detect a weakness in the Soviet defenses. An attack on the following morning, 22 January, by the 1st Panzer Division broke into the center of Székesfehérvár from the south. The appearance of enemy tanks in the city center caused a panic and the hasty retreat from the positions on the approaches to it. Already that same day, defensive positions to the east of Székesfehérvár began to be prepared at Zakharov's order. At 18.00 22

January, the city which had been taken with fighting back in December 1944 was abandoned by its Soviet defenders.

The situation by the end of 22 January could to a certain degree be characterized by the following words from a report of the 3rd Ukrainian Front's deputy chief of the Political Department, Katunin: "The overall disorderly retreat by the units of the 21st Guards Rifle Corps continued until nightfall. Blocking detachments that were deployed restored order and returned those who were fleeing back to their units. Control over the troops at lower levels of command are as before absent; individual commanders, especially artillerymen, have lost their units."

In order to restore the front near Székesfehérvár, the 4th Guards Army commander was given the 223rd Rifle Division from the 46th Army. In this manner, yet one more potential reserve was expended in order to avert a crisis on a previously quiet sector of the front.

However, it mustn't be said that the assessment of these events on the enemy's part was unanimous. The offensive toward Székesfehérvár from the south was conducted at the order of the IV SS Panzer Corps command. Subsequently Gille's decision was subjected to sharp criticism on Balck's part. He argued that the storming of Székesfehérvár was a diversion and a waste of time that could have been used by the 1st Panzer Division instead for pushing forward before a solid line of defense could be built between Lake Velence and the Danube from the reserves of the 3rd Ukrainian Front. However, this disregards the vital necessity of seizing Székesfehérvár in view of its location astride the IV SS Panzer Corps' lines of communication. Balck was clearly aware of this. He had been informed of the situation by the *Oberquartiermeister* of the German Sixth Army back on 20 January 1945: "In the area of combat operations southeast of Stuhlweissenburg [Székesfehérvár], the movement of supplies is often interrupted due to the heavy action of hostile fire. Because of this, delays are being created in the delivery of food and ammunition."[3]

With the capture of Székesfehérvár, this threat was eliminated. Moreover, *Armeegruppe Balck* was now able to reduce its front substantially and to eliminate a threat from the flank. However, General Balck was unquestionably correct regarding one point: the need to regroup the 1st Panzer Division forced the postponement of the start date for the decisive offensive toward Budapest through the corridor between Lake Velence and the Danube River. During the blitzkrieg era, the secondary task of expanding the hole torn in the enemy front by the panzers would have been taken on by the infantry. However, Balck didn't have an adequate amount of infantry under his command.

On the whole, though, Balck's carping and concerns regarding the loss of time were unfounded. The defense of the 5th Guards Cavalry Corps in the neck of land between Lake Velence and the Danube was steadily being reinforced. The 1st Guards Mechanized Corps, while remaining subordinate to Front command, was parceled out by brigade among the various sectors of the 4th Guards Army's defense. As already noted above, one brigade was in Székesfehérvár, and the 3rd Mechanized Brigade had been transferred to the 46th Army. The remaining two brigades of the 1st Guards Mechanized Corps were assembled on the axis of the SS IV Panzer Corps' main attack. By 8.00 on the morning of 21 January, the 2nd Mechanized Brigade had taken up a defense in the Kápolnásnyék – Baracska area. These villages soon became the scene of fierce combat. Despite their rural locations, they consisted of stone houses, often with deep cellars, while brick enclosures provided additional benefits to the defenders.

One of the veterans of that fighting briefly, but succinctly described the occupied positions: "Baracska was distinguished by its particular geographic location. From the village, it was just a stone's throw to Budapest: 30 kilometers over an excellent paved road. In other words, in a strategic respect Baracska was a key point on the approaches to the Hungarian capital."[4] In a word, there was a clear motivation to hold the designated positions. In addition to the Sherman tanks of the 2nd Guards Mechanized Brigade, two batteries of SU-100 tank destroyers and anti-tank artillery moved into the streets of the Hungarian villages. The 1st Guards Mechanized Brigade

A bogged down and abandoned Tiger of the *Totenkopf* Division.

together with a regiment of SU-100 tank destroyers took up a defense in the neighboring sector on the Vali River. A day later the defense of the 5th Guards Cavalry Corps received a "safety cushion" behind its positions in the form of the 252nd and 113th Rifle Divisions, which had been shifted from quieter sectors of the front. The 252nd Rifle Division moved into its positions behind the 5th Guards Cavalry Corps already by 10.00 22 January, several hours before Székesfehérvár fell. The defense cobbled together by Tolbukhin was ready to withstand the next attack.

It shouldn't be thought that while the assault against Székesfehérvár was underway, the two SS panzer divisions of Gille's IV SS Panzer Corps had been sitting idly by. They weren't even discouraged by the march of the 509th Heavy Panzer Battalion of King Tigers toward Felsöbesnyö on 21 January, when as a result of the marshy terrain and engine stress 6 of the 12 heavy tanks broke down. The SS undertook an attempt to break through to the Vali River and to seize a bridgehead across it. *Totenkopf* struck on the left flank by Lake Velence, while *Wiking* attacked on the right, closer to the Danube. On 21 January, *Totenkopf*'s attack cut off a regiment of the 63rd Cavalry Division from the remainder of the division's forces and pressed it back against the lake. A much stronger attack followed on 22 January. The SS Panzer Division *Wiking* struck the boundary between the 11th and 12th Cavalry Divisions. The defenders estimated the strength of the enemy's attacking force as "more than 100 tanks and self-propelled guns." According to a report from *Wiking* for 21 January, however, it had just 3 Pz IV, 5 Pz V, and 4 Jagdpanzer IV still serviceable, though it also had the attached 303rd Assault Gun Brigade numbering 34 self-propelled guns (26 StuG and 8 StuH). Thus, the SS armored battering ram at that moment consisted primarily of *Sturmgeschütz* assault guns. The Germans managed to drive a narrow wedge into the Soviet defenses, 3 kilometers wide and 5 kilometers deep. SS *Wiking*'s spearhead reconnaissance battalion reached the area of Agg. Szentpéter and even forced a crossing of the Vali, where it became isolated. On 23 January, after several attacks, the Germans re-established connection with it and tenaciously clung to Agg. Szentpéter.

The next powerful attack came at 22.00 on 23 January, when the 1st Panzer Division and the 403rd Volks Artillery Corps, having regrouped from Székesfehérvár joined the offensive. The newly arriving forces didn't achieve great successes, but enabled *Totenkopf*, which had turned over part of its sector to them, to break through toward Baracska from the southwest. A report from the commander of the 5th Guards Cavalry Corps at 6.00 24 January 1945 conveys the atmosphere of what was happening: "Remnants of the combat formations are fighting piecemeal. Contact exists with the 11th and 12th Cavalry Divisions but not with the 63rd Cavalry Division. It managed to transmit "Approaching the command post – 20 [enemy] tanks." As a result of the deep German penetrations into the Soviet defenses, the commander of the 5th Guards Cavalry Corps General Gorshkov ordered a withdrawal of the units and formations subordinate to him to the second line, which was located on average 4 kilometers behind the first.

At last, on 24 January there came a general German offensive with the participation of the three panzer divisions of Gille's IV SS Panzer Corps. However, the attackers were unable to achieve a decisive result in the day's fighting. An important advantage of the second line of defense was a swampy valley with a broad and deep canal flowing down the middle of it that obstructed the approaches to Baracska from the south. The Soviet defensive positions overlooked this valley and canal. Four German tanks attempted to cross it, but became stuck and were left burning by Soviet artillery.

It seemed at last that a firm barrier had been erected in the path of the relief offensive toward Budapest. The German command had the same impression. At the command post of the IV SS Panzer Corps, Army Group South commander Wöhler and the commander of *Armeegruppe Balck* held a meeting to discuss what to do next and who was to blame. Gille, whose name was on Balck's tongue as the answer to the latter question, was absent from the meeting – he was up at one of the forward *kampfgruppe*. Thus, the commander of the army group and the commander of the group of armies reached a decision without him. There is an entry in the journal of combat operations of Army Group South regarding the results of the discussion: "As today's experience showed, a frontal attack upon the firm and deeply echeloned enemy defense beyond the Vali provides no chance for a successful breakthrough." In addition, the commander of Army Group South was troubled by the presence of the grouping of Soviet forces to the north of Lake Velence that was looming over the left flank. As a result, the decision was made to turn the spearhead of the attack to the northwest. The IV SS Panzer Corps now was to pivot 90 degrees. It was directed to attack toward Bicske and to encircle the Soviet forces to the north of Lake Velence in conjunction with Breith's III Panzer Corps and the Hungarian VIII Corps.

The motivations for such a decision are rather obvious. Retaining the initiative and launching an encircling attack, the attacker would thereby tear a hole out of the defender's front and force him to rebuild anew an intact front. The defensive arrangement would thereby dissolve, and a hope for a successful breakthrough on the desired axis would appear. However, Balck's and Wöhler's joint decision would later be subjected to sharp criticism, in particular from the historiographer of the Sixth SS Panzer Army Georg Maier, who argues that staying on the former direction of attack better corresponded to resolving the main task – a breakthrough to Budapest. It is also doubtless that time was an important factor. It makes sense to punch through and roll back a sector of the enemy's defensive front in those conditions when the defending grouping is static and cannot be reinforced. However, in the case with the 3rd Ukrainian Front, this wasn't so – reserves, taken from the neighboring 2nd Ukrainian Front, were already approaching.

Gille, who believed it necessary to attack not to the northwest, but to the northeast (toward Budapest), knew better than the others the situation facing his panzer divisions, as well as their own capabilities. The fighting on 24 January not only demonstrated the stoutness of the defenses along the Vali River. The 5th Guards Cavalry Corps' first line of defense had extended for 18 kilometers, but the second line stretched for 24 kilometers. After the pullback to the second line, the defensive front became extended, but the troops defending it had suffered losses and their capabilities had decreased. The 252nd Rifle Division, which had been shifted in order to reinforce the cavalrymen, had been badly battered already on the first day of the German offensive. One of the primary principles of German offensives was to attack on a narrow front. In so doing, efforts are focused on a single point within the salient of a penetration in the Soviet defense. In contrast, the defenders are compelled to cover the entire perimeter of the inner salient in their lines relatively equally, with no prior knowledge of where the attack would come. In this situation, the attacker would be guaranteed to secure a large numerical superiority on the chosen direction of his main attack. The stretching of the Soviet defensive front with practically no changes in the forces available to hold it would increase the Germans' chance for success with their next attack.

Subsequent events quickly demonstrated the strengths and weaknesses of 5th Guards Cavalry Corps' defense. The pivoting of the attacking spearhead by 90 degrees didn't happen right away – most of the day of 25 January was spent regrouping the forces. Once again, as in the course of *Konrad II*, the SS units had to assume a defensive posture 18 kilometers outside of Budapest and regroup for a new attack. Now the axis of the main attack was directed toward the Pettend farmsteads, which lay along the road running northeast to Budapest between Lake Valence and Baracska. The farmsteads had been converted into a defensive strongpoint. It was being defended by units of the 63rd Cavalry Division, as well as a submachine gun company, 5 Sherman tanks and 5 SU-100 tank destroyers from the 1st Guards Mechanized Corps. They held out for seven hours in the battle which started before sunup, and in the end almost all the defenders were killed. It must be said that the casualties of the 1st Guards Mechanized Corps in these battles were rather heavy; altogether between 19 and 25 January, the corps lost 54 Sherman tanks and 17 SU-100s.

Having broken through along the highway leading to Budapest, the Germans overran the defenses of Gorshkov's group to its entire depth. German tanks even broke into the firing positions of the 877th Howitzer Artillery Regiment. They also managed to outflank the Soviet strong point in Baracska further along the road to Budapest. Nevertheless, the SS troops failed to take Baracska. Here, the Soviet air force played a major role in repelling the enemy attacks. The commander of the 5th Guards Cavalry Corps subsequently even wrote a message of gratitude to the Il-2 crews of the 136th Ground Attack Aviation Division:

> On the difficult day of 25.1, when a crisis set in during the battle for Baracska, the Il-2s that appeared above the battlefield turned the battle in our favor. Despite the poor meteorological conditions – snowfall and limited visibility – the bombing was exceptionally accurate and the enemy's decisive attack was broken up. All the Cossacks, sergeants, officers and generals of the Cossack Corps [5th Guards Cavalry Corps] are in admiration of the work of your crews on 25 January 1945.[5]

The ground attack aircraft of the 10th Ground Attack Aviation Corps operated rather energetically in the area of Baracska. Its 58 Il-2s conducted 164 individual combat sorties, which yields 3 sorties a day for the majority of the aviation corps' aircraft. The losses suffered could be considered insignificant – just one Il-2 was shot down by German anti-aircraft fire.

However, on the whole the German attack on 25 January could be assessed as a tactical success. Though it was only in a narrow sector, the IV SS Panzer Corps managed to break out of the "gap" between Lake Velence and the Danube. That night, the attackers from the march took Pázmánd, and at 4.00 on 26 January, the German panzers broke into Vereb. That dawn, German panzer reconnaissance vehicles even broke through to the town of Vál, where the headquarters of the 4th Guards Army was located. In order to contain the extent of the German breakthrough into the rear of the 4th Guards Army, the last reserve had to be thrown into the fighting – a composite brigade of the 7th Mechanized Corps.

Despite the success of the IV SS Panzer Corps on 25 January, the hopes for closing the jaws around the 4th Guards Army were more than illusory. The attacks of the III Panzer Corps at Zámoly and of the 1st Cavalry Corps at Bicske made no headway. Gille's panzer corps had made a penetration of 10 kilometers in the Soviet defenses on a front of approximately 5 kilometers. It would have to make a similar advance in order to reach Zámoly, and it was even a little farther to Bicske. It can't be ruled out that an analogous success might have been achieved by the Germans had the efforts been concentrated toward the northeast, which is to say that Gille's option to continue to direct the offensive toward Budapest was perhaps more appropriate than Balck's idea about encircling the Soviet forces to the north of Lake Velence.

In the middle of the day on 26 January, the following intriguing discussion took place between the commander of the Sixth Army Balck and the commander of the IV SS Panzer Corps Gille:

> Balck: "We must cope with our assignment here. This now has decisive significance. What's the situation here [at Kajászó – Szentpéter]?"
> Gille: "This bridge, contrary to initial reports, is passable for panzers. We have a small bridgehead here."
> Balck: "That is very good and very important. How's your progress here?"
> Gille: "Contact was established between both *kampfgruppen* at 12.10. The last dispatch arrived at 13.50."
> Balck: "We must break through here. This decides everything, or here we will die."

Kajászó-Szentpéter is a settlement south-southeast of Vál. Judging from the evidence, the discussion was about the crossing of the Vali River, which is to say that a small bridgehead had been seized on its eastern bank, a little north of the highway leading to Budapest. This indicates that Gille had continued to search for a route leading to Budapest, even though his orders were to attack to the west and link up with Breith's III Panzer Corps; yet in this conversation, Balck gives his full support to Gille.

Interestingly, Balck would later attack Gille with accusations that the bridge at Kajászó-Szentpéter had been taken against his orders and that thereby the offensive forces became "dispersed". Balck also accused Gille of holding up the offensive for 36 hours. However, all of this remained a "paper" controversy, because the situation soon changed fundamentally.

If the German command had set for itself the limited task of extracting the Budapest garrison out of encirclement, then it made more sense not to alter the direction of attack of Gille's IV SS Panzer Corps to the northwest. A concentrated attack in the direction of Budapest, most likely, would have led to the same 10-kilometer penetration, but days earlier. The German and Hungarian units remaining in Buda might have been able to organize a breakout and might have linked up with units of Gille's panzer corps. A raid by an armored group from one of the panzer divisions of the IV SS Panzer Corps, analogous to Pieper's raid at Kharkov in February 1943, might have reinforced the grouping coming out of the encirclement. In principle, the possibility of a breakout by the Budapest garrison remained even after the pivot by the bulk of the IV SS Panzer Corps to the northwest. However, in this breakout, plainly only a small portion of the garrison would have reached the Vali River. In either of these two alternatives, the battle for Budapest might have ended as an effective "less than defeat" (or semi-victory), which could have become a source of pride and rhapsodized about in the memoirs about the "lost victories" after the war.

However, Balck and Wöhler set for themselves far more ambitious tasks. Here, it is impossible not to rebuke Balck for having an excessive and unfounded optimism in his assessment of the situation. He knew about the assembly of forces opposite his southern flank (the 18th Tank Corps), as well as about the movement of fresh Soviet forces across the Danube at Budapest. A logical inference to draw from this information would have been to conclude that the prospects of holding the occupied positions as far as the Danube were dubious. Accordingly, a more sensible scenario would become to "hit and run", that is to say, to free the Budapest garrison and to withdraw together with it to the offensive's start line. However, there was no change in the German strategy prior to the start of the Soviet counteroffensive. If you will, the only justification for Balck might be to view his actions as attempts to improve the overall situation through the reserves that had been sent to him (the IV SS Panzer Corps) before they could be taken away from him. With the inevitable fall of Budapest, the SS Panzer Corps might have been removed from Army Group South and sent somewhere else. At the end of January 1945, when the German defensive front along the Vistula River collapsed, the Germans had an abundant number of suitable places where the elite SS divisions were needed. In this case, the destruction of the maximum number of enemy formations might ease the life of Army Group South after the gift in the form of two SS panzer divisions was removed from it.

Be that as it may, there was now no longer time to realize either of the possible German objectives (the relief of Budapest or the encirclement of the 4th Guards Army). From 9.00 25 January, G.F. Zakharov took operational control of the 104th Rifle Corps (the 66th and 151st Rifle Divisions, and the 3rd Guards Airborne Division) and the 23rd Tank Corps. These formations had been transferred from the 2nd Ukrainian Front and had crossed the Danube to the western bank south of Budapest. With their help, it was being proposed to launch a powerful counterattack in order to liquidate the threat of breaking the ring around the Budapest garrison. By plan, the counteroffensive was to begin on 28 January, but the German breakthrough on 25 January somewhat upset the plans of the 3rd Ukrainian Front command. Two brigades of the 23rd Tank Corps were immediately thrown into the fighting in order to eliminate the German penetration. The battle shifted into its next phase.

5

The Front is Restored

The concluding phase of battles of many operations often remains in the shadow of the turning points. The turning point of defensive battles, a decisive counterstroke or the enemy's adoption of a defensive posture is similar to the final scenes of a melodrama – the hero and heroine come together in a kiss, and the closing credits begin to roll across the screen. The further lives of the heroes, their time together and their trips to the supermarket are of no interest to anyone. War is more similar to a film production than to a love novel. In the given case, the restoration of the front is not only emblematic in itself; it is also a necessary prelude to the next clash – the March 1945 fighting to repel the attack by the Sixth SS Panzer Army. In addition, successfully pushing the Germans back from Budapest sealed the unenviable fate of the remnants of the city's garrison.

Sometimes, the battles in the area of Lake Balaton are called a "second Kursk". However, according to the rules of the genre, a "Prokhorovka" must be present, that is to say, a counterattack against a tough enemy grouping, which results in heavy losses. As in the case of Prokhorovka, the Soviet counterattack here was launched by a fresh formation that had just arrived to join Tolbukhin's Front. A.O. Akhmanov's 23rd Tank Corps, which had passed to Tolbukhin's control from the 2nd Ukrainian Front, received an order to cross to the western bank of the Danube River by the end of 24 January. However, in connection with the moving chunks of ice in the river, the majority of the corps had assembled on the western bank only by the morning of 25 January. In comparison with the badly battered mechanized formations of the 3rd Ukrainian Front by the end of January, the newly arrived corps appeared more than impressive – 153 T-34s and 21 ISU-122s.

It was decided to employ the 23rd Tank Corps and the 104th Rifle Corps for a major counterattack by the Front. According to Tolbukhin's plan, two converging attacks would be launched from the north and south. The northern assault grouping would consist of the two newly arrived corps, which were assembled in the area to the northeast of Lake Velence. The reinforced 18th Tank Corps was to attack from the south together with two rifle corps. The road hub of Sárosd, lying between the northern tip of Lake Balaton and the Danube River, was chosen as the point where the pincers would close. Thereby, the German units in the area to the east of the Sárviz Canal that had reached the Danube would be cut-off from the main forces of the Sixth Army. The attacking forces would move into their jumping-off positions on the night of 27/28 January and launch the attack on the morning of 28 January. It should be noted that Tolbukhin opted not to deploy the northern assault grouping of two fresh corps further westward to the Székesfehérvár area in order to try to cut off the entire enemy penetration, although Gille, when giving his troops their assignments as part of Operation *Konrad III*, was anticipating counterattacks precisely from the Székesfehérvár area. However, Tolbukhin believed the shifting of the armored fist to Székesfehérvár contained the risk of losing control over the situation between Lake Velence and the Danube. The Soviet command chose not to take such a risk. The arriving reserves were concentrated against the enemy's offensive spearhead – just in case.

Such a case soon showed itself in view of the German breakthrough to the town of Vál, where the 4th Guards Army's command post had recently been located. The prerequisites for either a turn toward Budapest or the encirclement of the 4th Guards Army' units that were defending in the Zámoly area were now in place. Zakharov requested authorization from the Front commander to use the brigades of the 23rd Tank Corps in order to parry the emerging crisis. Already at 10.30 26 January, an order was issued for a counterattack by the 3rd and 135th Tank Brigades of Akhmanov's 23rd Tank Corps. They were to move against the tanks and self-propelled guns of the German assault wedge's spearhead. The 3rd Tank Brigade (42 T-34s) already at 14.00 was attacking the forward German units in Vál. They had been estimated as being 3 tanks and 8 armored halftracks with infantry. After a two-hour battle, the brigade drove this enemy group out of Vál, and by 23.00 26 January, it had taken full control of the town. This success cost the brigade 3 T-34 tanks burned out. That same evening, the 135th Tank Brigade attacked the bridgehead that had been seized by the SS troops at Kajászó-Szentpéter. The counterattack by the two tank brigades had no decisive result, but they halted the enemy's further advance into the depth of the 4th Guards Army's defenses. In these combats, the 23rd Tank Corps suffered its first losses – at the end of 26 January, it now numbered 126 T-34s and 19 ISU-122s, which was 27 T-34s and 2 ISU-122s less than it had on the morning of 25 January.

The next step was to be a powerful counterstroke with forces of the 23rd Tank Corps and 104th Rifle Corps into the flank of the German grouping that had broken out of the "gap" between Lake Velence and the Danube River. The Soviet command recognized the weakness of the tank corps' own artillery component, and thus the attack of the 23rd Tank Corps was to be supported by the 9th Artillery Breakthrough Division (54 152mm howitzer cannons). In order to strengthen the infantry component of Akhmanov's corps, the 151st Rifle Division was operationally attached to it. There would be no air support in view of the bad weather that was keeping the aircraft grounded.

The 23rd Tank Corps' attack against the SS Panzer Division *Totenkopf* began at 10.00 27 January. Initially the 135th Tank Brigade, which at 11.00 broke through to the Pettend farmsteads, achieved the greatest success. However, the Germans couldn't tolerate the loss of this key strongpoint at the base of the salient they had driven into the Soviet defenses and they fiercely counterattacked. The King Tigers of the 509th Heavy Panzer Battalion became the greatest inconvenience to the Soviet tankers. As it happened, prior to Tolbukhin's counterstroke, the 509th Heavy Panzer Battalion had been withdrawn to Seregélyes for rest and refitting. News of the Soviet counteroffensive prompted it to conduct an immediate counterattack against the Pettend farmsteads with 3 of its heavy panzers, which were later joined by the battalion commander in his own heavy panzer. Norwegians of the SS *Norge* Battalion provided them with infantry support. The ponderous King Tigers didn't often rush to the battlefield in the first hours of repelling counterattacks, but they nevertheless could be found close to the spearhead of an attacking armored wedge. In contrast, the 151st Rifle Division, which was supposed to attack toward Pettend together with the 135th Tank Brigade, didn't come up in time and remained back in the vicinity of Kajászó-Szentpéter. In the course of two hours of hard fighting, the 135th Tank Brigade lost a significant number of its tanks and was forced to fall back to its jumping-off positions. This is one of the few confirmed episodes of the effective use of King Tigers in battle. The crews of the four German heavy tanks claimed the destruction of 41 T-34/85 tanks. According to the records of irrecoverable losses, the 135th Tank Brigade left 27 T-34 tanks burned out on the battlefield at Pettend on 27 January 1945.

The other brigades of Akhmanov's tank corps were greeted with heavy fire, but after several repeat attacks, the 3rd Tank Brigade nevertheless broke into Vereb by 21.00 and became tied up in street fighting for the possession of it. All of the 39th Tank Brigade's attacks toward Pázmánd were unsuccessful.

The results of the counterattack against the main forces of the IV SS Panzer Corps were disappointing, but predictable. Over the course of 27 January 1945, the 23rd Tank Corps lost a total of 61 tanks and self-propelled guns, including 45 T-34s burned out, 13 T-34s knocked out, 1 ISU-122 burned out and 2 ISU-122 knocked out, which is equivalent to 42% of its available armor before entering battle. Human losses amounted to 160 men killed and 220 wounded. This, of course, was substantially less than the losses suffered by the tank corps of P.A. Rotmistrov's 5th Guards Tank Army at Prokhorovka. I'll remind you that on 12 July 1943, the 29th Tank Corps lost 153 tanks and 17 SU-76 and SU-122, which amounted to 77% of the armored vehicles that took part in the attacks. The 18th Tank Corps on that same day lost 84 tanks, which was 56% of its complement before the start of the counterattack.

In addition to the lower level of losses, there was an additional substantial difference. Justified doubts have been put forward regarding the decisive influence of the fighting on the Prokhorovka tank field on 12 July 1943 on the outcome of the entire Kursk battle. On the contrary, the effects of the attack of Akhmanov's tank corps on the enemy have been precisely noted in German documents. In his order to the IV SS Panzer Corps on 27 January, Gille stated:

> The enemy today attacks our forward panzer detachments in the Vereb area and south of Vál with major forces of tanks and infantry. The 23rd Tank Corps went on the offensive out of the enemy bridgehead in the Baracska area to the southwest and south, having the assignment to block the defile between the Vali River and Lake Velence in the rear of our attacking forward detachments. In the course of bitter fighting, a total of 122 enemy tanks were destroyed today.

Having finished his description of the situation with the stirring phrase regarding the number of destroyed tanks, the commander of the IV SS Panzer Corps then issued assignments that didn't inspire optimism. Gille ordered:

> Following orders, the panzer corps is to withdraw its units that are located in the area west of the defile between the Vali River and Lake Velence, and on the night 27/28 January will temporarily take up a defense on the line Baracska – Pettend – Kápolnásnyék, positioning the 5th SS Panzer Division *Wiking* between the Danube River and the line of the Vali River, the 3rd SS Panzer Division *Totenkopf* on both sides of Lake Velence and *Gruppe Holst* (which is subordinate to the corps from 7.00 28.01.45) between Székesfehérvár and the southern extremity of the Vérteshegység mountain massif.

Thus, already after the first attack by the fresh Soviet tank corps, Gille ordered a withdrawal of the units that had broken out beyond the defile, and went over to a defense. The assault capabilities of the SS corps had already reached its limits, and the change in the correlation of forces compelled the cancellation of the offensive. Simultaneously with the assumption of a defensive posture, there was a force regrouping. The 1st Panzer Division was removed from subordination to the IV SS Panzer Corps and became directly subordinate to the Sixth Army command. Thereby the German command dismantled the assault grouping and created reserves for repelling the pending Soviet counteroffensive. Simultaneously, the battalion of King Tigers, a battalion of Panthers, and the 303rd Assault Gun Brigade of StuG and StuH self-propelled guns were withdrawn from subordination to *Totenkopf*'s commander – they became the IV SS Panzer Corps reserve.

The 3rd Ukrainian Front's counterattacks weren't limited to those conducted against the German salient near Lake Velence. An offensive into the rear of the German assault grouping from the south was a simple and obvious decision, the realization of which the Soviet command embarked upon immediately after the accumulation of forces for it. The forces that had fallen back from the Sió Canal were used for the counterattack. Here, a group was organized under the overall leadership of Colonel General A.S. Zheltov, a member of the 3rd Ukrainian Front's Military Council. Zheltov's group included the 18th Tank Corps and the newly arrived 30th and 133rd Rifle Corps. Later, with the arrival of the 26th Army headquarters under the 3rd Ukrainian Front's command, these formations together with the 57th Army's 135th Rifle Corps (the 233rd and 236th Rifle Divisions) were made subordinate to the new army headquarters.

The general offensive on the southern sector of the front was timed to begin simultaneously with the counterattack of the 23rd Tank Corps and 104th Rifle Corps – at 10.00 on 27 January 1945. The 18th Tank Corps, after receiving replenishments from trains, had been brought back up to a fully satisfactory condition – at the start of the offensive, it numbered 88 T-34, 8 ISU-152, 28 ISU-122, 1 SU-85 and 34 SU-76, for a total of 159 armored vehicles. The 1202nd Self-propelled Artillery Regiment, which had received another 20 SU-76 from the factory, was also supposed to support the infantry.

The offensive began with great promise. After an 8-hour battle, Herczegfalva was taken, and by the end of the day the attackers were closing on the road hub of N. Perkáta. With its capture, the German units along the Danube riverbank would become virtually encircled. Indeed, with the arrival of Soviet forces outside of N. Perkáta, the road to Dunapentele [Dunaúváros] was cut, and the German garrison holding N. Perkáta became isolated. Thus, this village was defended with particular stubbornness. Units of the 18th Tank Corps together with infantry attacked it from several directions, and in response the Germans launched desperate counterattacks. In this area, the Soviet forces were opposed by the 3rd Panzer Division, and west of it, the 23rd Panzer Division. The main forces of the 1st Panzer Division were also operating in the Dunapentele [Dunaúváros] area. These divisions were organized under the command of the III Panzer Corps. Thus, the Germans had committed rather major forces on the southern flank of the corridor that had been driven to the Danube River, which were fully capable of checking the 26th Army's offensive. On 28 January, the Soviet 30th Rifle Corps numbered 16,832 officers and soldiers, the 133rd Rifle Corps -- 15,139 men. Meanwhile, the German 3rd Panzer Division had 14,000 men on its roster for 1 February 1945, while the 23rd Panzer Division had approximately 14,500 men (though not all of these were combatants). In addition, whereas the Soviet side had one mobile formation, the German grouping opposing the 26th Army consisted entirely of mobile divisions. Nevertheless, the Front leadership was dissatisfied with the actions of the 26th Army commander Lieutenant General L.S. Skvirsky, who had led the army since May 1943. On 30 January 1945, Lieutenant General N.A. Gagen assumed command of the 26th Army.

As is known, at Kursk the process of shoving the Germans back to their jumping-off positions had cost the Voronezh Front quite dearly. This pattern of "Kursk II" was retained at Balaton. The combat against the German panzer divisions primarily led to rather heavy armor losses in the 3rd Ukrainian Front's southern assault grouping. From 27 January to 30 January 1945, the 18th Tank Corps lost 95 armored vehicles (73 T-34, 6 ISU-122, 5 ISU-152, and 15 SU-76) burned out or knocked out. In this fighting, the commander of the 1438th Self-propelled Artillery Regiment Colonel F.A. Zatylkin was killed; he had commanded this regiment without interruption since 1943 and had traveled the long path from the Ukraine to Hungary together with the 18th Tank Corps. In addition, here a rather unusual episode took place, which demonstrates the features of maneuver warfare rather well. Two tank brigades of the 18th Tank Corps that were advancing to the north in bypass of N. Perkáta wound up cut-off by an enemy counterattack. Showing no panic and continuing their attack, on 1 February they continued on to Adony and seized that town. On the morning of 2 February, the formally encircled brigades were "freed" – they linked up with the 4th Guards Army's 3rd Guards Airborne Division, which had been attacking from the north to meet them.

The measured successes of the 26th Army in its offensive from the south, of course, were disappointing, but the other axis created greater anxiety. Pushing the enemy relief grouping, which had gone over to the defense, away from the approaches to Budapest remained the most important task for the 3rd Ukrainian Front in the last days of January and first days of February 1945. After pulling back the panzers that had broken out of the defile between Lake Velence and the Danube River, the positions of the IV SS Panzer Corps on this axis no longer had any vulnerable locations. The assault grouping of the 4th Guards Army operating against it was unable to make any rapid progress. The danger of a German breakthrough to Budapest was eliminated, but the counteroffensive by the 23rd Tank Corps and 104th Rifle Corps progressed slowly. This wasn't surprising – the German assault grouping, which was quite strong even after the order about redistributing the forces, was being attacked head-on. The shifting of the axis of attack on 29-30 January to the sector between Baracska and the Danube, where the 5th SS Panzer Division *Wiking* was defending on a relatively broad front, brought no success. Some sort of solution, which would jolt the battle out of its situation of a tottering balance that didn't give either side a decisive advantage, was necessary. Such a solution was soon found. The successful actions of detachments of the 20th and 21st Guards Rifle Corps near Székesfehérvár, as well as intelligence that the Germans had shifted the 23rd Panzer Division to the southern flank to counter the 26th Army, caused the Soviet command to begin to ponder changing the axis of attack to that location.

Without giving the idea a long thought, on 30 January Tolbukhin made the decision to switch the 1st Guards Mechanized Corps and 5th Guards Cavalry Corps to the area north of Székesfehérvár. The Front commander issued the order for an enveloping attack around Székesfehérvár with the forces of these two mobile corps, together with three rifle divisions of the 20th and 21st Guards Rifle Corps, with the aim of cutting the lines of communication leading from that city to Mór. The attackers would then screen Székesfehérvár from the north and attack the city itself. This was the plan that Gille had expressed specific concerns about in his orders for Operation *Konrad III*. However, the attackers still had a chance to shake the enemy's defenses – the 1st Guards Mechanized Corps on the evening of 30 January still had 71 Shermans and 17 SU-100 tank destroyers operational.

The 1st Guards Mechanized Corps and 5th Guards Cavalry Corps faced a march of 45 kilometers to reach their jumping-off positions. The night was dark, and snow was falling, driven by a strong wind. The cavalrymen and motorized infantry were moving along the same road. Because of traffic jams and snow drifts, there were frequent halts and gaps appeared in the column. There could no longer be any talk about completing the assembly of units for the offensive by the early morning of 31 January. The two corps completed arriving in the designated area only by mid-day. The attack began at 14.00. The Soviet troops were opposed by *Gruppe Holst*, which was composed of dismounted cavalrymen and the 356th Infantry Division, which had recently arrived at the front. Previously it had been located in Italy, and only in January 1945 was it shifted to Hungary.

It shouldn't be thought that only the 3rd Ukrainian Front was receiving fresh formations. The German 356th Infantry Division had arrived in subordination to the IV SS Panzer Corps just before the described events – on 28 January. It was immediately placed in the front line in the most vulnerable sector from the point of view of the German command – at Székesfehérvár. It is impossible not to note the revealing confluence of events. The 23rd Tank Corps and 104th Rifle Corps arrived in the 4th Guards Army on 25 January. If Tolbukhin had reached the decision to move these units promptly to the Székesfehérvár area, then it is fully possible that the attack could have been launched prior to the arrival of the fresh German division in its defensive positions on the approaches to the town. The Soviet armored battering ram consisting of 150 tanks of Akhmanov's tank corps would have fallen upon the relatively weak defense by the dismounted cavalrymen of *Gruppe Holst*. However, this decision would have required iron nerves. It is rather difficult to condemn the 3rd Ukrainian Front's command for the cautious regrouping of the arriving reserves in closer proximity to the enemy's armor spearhead. If the German panzers had broken out of the defile between Lake Velence and the Danube River, this would have unquestionably raised alarms and would have required a rapid decision.

The transfer of the 3rd Ukrainian Front's point of attack on the final day of January, however, took place under completely different circumstances. The German command correctly assessed the strong probes by the 20th and 21st Guards Rifle Corps, the results of which had prompted Tolbukhin to shift the 5th Guards Cavalry Corps and 1st Guards Mechanized Corps to the Székesfehérvár area. In addition, the implementation of the hasty regrouping according to the

Commander of the 26th Army Lieutenant General
N.A. Gagen.

A T-34/85 tank with tank riders aboard. In view of the almost complete absence of armored
personnel carriers in the Red Army, tanks were often used to transport infantry.

A German 75mm PAK-40 anti-tank gun left behind in its position in the
Budapest area. (TsAMO)

A StuG III self-propelled gun with its gun removed. Most likely, this machine was abandoned
and cannibalized for its useful parts in order to repair other StuG IIIs.

A knocked-out Panzerjäger 38(t) Ausf.M (Marder III) 75mm self-propelled anti-tank gun.

A knocked-out Panther, Hungary, January 1945. Shell holes are clearly visible in the side armor of the turret. (TsAMO)

A StuG 40 abandoned on the street of a Hungarian village.

3rd Ukrainian Front commander's order wasn't kept concealed from enemy aerial reconnaissance: "The attacks undertaken today in the sector of divisional *Gruppe Holst* should be taken as a reconnaissance in force. In connection with the bringing up of reserves to this area, which was detected by aerial reconnaissance, major attacks should be expected in this area."[1]

However, it was through the combat dispositions of the fresh 356th Infantry Division that the units of the 1st Guards Mechanized Corps succeeded in breaking through toward Székesfehérvár. Wintertime combat on the Eastern Front must have come as a shock to the men of this German infantry division, fresh from Italy. As the IV SS Panzer Corps headquarters reported to the Operations Department of *Armeegruppe Balck*: "In the opinion of the division commander based on the experience of today, the 356th Infantry Division in no way corresponds to the demands of warfare on the Eastern Front, particularly in winter. The conduct of II/871 Grenadier Regiment on the battlefield threatened to undermine the combat morale of the neighboring units."[2]

After the defeat of the units that were targeted by the new Soviet offensive, German hopes for retaining the occupied positions began quickly to melt away. The dismantling of the German assault grouping continued. One of *Totenkopf's* regiments, the 6th SS Panzer Grenadier Regiment *Eicke*, was sent to Székesfehérvár as a reserve. On the second day of the offensive, 1 February, the 1st Guards Mechanized Corps managed to break into the northern and northwestern outskirts of Székesfehérvár, where it became tied up in street fighting. Thanks to the arrival of *Totenkopf's* regiment, the Germans managed to hold on to Székesfehérvár, and the units of the 1st Guards Mechanized Corps were pushed back to the outskirts.

As was the case in December 1941 in front of Moscow, the failure of the German offensive meant serious difficulties for the Germans in the event that the Red Army went over to the offensive. There was simply nothing left with which to parry the Soviet attacks against the sectors that had been weakened in order to reinforce the assault grouping. As the result of the nearly two weeks of intensive combat, the assault grouping of Gille's IV SS Panzer Corps had suffered heavy armor losses. Information about the IV SS Panzer Corps armor park is shown in Table 3:

Table 3 Condition of the Divisions of the IV SS Panzer Corps on 1 February 1945

	3rd SS Panzer Division *Totenkopf*	5th SS Panzer Division *Wiking*	1st Panzer Division	3rd Panzer Division
Pz. III	1	-	–	3 (1)
Pz. IV	5 (11)	3 (2)	4 (2)	8 (21)
Pz. V	3 (11)	6 (11)	6 (14)	10 (20)
Pz. VI	2 (11)	–	–	–
StuGs	7 (8)	0 (5)	2	5 (2)
Jg.Pz. IV	3 (6)	–	–	16 (7)
SdKfz Half Tracks	57 (19)	116 (36)	51 (31)	156 (109)
Guns	35 (17)	37	27 (10)	31 (6)
Mobility	85%	45%	50%	65%

Note: The numbers in the parentheses indicates the number of vehicles under short-term repair.

The 509th Heavy Panzer Battalion of King Tigers had only 11 operational tanks on 1 February 1945. Having available only a limited quantity of serviceable armor, Gille could not count upon holding the broad area extending from Lake Balaton and Székesfehérvár to the Danube. Moreover, the attack in the Székesfehérvár area threatened the main lines of supply that fed the German grouping that was extended in the direction of the Danube. On the other hand, the further dismantling of the assault grouping in order to support the defense of Székesfehérvár was weakening the positions in the interval between Lake Velence and the Danube, as well as the southern flank of Gille's IV SS Panzer Corps.

On 2 February, equilibrium was established at Székesfehérvár. The 1st Guards Mechanized Corps and the rifle units that were operating with it dug in on the outskirts of the city and repelled German counterattacks. On this same day, a German staff car was ambushed by a reconnaissance patrol from the 1st Guards Mechanized Corps. Inside the car was the Deputy Chief of Staff for Operations of the IV SS Panzer Corps and a lieutenant-interpreter. They had been driving out along the road to Seregélyes to visit one of the forward units in order to interrogate a prisoner. The senior officer was killed in the exchange of fire, and the interpreter was taken prisoner. Unfortunately for the Germans, the deputy chief of the Operations Department happened to be carrying with him operational materials of the IV SS Panzer Corps, including the plan for Operation *Konrad III*, and a printed transcript of the discussions between Gille and Balck. It was information from these particular captured documents that was cited above.

If the divisions of the IV SS Panzer Corps literally had only a handful of operational panzers, the situation on the opposite side of the front also wasn't rose-colored. The 23rd Tank Corps had suffered heavy losses in its counterattack against the main forces of the German's assault grouping. On 1 February 1945, it had serviceable only 24 T-34/85 tanks and 13 ISU-122 self-propelled vehicles. The irrecoverable losses in armor from the moment it entered battle amounted to 84 T-34 tanks and 3 ISU-122 self-propelled guns, while an additional 24 T-34 and 5 ISU-122 required medium-term repairs. Another 11 T-34 tanks needed major overhauls. The 23rd Tank Corps had also left behind T-34s subordinate to the 2nd Ukrainian Front, and they were involved in the street fighting in Budapest. Given such a decline in armor numbers, the strike capabilities of the tank brigades were substantially reduced. For example, the 9th Guards Tank Brigade had only 9 tanks in formation. However, the overall situation smiled upon the offensive operations of the 23rd Tank Corps and the 104th Rifle Corps, when after the successful attack of the 1st Guards Mechanized Corps at Székesfehérvár, the German forces between Velence and the Danube were compelled to break up their assault grouping and to begin a gradual retreat.

The attacking forces of the 4th Guards Army encountered serious resistance on the approaches to the road hub of Seregélyes. The 23rd Tank Corps pushed toward the town on 2 February, but the infantry of the 66th and 151st Rifle Divisions moving in its wake were lagging behind. However, the Germans had no intention to yield the road hub without a fight; moreover, they launched a counterattack. The brigades of Akhmanov's tank corps that were approaching Seregélyes were counterattacked in both flanks and the rear. As a result of two days of maneuvering combat, the 23rd Tank Corps was compelled to fall back, but then was sent to outflank Seregélyes to the north. Moreover, the tank corps was given an ambitious assignment: it was to seize Székesfehérvár by the end of 4 February.

On the path of the outflanking maneuver in the space between Seregélyes and Lake Velence lay a canal, with a depth of 2 meters and a width of 6 meters. The 23rd Tank Corps was unable to force a crossing of it from the march, but with the onset of darkness a bridgehead was seized on the other side, and by the morning of 5 February, a temporary bridge had been laid across the canal. However, the canal passed through a broad, swampy meadow, and it was possible to reach the bridge only via a narrow dike that stretched for approximately 2 kilometers. The absence of maneuver possibilities and the lack of natural cover meant that on the approach to the bridge crossing the canal, the Soviet tanks were simply shot up. It was necessary to expand the bridgehead, but this required infantry. Only on the night of 5/6 February did the few remaining tanks of Akhmanov's tank corps cross over into the bridgehead. At that moment, the 3rd Tank Brigade had only 8 serviceable tanks, the 39th Tank Brigade – 6, the 135th Tank Brigade – 5, and the 1443rd Self-propelled Artillery Regiment – 9 ISU-122, for a total of just 28 operational vehicles in the 23rd Tank Corps.

Together with the 66th and 151st Rifle Divisions, the 23rd Tank Corps began to break out of the bridgehead to the northwest toward Székesfehérvár on 6 February. That day, the town of Börgönd, which was just a stone's throw away from Székesfehérvár, fell to the attacking Soviet forces, as did Seregélyes. The simultaneous appearance of a Soviet bridgehead to the north of Seregélyes facilitated the Soviet assault on Székesfehérvár. In addition, prior to this the city had been enveloped from the south by the 26th Army's 155th Rifle Division. Infantry of the 4th Guards Army that were attacking from the east broke into the nearly enveloped city and seized this important road hub before nightfall on 6 February.

However, the German command had no intention to settle with the loss of this favorable line of defense. On 7 February, the Germans counterattacked. For this, the 509th Heavy Panzer Battalion, which at that moment possessed 16 King Tigers, was summoned in response to an alarm and was thrown back into the fighting. The Soviet bridgehead, which extended in the direction of Székesfehérvár, was attacked from the flank. The target of the attacking German panzers was the bridges that the Soviets had built across the canal. This attack at a sensitive place forced a regrouping of the 23rd Tank Corps in order to defend the territory that had been gained. Two of its tank brigades were withdrawn from the bridgehead and sent to the southeast to defend Seregélyes.

On 8 February, a counterattack by the 5th SS Panzer Division *Wiking* eliminated the Soviet bridgehead across the canal and retook Székesfehérvár. Having overrun the infantry of the 151st Rifle Division's 581st Rifle Regiment, the German armor and panzer grenadiers cut off the 23rd Tank Corps' 56th Motorized Rifle Brigade. The brigade spent the entire day fighting in encirclement and fell back to the eastern bank of the canal with the onset of darkness. Up to 65% of the soldiers and officers that came out of the encirclement were wounded. Under the threat of encirclement, the 3rd Tank Brigade abandoned the bridgehead and withdrew across the canal. The bridges across it were blown up.

Over the course of 7-8 February, the 23rd Tank Corps lost 12 T-34 tanks knocked out, and 2 ISU-122s. It now had serviceable only 14 tanks and 5 self-propelled guns. The adversary of Akhmanov's tankers, the 509th Heavy Panzer Battalion of King Tigers, had just 5 operational tanks after the elimination of the Soviet bridgehead. However, on the whole, the front began to stabilize. The lost bridgehead would have to be seized once again, but there was no longer the strength to do it. It was necessary to abandon the idea of taking Székesfehérvár for a while. The capture of Seregélyes remained the last major success of the Soviet counteroffensive.

Despite the fact that the lines of defense that had existed prior to 18 January could not be fully re-established, the Soviet counteroffensive was an undoubted success. The IV SS Panzer Corps was pushed back away from Budapest. The garrison of the encircled city lost its last remaining hope for relief. The German command also lost favorable positions for the further development of an offensive. From the staging area that had been created as far as the Danube at the height of *Konrad III*, it might have been possible to strike either to the south into the rear of the 57th Army and 1st Bulgarian Army, or to the north into the rear of the 4th Guards Army. The Germans no longer held this advantageous position.

Following the counteroffensive, the subsequent Soviet withdrawal to the positions between Lake Velence and Lake Balaton made the defensive front more compact, and enabled it to be defended with an adequate amount of strength and means. Even though Székesfehérvár had not fallen to the 4th Guards Army, it now had only extremely limited use as a logistics hub – Soviet troops were holding the heights to the east of the city that overlooked it, and were keeping it under artillery fire.

6

The Storming of Budapest

The epopee of the storming of the Hungarian capital began on 27 December 1944, when the ring of encirclement around Budapest finally snapped shut. Caught in the encirclement were the 8th and 22nd SS Cavalry Divisions, the 13th Panzer Division, the SA Panzer Grenadier Division *Feldherrnhalle*, a portion of the 271st Volksgrenadier Division, the 10th Hungarian Infantry Division, the 12th Hungarian Reserve Division, a Hungarian armor division, a portion of the Hungarian 1st Hussar Division, and a number of separate battalions of infantry and artillery, including Hungarian volunteer corps.

According to information cited in the book *The Siege of Budapest: 100 Days in World War II* by the Hungarian historian Kristián Ungváry [which has been translated into English by Ladisláus Löb and published by Yale University Press], the total ration strength of the Hungarian units and formations, police combat groups and volunteer corps that were encircled in Budapest amounted to 55,100 men. The German units and formations numbered a total of 42,600 men, including 1,600 wounded or sick in Budapest hospitals.

The Soviet forces had to overcome several concentric lines of defense, which ran along the ring streets of the city, with their flanks resting on the Danube. There were four such lines of defense in Buda, the western half of the city. In Pest, the eastern half of the city, there were 6 main, concentric lines of defense. The first, which could already be viewed by soldiers on the front line, ran along the Rákos Canal. This canal, which was 15-20 meters wide and had a depth of 2.5 meters, represented a serious anti-tank obstacle. All the bridges across the canal had been blown up, and the approaches to it were covered by fire from the residential and factory buildings located along the canal bank. The homes and buildings on the outskirts of the city and in the city itself had been converted into machine-gun positions. The eastern suburbs of Budapest consisted of dense blocks of one- and two-story brick homes. Between the homes there were small gardens and fences, which facilitated the infiltration of assault groups.

The central part of the city was strikingly different from the outskirts and consisted primarily of densely-packed, multi-story buildings with very narrow and straight streets. Here, the conditions for the attacker were much worse. Fortified shelters had been set up at street intersections, in which the gendarmes took cover during air raids. In the course of the assault, these shelters became improvised pillboxes. The large stone buildings and enclosures were adapted for a lengthy defense; loopholes were created in the walls of the buildings for rifles and small-caliber guns. The streets were blocked by barricades of rubble and sandbags. The barricades were constructed according to the materials in the given area in peacetime. For example, at the crematorium, the street was blocked by a barricade made from cut stone. The approaches to the crematorium were blocked by a barricade made from tombstones with an anti-tank ditch in front of it. On Zsygmond and Keresztyén Streets, barricades made from large-caliber guns that were partially covered with earth and piled sandbags were encountered. In the center of Buda, there were a large number of barricades consisting of overturned trucks, cars and even armored personnel carriers.

In view of the necessity of regrouping forces for the defense of Buda, the German-Hungarian grouping defending Pest had left to it:

- Panzer Grenadier Division *Feldherrnhalle*;
- 13th Panzer Division;
- 10th and 12th Hungarian Infantry Divisions;
- Hungarian armor division;
- 22nd SS Cavalry Division.

The divisions have been listed in the order of their location around the perimeter of defense of the eastern half of the city. Separate battalions were also scattered along the perimeter of defense.

The Soviet attackers employed the classic principle "Break up and destroy" in the assault on Budapest. First it was decided to tackle the eastern half of the city. By 1 January 1945, the following formations of the 2nd Ukrainian Front were standing outside the walls of the city in readiness to storm Pest:

> 30th Rifle Corps (25th Guards, 151st and 155th Rifle Divisions) with attached assets: the 16th Artillery Division, the 18th Howitzer Artillery Brigade, the 49th Guards Cannon Artillery Brigade, and the 115th Destroyer Anti-tank Artillery Regiment;
> 7th Romanian Army Corps consisting of the 2nd and 19th Infantry Divisions and the 9th Cavalry Division;
> 18th Guards Rifle Corps (66th and 68th Guards, 297th and 317th Rifle Divisions) with attached assets: the 17th Cannon Artillery Brigade, the 95th Howitzer Artillery Brigade, the 27th Mortar Brigade, the 152nd Cannon Artillery Brigade, the 48th Guards Mortar Regiment, and the 14th Assault Engineer-Sapper Brigade.

The reader will not find on this list a single tank corps or even one tank brigade. One of the features of the battle for Budapest was the sparing use of armor in the storming of the city. Whereas in Berlin the tanks and self-propelled guns were almost the main shock force of the attackers (three full tank armies and the infantry support tank units of the combined-arms armies entered the city), in the storming of the Hungarian capital primarily infantry, combat engineers and artillery were involved. One tank battalion of the 3rd Tank Brigade and one tank company of the 39th Tank Brigade (both from the 23rd Tank Corps) took part in the assault on Pest. There were not more than 22 tanks in these units. The Soviet infantry of the 46th Army assaulted Buda, with the support of two self-propelled gun regiments, which had 30 SU-76 as of 1 January 1945. Later, when the assault on Buda was already underway, a company of tanks of the 5th Guards Tank Corps was committed into the city.

The limited use of tanks was determined by both the need for tanks in the fighting around the outer ring of encirclement and the impossibility of deploying major armored forces in street fighting conditions. In connection with this, the claims found in foreign sources, in particular in Ungvári's book, regarding the destruction of 200 Soviet tanks in Budapest looks in the best case like a bad joke. Soviet tanks in Budapest operated alone or in pairs that supported the infantry assault groups.

In view of the very limited number of tanks used by the Soviet forces in the storming of Budapest, the strength of the defenders was fully comparable with the strength of the attackers in this regard. On 5 January 1945, the units of the German 13th Panzer Division in Pest had 7 Pz. IVs and 7 Pz. V Panthers, while the *Feldherrnhalle* Division had 9 Pz. V Panthers and 13 StuG assault guns. The Hungarian battalions of assault artillery had approximately 30 self-propelled guns, while the Hungarian armor division had 7 tanks. Thus, the 13th Panzer Division and *Feldherrnhalle* Division in Pest alone had more tanks than the attackers, even setting aside the Hungarian armored vehicles of the besieged garrison. At the same time, of course, the lack of fuel substantially constrained the use of heavy combat equipment by the defenders of Budapest. Primarily, the tanks and self-propelled guns were used in Budapest for firing from fixed positions and for ambushes.

The tanks, despite their leading role in many battles of the Second World War, were only one of the available combat means. There were also the infantry, artillery, combat engineers and chemical troops. The main "music" of the assault was not the squeaking of tracks and the howl of shells fired by the main guns of tanks, but the explosions of the demolition charges of the combat engineers and of artillery shells. As of 1 January 1945, the forces of the 2nd Ukrainian Front in Pest possessed 48 203mm howitzers, 172 152mm guns, 294 122mm guns, 191 76mm divisional guns, 174 76mm regimental guns, and 158 45mm and 57mm anti-tank guns.

This ensured a more than three-fold superiority in the amount of artillery over the defenders. At the same time, the majority of the German and Hungarian artillery was compelled to remain silent in view of the lack of ammunition. As noted above, some of the heavy guns, lacking shells, were even used for building barricades across city streets and boulevards. The main tactic employed by the artillery was firing over open sights. Up to 80% of the guns involved in the battle were used this way.

However, the primary motif in the concert of the storming of Budapest became the hissing sound of the streams of flames emanating from flamethrowers. In contrast to the insignificant number of tanks storming the Hungarian capital, the divisions of the 2nd Ukrainian Front possessed a very impressive number of flamethrowers. On 6 January 1945, the 30th Rifle Corps was being supported by an army-level battalion of LPO-50 flamethrowers and the 173rd Separate Company of ROKS flamethrowers, which numbered a total of approximately 150 flamethrowers. Correspondingly, the 39th Separate Battalion of ROKS flamethrowers was attached to the 18th Guards Rifle Corps.

Interestingly, in one of the street battles, a flamethrower was employed against an enemy tank. A tank that was cruising down one of Budapest's streets became the victim of the flamethrower Filatov, who made his way to the street the tank was using through a shattered building. There, Filatov took up an ambush position, and when the tank passed by him, he set it afire with a long squirt. Such an incident, of course, wasn't typical for the battles for Budapest. Much more commonly, the flamethrowers would cooperate with the assault groups when taking buildings. The engineers would blow holes in walls with a demolition charge, and the flamethrowers would immediately dash up to the opening that had just been created and release a stream of fire inside the building. The same tactic was employed to dig the enemy out of cellars. Explosive charges would be detonated on the floor of the ground level, and then the flamethrowers would squirt fire down through the openings.

In fact, the artillery tactics radically changed with the onset of the assault on the city blocks. Whereas on the approaches to the city, the artillery was deployed according to the principle of breaking through a regular sector of fortifications and used mostly in the indirect fire role, with the start of street fighting up to 80% of the artillery fired over open sights. In order to protect the guns and crews from being struck by enemy fire, a sheltering wall of stone rubble would be built up in front of the gun. Since in the initial phase of the assault the German and Hungarian artillery remained silent in order not to reveal themselves, the guns and crews tended to be sheltered behind the walls of buildings to prevent them from being subjected to enemy fire.

During the assault, initially the tanks too often forged ahead and lost contact with the supporting infantry. As a result, over 2 and 3 January 1945, the small detachments of tanks of the assault force lost 7 armored vehicles burned out and 5 more disabled. In the future, close cooperation with the infantry and artillery was organized, which allowed a more effective use of tanks in the city.

One of the variants of tank employment in the city, we'll say directly, was unusual. By the end of 3 January, the attacking troops reached the Rákosszentmihály train station on the northeastern edge of Pest. In order to continue the offensive, on the night of 3/4 January, the railroad cars of the trains that were standing at the station were unhitched, and with the help of tanks of the 3rd Tank Brigade, the cars were pulled apart, thereby creating passages for the infantry attacks. In the course of fighting on 4 January, the tank battalion of the 3rd Tank Brigade lost one tank disabled. Subsequently, the tanks operated as part of assault groups, and targeted enemy firing points in the buildings.

The tanks that took part in the assault were split into detachments of 1-2 vehicles and were subordinated to the rifle battalions. The assault groups ground slowly forward against fierce resistance. By 8 January, the tank company of the 39th Tank Brigade didn't have a single serviceable tank; the two remaining T-34s were under repair. The tank battalion of the 3rd Tank Brigade continued to attack.

Up until 5 January, the Soviet forces in Pest, battling their way through enemy fortifications, made slow headway across the entire front. Soon, the strategy had to be changed. On 7 January, the commander of the 2nd Ukrainian Front R.Ia. Malinovsky decided to reallocate his forces around the perimeter of defense in order to concentrate them for key points of attack. Equal pressure along the front was suitable only against light enemy resistance. The stubborn and organized defense of Pest required breaking up the defenders into isolated groups and destroying them in turn through a concentration of force. Asserting in the introductory section of his Order No. 0020/op, "… forces are distributed evenly, which doesn't allow a powerful attack with the aim splitting the [enemy] front into separate pieces," the Front commander went on to order:

1. To the commander of the 7th Guards Army: Launch a main attack with the strength of three divisions in the general direction of Hajtsár Street and Liszt Ferenc Square, and reach the Danube River no later than 11.1.45.
2. To the commander of the 18th Guards Rifle Corps: Launch a main attack with the strength of not less than one and a half divisions in the general direction of Valéria and further on toward the railroad bridge, and reach the Danube River no later than end of day 11.1.45.

Thus, according to Malinvosky's plan, the entire Pest group would be split in two. Since at this time the battle between the forces of the 3rd Ukrainian Front and the IV SS Panzer Corps that was advancing to link up with the city's garrison was raging to the west of Budapest, the situation in Buda was relatively calm. Theoretically, this allowed the defenders to maneuver reserves and to strengthen the defense of Pest by shifting units from Buda. In connection with this, Malinovsky ordered the destruction of the remaining bridges across the Danube, which linked Buda and Pest. Aviation, 203mm howitzers and 152mm howitzer-cannons were committed to this mission in order to fulfill this order. Because the primary type of strike aircraft of the 5th Air Army was the Il-2, the destruction of the bridges ran into serious difficulties. The bombs that the Il-2 could carry weighed only up to 250 kilograms, and thus were unable to cause serious damage to the strongly-built stone and iron bridges across the Danube. The first air attacks proved ineffective. The long-range artillery fire also at first didn't yield the desired result.

In order to improve the organization of the assault on the city, on 11 January 1945 the so-called Budapest Group of Forces was created under the leadership of the commander of the 18th Guards Rifle Corps Major General I.M. Afonin. It included the 18th Guards Corps, the 30th Rifle Corps, and the Romanian 7th Army Corps with attached units. The formation of the Budapest Group could be considered as the start of the serious storming of Budapest according to all the principles of urban warfare and with application of all the previously acquired experience.

The Romanian corps advanced more slowly than its neighbors, and on 15 January their flanks linked up, leaving the Romanians in their rear. At the order of the commander of the 2nd Ukrainian Front, the Romanian 7th Army Corps was withdrawn from the city and was subsequently sent to north Hungary. The casualties suffered by the Romanians in the fighting for Budapest can be considered insignificant – 2,548 men killed, wounded or sick.

Commander of the 2nd Ukrainian Front Marshal R.Ia. Malinovsky.

Commander of the 3rd Ukrainian Front F.I. Tolbukhin at work in his headquarters.

A Wespe self-propelled artillery vehicle abandoned by its crew. The machine presumably belonged to the 13th Panzer Division.

A knocked-out Panther. The blotches on the turret are most likely the results of the fire.

A flame-throwing Flammpanzer III tank, abandoned by its crew during the fighting in
Budapest.

A knocked-out and burned-out Panther Ausf.G; Budapest area, January 1945.

A view of a Budapest street after the storming of the city – burned-out vehicles and building walls riddled by shells and bullets. (TsAMO)

The wreckage of a German 88mm anti-aircraft gun on a Budapest street.

An armored wagon on a Budapest street. The recognition symbol of the Hungarian Army is clearly visible on the side of the wagon. (TsAMO)

An SdKfz.250 of one of the German motorized units abandoned on a Budapest street. (TsAMO)

Hummel self-propelled howitzers, left abandoned on a Budapest street. (TsAMO)

An 88mm gun mounted on the chassis of a Bussing Nag on a Budapest Street. Note the white rings around the barrel of the gun, denoting the number of knocked-out tanks.

Soviet tankers examining the abandoned Hummels shown in the photograph on the previous page. (TsAMO)

The same self-propelled howitzers pictured from above. (TsAMO)

A Hungarian Nimrod self-propelled anti-aircraft gun on a Budapest street, February 1945. (TsAMO)

The wreckage of a German self-propelled anti-aircraft gun in front of the Calvinist Church in Budapest. (TsAMO)

A German Flakpanzer IV abandoned on a Budapest street. In the background, a German glider that has crashed into the wall of a building is visible. These gliders were used to bring in supplies to the city's garrison.

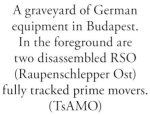

A graveyard of German equipment in Budapest. In the foreground are two disassembled RSO (Raupenschlepper Ost) fully tracked prime movers. (TsAMO)

A Hungarian-manufactured Turan I tank abandoned in a Budapest suburb.

A snow-covered 88mm anti-aircraft gun in one of Budapest's parks. (TsAMO)

Obergruppenführer der Waffen-SS Karl von Pfeffer-Wildenbruch, commander of the Budapest garrison. (Bundesarchiv, Bild 101III-Ege-237-06A, photo: Hermann Ege)

Generalmajor Gerhard Schmidhuber, commander of 13th Panzer Division. (Bundesarchiv, Bild 101I-088-3743-15A, photo: Fischer)

The casualties of the Soviet forces involved in the assault were also on the level of several thousand men. For example, between 1 and 10 January 1945 the 18th Guards Rifle Corps had 791 men killed, 2,567 wounded, 50 missing in action, 72 sick, and 1 non-combat injury (an officer was wounded by the careless handling of a weapon), for a total of 3,841 men. These losses were distributed across four rifle divisions. The tank battalion of the 3rd Tank Brigade, and the tank company of the 39th Tank Brigade lost 20 tanks destroyed by 18 January, virtually their entire complement.

The two attacking Soviet corps kept stubbornly advancing, splitting the defense of the German and Hungarian units. On 16 January the Franz Joseph Bridge collapsed under constant attacks. According to German records it was destroyed by a bomb dropped from the air, but Hungarian records state that it was simply blown up. On the evening of 17 January, the overall commander of the Budapest garrison, SS *Obergruppenführer* Pfeffer-Wildenbruch received authorization to evacuate Pest. The withdrawal to the bridges across the Danube turned into a genuine judgment day. At that moment, two bridges remained intact: a suspension bridge and the Elizabeth Bridge. They both had been serious damaged by artillery and bombs, but they were still standing.

When the bridges were finally blown up at 7 o'clock in the morning on 18 January, people were still crossing it. Later that same day, the 18th Guards Rifle Corps and 30th Rifle Corps finally linked up in the center of the city on the Danube riverbank. A large enemy grouping wound up isolated from the river crossings. Employing part of their force in order to defend along the eastern bank of the Danube, the two rifle corps began methodically reducing the encircled enemy. Over the course of the afternoon, this German and Hungarian grouping in Pest was wiped out – the enemy troops were either killed or taken prisoner. Altogether over the day, 18,519 prisoners were taken, including 320 officers and one general. It should be noted that many of the Hungarian troops deliberately chose to remain in Pest; they even refused to fuel up their vehicles, in order to avoid being evacuated to Buda. They believed that the war for them was already over.

The storming of Buda by the forces of the 3rd Ukrainian Front's 46th Army began back at the end of December 1944. By the start of January, the Front was involved in heavy fighting on the outer ring of encirclement against the IV SS Panzer Corps' efforts to relieve the defenders of Budapest. As a result, the attacks against the western part of the city were sporadic in nature and were unable to crack the defenses. By the decision of the *Stavka* of the Supreme High Command, on 18 January the leadership of the operations to destroy the enemy grouping in Buda was handed over to the 2nd Ukrainian Front. Accordingly, its headquarters took control of the 3rd Ukrainian Front's 75th Guards Rifle Corps (113th and 180th Rifle Divisions, and two regiments of the 109th Rifle Division), the 37th Guards Rifle Corps (the 108th, 316th and 320th Rifle Divisions), and the 83rd Naval Infantry Brigade, which were besieging this part of the city. The transferred rifle corps and brigade were made subordinate to Major General I.M. Afonin's Budapest Group of Forces. Simultaneously, there was a shift of forces in the opposite direction – the 30th Rifle Corps, which had been assaulting Pest, was taken from Malinovsky's command and given to Tolbukhin. Later, the 337th Rifle Division was transferred to the Budapest Group of Forces, but it was placed in the second echelon of the forces' guarding against a possible breakout from Budapest.

As a result of all this reshuffling, on 21 January 1945 the Budapest Group of Forces had the 18th, 37th and 75th Guards Rifle Corps. They numbered respectively 13,140, 16,645, and 14,179 men. The three rifle corps were reinforced by the 5th, 7th and 16th Artillery Divisions, the 462nd Mortar Regiment, and the 12th and 14th Assault Engineer-Sapper Brigades. Two tank companies were committed to the assault on Buda: one from the 23rd Tank Corps (8 T-34 tanks) and one from the 5th Guards Tank Corps (11 T-34 tanks). The initiation of the assault on the western half of Budapest was delayed by the start of *Konrad III*. The IV SS Panzer Corps broke through to the Danube south of Budapest and arrived in force near the temporary bridge at Ercsi, across which all of the Budapest Group of Forces' supplies was flowing. The final and decisive assault on Buda had to be postponed until the situation on the 3rd Ukrainian Front became stabilized.

However, Ivan Mikhailovich Afonin wasn't in command of that assault when it began. On the night of 21 January, while crossing the bridge at Ercsi, his vehicle was strafed by a German aircraft, and the general was severely wounded. He managed to return to service before the war ended, commanded a corps in Czechoslovakia, and later in the brief Manchurian campaign against Japan. The commander of the 53rd Army Lieutenant General I.M. Managarov assumed command of the Budapest Group of Forces.

A report by the German IX SS *Gebirgs* [Mountain] Corps to *Armeegruppe Balck* gives a notion of the Budapest defenders' numbers by the second phase of the assault on the city:

> In order to give an impression of the personnel's condition on 20.1, the Corps command
> after thorough checking reports:
> Ration strength of 43,500 (including Hungarian units)
> Number of wounded: 10,542 (only Germans)
> A total strength of 25,667 (not counting the wounded), including 17,661 Germans; the
> corps' has just 15,149 combat effectives, including 11,130 Germans.[1]

Thus, the attackers were superior to the city's defenders in numbers by approximately 1.7 to 1.

Prior to 30 January, the units of the Budapest Group of Forces were involved in combats of only local significance in Buda, and making only insignificant advances. With the 3rd Ukrainian

Front's launching of the counteroffensive and the elimination of the German threat to the temporary bridge in Ercsi, the time arrived for a decisive assault. As in the case of the storming of Pest, the artillery was to play the key role. As of 1 February 1945, the Budapest Group of Forces had:

114 45mm guns;
60 76mm regimental guns;
245 76mm divisional guns;
30 57mm guns;
160 122mm guns;
116 152mm guns;
69 203mm guns;
307 82mm mortars;
213 120mm mortars;
24 *Katiusha* rocket launchers.

Thus, the number of artillery barrels had even somewhat decreased since the assault on Pest. Only the quantity of 203mm howitzers had noticeably increased. This can be explained on one hand by the fact that the buildings in the city's old quarter on the western bank of the Danube were on average more solidly built, and on the other hand, the flat topography in Pest wasn't favorable for the concentration of artillery firing over open sights. In the hilly topography of Buda, the guns could be deployed in several belts while preserving their ability to fire upon the same target.

In the city's old quarter, there was a large quantity of stone and iron walls around the buildings. The walls were kept under fire from neighboring buildings. It was possible to overcome them only after the use of demolition charges or their destruction by artillery. The demolition charges would be emplaced at night under cover of darkness, or in the daytime under the cover of smoke or even the fire of neighboring units. Tanks always advanced behind the infantry, supporting them with fire from protected locations. The assault groups consisted of 1-2 tanks, a submachine gun platoon, a combat engineer squad, and 3-4 flamethrowers. The tanks of the assault groups advanced in a single file, or staggered 50-60 meters behind the infantry. The overall operational principle of the Budapest Group of Forces remained unchanged – breaking up the enemy defenders into several isolated groups with their subsequent gradual annihilation.

One can cite the attack by the 23rd Tank Corps' tank company on 4-5 February as an illustration of tank operations in Budapest. The road ahead for the attacking Soviet units was blocked by an anti-tank ditch. The tanks took up suitable positions on the approaches to it and placed the adjoining streets under fire from their main guns and machine guns. Meanwhile, the combat engineers and infantrymen began filling the ditch with rubble and to level its earthen parapet. Enemy firing points hindering this work were quickly suppressed by the tanks. When the passage was ready, the tanks crossed over it and the attack was resumed.

The casualties of the units and formations that were assaulting the city can be regarded as moderate. From 1 February to 10 February 1945, the Budapest Group of Forces lost 1,044 men killed, 3,047 wounded, 52 missing in action, 276 sick, and 4 due to non-combat reasons (careless handling of a weapon, etc.), for a total of 4,783 men.[2] The tank company of the 23rd Tank Corps lost 4 tanks destroyed and 1 disabled in the course of fighting for Buda, while the tank company of the 5th Guards Tank Corps lost 5 tanks and had 2 disabled.[3]

The day of 11 February became the turning point, when the 18th and 37th Guards Rifle Corps isolated the southern portion of the main enemy grouping in Buda. Pfeffer-Wildenbruch decided to launch a break out. He reported his intentions by radio to the headquarters of Army Group South, and as he had been ordered, also to *Führer* headquarters, only at the last possible moment, at 15.50 11 February. He transmitted the following:

1. Rations are used up, the last round is in the barrel. The choice is capitulation or the defenseless massacre of the Budapest garrison.
   As a result, I have decided to take to the offensive with the remaining combat-effective German elements, *Honveds* and Arrow Cross members to fight to a new combat and supply position.
2. Breakout with the fall of darkness on 11 February.
   Request passage between Szomor – Máriahalom.
   If passage is not possible there, I will advance into the Pilis Mountains. Request passage there in the area north of Pilisszentkereszt.
3. Recognition signals: two green flares – our own.
4. Present strength 23,900 Germans, of which 9,600 are wounded; 20,000 Hungarians, of which 2,000 are wounded.

Immediately after this message was transmitted by radio, the radio operators destroyed all the radios. Pfeffer-Wildenbuch was afraid that he would be overruled. He wanted nothing that could hinder his operation now.

The encircled forces on 11 February 1945 had remaining 12 Panthers, 9 Hetzers, 6 assault guns, 10-15 tanks of unknown types, and 50-60 guns. Those that could not be pulled out of their present positions stealthily and without betraying the breakout plan in advance were blown up in place. It is possible to assume that not more than 10-12 armored vehicles were gathered together for the breakout attempt. The arrangement of forces for the breakout was as follows: In the first wave were units of the 13th Panzer Division and 8th SS Cavalry Division. They were split up into groups of 30 men, each of which had a Hungarian guide who was knowledgeable of the local area; in the second wave were the SA Division *Feldherrnhalle*, the 22nd SS Cavalry Division, and the Hungarian units.

The plan was kept in deep secrecy. Division commanders were made aware of it at 14.00, regiment commanders – at 16.00, and lower-level officers – after 18.00. Hungarian commanders were informed of it at the last possible moment, since the German command was concerned about leaks of information through them. According to prisoners taken later by the Soviet troops, at 18.00 all the units received an order to prepare for a march and to destroy everything unnecessary for it. Having assembled the forces on a narrow sector in the northern part of the city center, at 20.00 11 February the remnants of the IX SS *Gebirgs* Corps began the breakout operation. Having broken through the front of the 180th Rifle Division, the encircled men began to spread out to the west and northwest, trying to make their way to friendly lines.

By the morning of 12 February, the breach that had been torn in the positions of the 180th Rifle Division was sealed, and units of the Budapest Group of Forces entered Buda. By the end of the day, the city of Budapest was completely in Soviet hands, and in the process, large amounts of materiel and approximately 20,000 prisoners were taken. On 14 February, the main forces of the Budapest Group (with the exception of the 297th Rifle Division and 83rd Naval Infantry Brigade, which were left behind to mop up the city) were sent in pursuit of the enemy's breakout forces. Several large groups of the encircled men were destroyed by forces of the 46th Army. The 2nd Guards Mechanized Corps and 5th Guards Cavalry Corps were also deployed against the enemy groups that were attempting to break out of the city. By 15 February, the vast majority of those trying to escape had either been rounded up or wiped out. Of the approximately 28,000 soldiers and officers attempting to escape the encirclement, only around 800 eventually made it to friendly lines.

Pfeffer-Wildenbruch, who was attempting to break out together with his headquarters by a special route along the so-called Czertovaya Canal, made their way out of the city, but soon after his group was encircled and he was taken prisoner. On 17 February, the Budapest Group of Forces was dissolved, and soon its divisions were distributed to the armies that were standing along the front that was facing to the west. With this, the somewhat prolonged epopee of the storming of the Hungarian capital, which had dragged on in part due to the relief attempts, came to an end.

7

Results and Conclusions

The January German offensive with the aim of freeing the Budapest garrison through the introduction of several fresh divisions, including panzer divisions, into the fighting can be called an attempt to reach an objective with far too inadequate forces. From the point of view of tank operations, the optimal route of attack around Lake Velence from the south required significant reserves in order to cover the extending flanks. However, this was no longer 1940, 1941 or even 1942. Thus the German command no longer had army corps with powerful infantry divisions. The panzer divisions of Gille's panzer corps simultaneously had to crack the Soviet defenses and to tend to threats to its flanks. All of this slowed the advance and allowed the Soviet command to set up a new line of defense.

Given all the ambiguities of such an indicator as casualties, they are still the yardstick for assessing many battles. The currently available data don't in any way permit the success of the Soviet forces in repelling the *Konrad* offensives to be called a pyrrhic victory. The personnel losses of the 4th Guards Army for January 1945 amounted to 3,588 killed, 11,552 wounded, 4,543 missing in action, 132 non-combat injuries, and 1,682 sick.[1] In total, G.F. Zakharov's army, which carried the main burden of repelling the German offensives, lost 21,467 men. According to the measures of 1945, these casualties are rather high, especially with respect to the missing in action. The overall losses of the 5th Guards Cavalry Corps, which was subordinate to the 3rd Ukrainian Front for January 1945, amounted to 2,165 men. The Front's 18th Tank Corps suffered 1,740 casualties, and the 23rd Tank Corps, in the course of the counteroffensive between 26 and 31 January lost 313 killed and 659 wounded.

The losses of *Armeegruppe Balck* for January 1945 (excluding those of the IX SS *Gebirgs* Corps in Budapest) amounted to 3,598 killed, 16,504 wounded, 1,520 missing in action and 12,751 sick.[2] The causes for the high number of sick are unknown; possibly, the lightly wounded were included in this category. It also isn't clear whether these figures include the Hungarian losses, but most likely they do not. Altogether, the losses of *Armeegruppe Balck* can be placed at 25-30,000 men.

The overall balance of losses between *Armeegruppe Balck* on the one hand, and the opposing armies of the 2nd and 3rd Ukrainian Fronts on the other, gives a doubtless advantage to the Soviet side, especially when the complete destruction and imprisonment of the Budapest garrison is considered. The losses of the troops that were assaulting the Hungarian capital were substantially lower than those of its garrison. For example, the total losses of the assaulting 18th Guards Rifle Corps for January 1945 was 2,357 men, and of the 7th Guards Army – 9,120 men (including combat operations outside of Budapest).

The 18th Tank Corps, which became the bulwark of the 3rd Ukrainian Front's defense, over the month of January 1945, lost 161 T-34, 21 ISU-122, 21 SU-76, 13 ISU-152, and 12 SU-85. The 23rd Tank Corps according to records of the Front headquarters lost 84 T-34 and 3 ISU-122 between 26 January and 31 January 1945.

When studying the January battles west of Budapest, the style of conducting the defensive operation by the 3rd Ukrainian Front command immediately catches the eye. Tolbukhin strove to keep the tank and mechanized corps under his immediate command. However, this wasn't done in order to launch counterattacks. Rather, the tank and mechanized corps became the "steel girders" of the defense. With the initiation of the *Konrad I* and *Konrad II* offensives, a new defensive line began to form 15-20 kilometers behind the crumbling original line. In order to reestablish a front, mechanized and cavalry corps moved out and took on the advancing German units. Comparable in their mobility to the tank brigades, the mechanized brigades also possessed artillery. Their arrival also substantially reinforced the newly created line of defense. Behind the mechanized units were the rifle divisions following in their wake, which cemented the front line. However, as before the "steel girders" of the newly built positions remained the tanks, which deployed in static positions would take on the enemy.

The evaluation of such an approach to the use of the tank forces was not unanimous. The *Stavka* criticized Tolbukhin for scattering his tanks across a broad front. In reality, the uncertain nature of the enemy's plans compelled Tolbukhin to "gird" several directions of attack simultaneously, with no concentration of strength on any particular one of them. However, we also have examples of other Red Army defensive operations, when the mechanized formations were hastily thrown into costly counterattacks and rapidly expended their combat effectiveness, after which they were also compelled to be used as "girders", but now with inadequate strength.

"Tolbukhin's system" suffered a setback only during *Konrad III*, when the front fell apart too quickly, before an adequately strong defensive line could be built 10-20 kilometers behind the initial line. The deploying anti-tank artillery regiments were crushed, while the tank corps was outflanked on both sides. Then the "girding" of the defenses of the 5th Guards Cavalry Corps again justified itself as a tactic, but there soon followed a second "Prokhorovka" with the head-on counterattack by Akhmanov's tank corps against the solidly built tip of the German panzer wedge. Incidentally, in the course of *Konrad III*, Tolbukhin nevertheless showed that he was a military commander who had mastered the art of the counterattack. He used the 18th Tank Corps, which had been quickly replenished with armor, for a stroke against the soft underbelly of the IV SS Panzer Corps.

On the whole, the adroitness with which the tank and mechanized corps were used is noteworthy. The brigade system of organization allowed the formation of combat groups (in the German terminology) around the kernel of the tank and mechanized brigades, strengthening them with self-propelled, rocket and tube artillery. Even when isolated from the main forces of its parent corps, the availability of a headquarters on the brigade level ensured command and control over such a combat group. With the organizational structure that the tank forces of the Red Army had back in 1941, such a tactic was practically impossible.

The air forces of the two sides played an important role in the January battles. It is sufficient to recall the heavy airstrikes by the German fighter-bombers in the area of Bajna, which cleared a path forward for the SS troops on 3-4 January.

The total losses for the 3rd Ukrainian Front's 17th Air Army for January 1945 amounted to 241 aircraft (47 La-5, 140 Il-2, 14 Lend-Lease Douglas A-20 Havocs, 30 Iak-3/9, 3 Pe-2 and 4 Po-2). The survivability of the Soviet aircraft in the January fighting is characterized by the following data on the number of combat sorties and hours of flight per 1 combat loss:

Table 4 Number of Combat Sorties and Hours of Flight per 1 Combat Loss

	Yak-9	La-5	Il-2	B-3	Pe-2	Po-2
Combat Sorties	60	71	45	52	40	2,380
Hours of Flight	48	56	38	73	60	2,588

If the figure for the losses of Pe-2 at just 3 aircraft (moreover reconnaissance aircraft) can be considered absurdly low, then the high losses of the Il-2 ground attack aircraft stand out among the losses of the other types. As the main strike aircraft of the 17th Air Army (the 3rd Ukrainian Front simply had no Pe-2 or Tu-2 acting as bombers), the Il-2s sustained losses from both enemy ground fire and as a result of enemy fighter attacks. Of the 140 Il-2s lost, 50 were downed by enemy anti-aircraft fire, 53 by enemy fighters, and 14 failed to return from combat missions. The remaining were non-combat losses. The Il-2s also logged more flight hours than any of the others; of the 12,000 individual combat sorties over the month of January, 6,000 were conducted by the *Shturmoviki*.

In the above text, the low effectiveness of the Il-2 in the role of bridge destroyers has already been noted. However, they inflicted painful strikes against the attacking German units. For example, on 20 January the 3rd SS Panzer Division *Totenkopf* made the following request to a *Luftwaffe* liaison officer: "I request the hasty covering of the Seregélyes 8844 area by fighters; constant raids by enemy ground attack aircraft."[3]

One of the novelties (relative, of course) of the *Konrad* offensives was the wide use of night actions by the Germans. Such night attacks had a substantial effect on the course of combat operations. This was reflected in a discussion that took place between the commander of the Sixth Army Balck and the commander of the IV SS Panzer Corps Gille on 26 January 1945, when the latter directly stated, "We are mainly acting at night."

It isn't totally clear what role that panzers equipped with night-vision optics played in this. It is reliably known that Panthers of the 130th *Lehr* [Training] Panzer Regiment of the *Panzer Lehr* Division, which were equipped with infrared optics, were operating in Hungary. The first combat use of night-vision optics belongs to Operation *Konrad I*. However, the number of tanks equipped with such optics for night operations was small. The rest used much more prosaic means for night fighting. For example, tankers of I/24th Panzer Regiment (Panthers) illuminated the battlefield with the help of illumination rifle grenades. They were discharged from launchers that were attached to a carbine barrel, and descending under a parachute, burned for around a minute.

For one reason or another, the Germans opted to employ night operations widely in the course of the *Konrad* offensives, and this required special measures in response from the Soviet side. In particular, flammable materials began to be piled in front of the anti-tank artillery positions in order to illuminate the area. It is interesting to note that back in the summer of 1941, the Soviet troops caught in a difficult position also made broad use of night operations.

In the defensive battles around Budapest, the Red Army's latest self-propelled gun, the SU-100 tank destroyer, was used for the first time. Despite their less than stellar debut at the beginning of January 1945, they played an important role and were highly regarded by their crews and the command. In a summary report from the commander of the 1st Guards Mechanized Corps' artillery Guards Lieutenant Colonel Zakharov dated 15 February 1945, he noted that despite the large size of the 100mm main gun, the crew's work conditions in comparison with those of the SU-85 were no worse. The self-propelled gun's maneuverability and the performance of its running gear had also not deteriorated in comparison with the SU-85. The combat rate of fire, despite a shell that was twice as heavy (32.6 kilograms versus 16 kilograms), remained acceptable – 4-5 shots per minute, against the SU-85's 7-8 shots per minute. He also noted that the ammunition storage and commander's cupola had improved over their previous versions. Regarding the SU-100's armor protection, Zakharov stated: "The frontal armor of the SU-100 is invulnerable to light and medium [anti-tank] artillery; against heavy tanks and 88mm guns, the frontal armor is inadequate and very frangible."[4] Among the SU-100's other shortcomings, he mentioned the ponderous operation of the gun laying mechanisms and the fact that the optics were often damaged by the shock of shell hits, whereas in the SU-85, the optics were unaffected by the shock of shell hits. Zakharov also observed that it would be desirable for the SU-100 to have a machine gun for self-defense against infantry. On the whole, the SU-100 self-propelled guns were evaluated as "a most effective means for combating the enemy's heavy tanks."

A German 150mm sFH 18 howitzer abandoned on the approaches to
Budapest. (TsAMO)

A Panzerjäger IV abandoned by its crew. A shell is embedded in the barrel of the gun.

Searchlights and sound detection equipment aboard platform cars seized by Soviet troops.
Hungary, end of 1944.

An abandoned Hummel self-propelled artillery vehicle. The gun's barrel is fixed in its travelling
position.

An anti-aircraft Flakpanzer IV Mobelwagen with the 37mm Flak 43 cannon, February 1945, Budapest area.

A captured Hungarian-manufactured Turan I tank on a railroad platform.

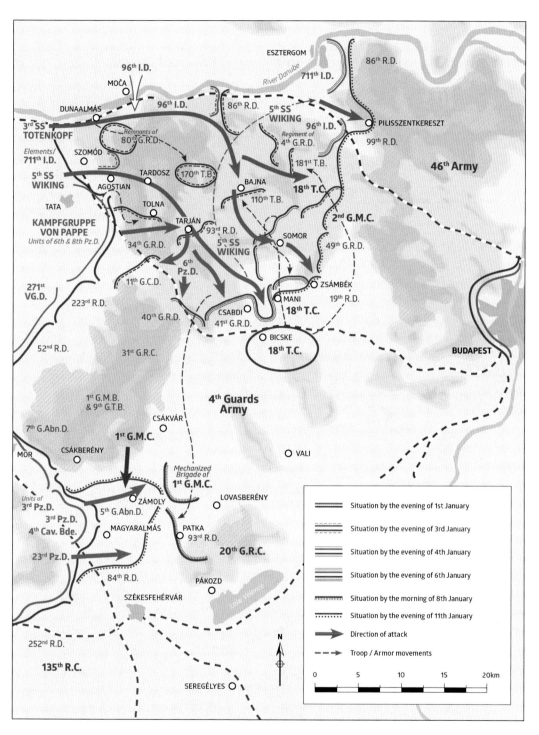

Map 1 Repulse of the German Counteroffensives *Konrad I* and *II*, 1-11 January 1945

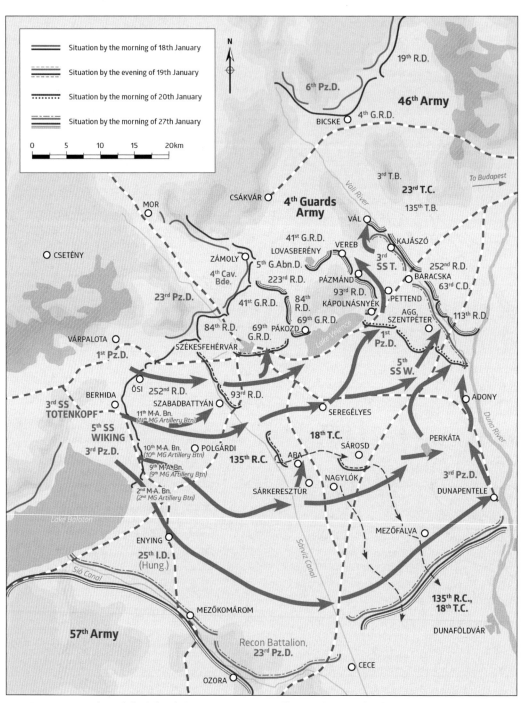

N

19th R.D.

6th Pz.D.

46th Army

BICSKE   4th G.R.D.

Váli River

3rd T.B.

To Budapest

CSÁKVÁR   4th Guards Army

23rd T.C.

135th T.B.

MOR

VÁL

KAJÁSZÓ

CSETÉNY

41st G.R.D.

LOVASBERÉNY   VEREB

3rd SS T.

252nd R.D.

ZÁMOLY   5th G.Abn.D.

BARACSKA

4th Cav. Bde.

223rd R.D.   PÁZMÁND

93rd R.D.

63rd C.D.

23rd Pz.D.

41st G.R.D.   84th R.D.

KÁPOLNÁSNYÉK

PETTEND

113th R.D.

84th R.D.   69th

PÁKOZD

AGG. SZENTPÉTER

VÁRPALOTA

G.R.D.   69th G.R.D.

Lake Velence

1st Pz.D.

1st Pz.D.

SZÉKESFEHÉRVÁR

5th SS W.

BERHIDA

ŐSI   252nd R.D.

93rd R.D.

ADONY

3rd SS TOTENKOPF

SZABADBATTYÁN

SEREGÉLYES

Duna River

11th M.A. Bn. (11th MG Artillery Btn)

5th SS WIKING

10th M.A. Bn. (10th MG Artillery Btn)   POLGÁRDI

18th T.C.   SÁROSD

PERKÁTA

3rd Pz.D.

9th M.A. Bn. (9th MG Artillery Btn)

135th R.C.   ABA

NAGYLÓK

3rd Pz.D.

2nd M.A. Bn. (2nd MG Artillery Btn)

SÁRKERESZTÚR

DUNAPENTELE

Lake Balaton

MEZŐFÁLVA

ENYING

25th I.D. (Hung.)

Sió Canal

Sárvíz Canal

135th R.C., 18th T.C.

MEZŐKOMÁROM

DUNAFÖLDVÁR

57th Army

Recon Battalion, 23rd Pz.D.

CECE

OZORA

Map 2 Repulse of the Third German Counteroffensive (*Konrad III*) 18-27 January 1945

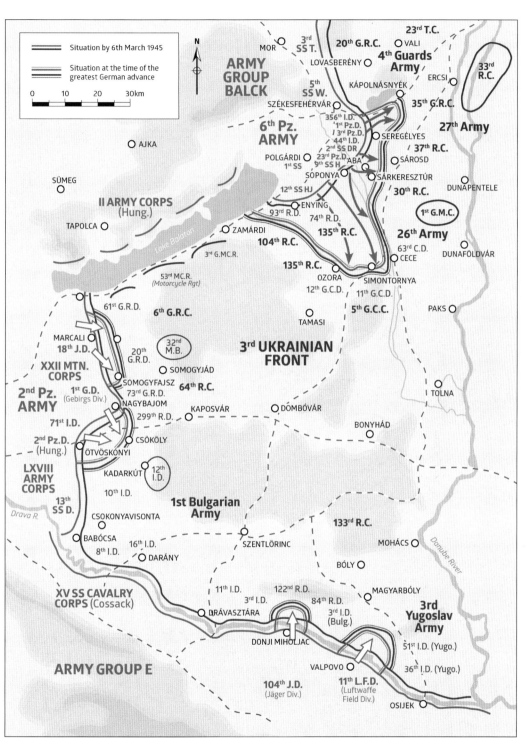

Map 3 The General Course of Combat Operations between 6 and 15 March 1945

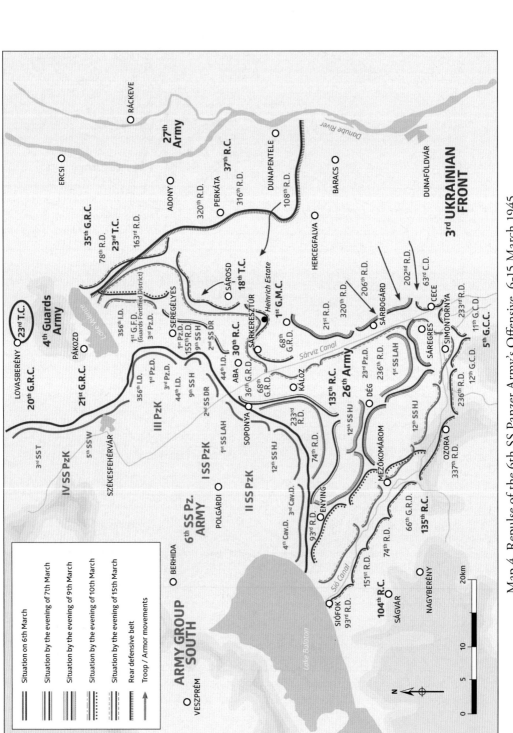

Map 4 Repulse of the 6th SS Panzer Army's Offensive, 6-15 March 1945

Soviet soldiers and officers inspecting a Panther, knocked-out on a Budapest street.

An abandoned Munitionsträger (ammunition carrier) Hummel in Budapest.
(TsAMO)

Amphibious Volkswagen Schwimmwagen abandoned in
Budapest. (TsAMO)

Part II

The Final German Offensive of the Second World War

8

Plans of the German Command

At the very beginning of 1945, Hitler had made a proposal to remove the Sixth SS Panzer Army from the Western Front, replenish it with equipment and troops, and transfer it to the Eastern Front. Already on 8 January 1945, the Chief of the General Staff General-Field Marshal Rundstedt received an order to begin redeploying units of the Sixth SS Panzer Army to central Germany. However, despite the opinion of a number of German generals, in particular Guderian, Hitler was proposing to use the SS panzer divisions not on the central sector of the Eastern Front in the area of the Oder River, but in Hungary. The main argument in support of such a position was the need to defend the oilfields in western Hungary, which at the time were producing up to 80% of the Third Reich's oil. Colonel General Jodl stated the following about Hitler's decision: "The *Führer* again pointed to the enormous significance of the oil producing sites located southwest of Lake Balaton. Control over them was decisive in the matter of the further continuation of the war."

However, the redeployment of the Sixth SS Panzer Army could not be implemented according to a tight schedule – many of its divisions were still locked in combat in the Ardennes. Moreover, because of the pressure of the Anglo-American troops, several of the SS divisions that had been pulled out of the front lines had to be thrown back into the fighting. For example, because of the sharpening of the situation on the front's right flank, on 14 January 1945 the German command had to re-commit the 2nd and 9th SS Panzer Divisions, which had been pulled into the reserve. Only by 22 January were the divisions of the Sixth SS Panzer Army completely disengaged from the battle, having been replaced by the Fifth and Seventh Armies.

Logistics became another obstacle in the transfer of the SS divisions – by this time the Allied air forces were systematically targeting the railroad hubs in Germany. In addition, the German rail system was experiencing a deficit of coal for its steam engines. At Hitler's personal order, elements of the III Flak Corps were allocated to cover the trains that were transporting the Sixth SS Panzer Army.

The movement of the SS divisions was conducted under the strictest secrecy, accompanied by an active disinformation campaign, the aim of which was to convince the Allied intelligence, and first and foremost Soviet intelligence, that the Sixth SS Panzer Army was reassembling in the area of Berlin. Even when the SS divisions began shifting from central Germany to Hungary, the German command continued to attempt to mislead the Soviets, striving to convince them that the Sixth SS Panzer Army was now positioned east of Berlin. The trains carrying the divisions of the Sixth SS Panzer Army southward were moving primarily at night, and at the order of the German command, the divisional insignia on the equipment had been painted over, and the registration numbers on the vehicles and prime movers covered up.

The assembly of the Sixth SS Panzer Army in Hungary was completed by 8 February 1945. In order to maintain concealment, its formations and units were given code names. For example, the Sixth SS Panzer Army's headquarters went by the code name "Headquarters of the Higher Pioneer Command of Hungary", while the headquarters of the subordinate corps and divisions were called "SS Replacement and Training Units". For example, the headquarters of the II SS Panzer Corps was known as "*Ersatz Stab* [Training Headquarters], Army Group South", the 1st SS

Panzer Division *Leibstandarte Adolf Hitler* was called *"Ersatz Stab Totenkopf"*, the 2nd SS Panzer Division *Das Reich* – *"Ersatz Stab Nord"*, etc. All of the divisions were instructed to observe strict radio silence, while the SS troops were forbidden to approach the front.

In this fashion, beginning from the moment of its arrival in Hungary until the start of the March 1945 offensive, the divisions of the Sixth SS Panzer Army had nearly an entire month for rest, refitting and reorganizing. In the process, they were brought back up to table strength in personnel. However, as Georg Maier, the former Deputy Chief of Staff for Operations of the Sixth SS Panzer Army pointed out in his book *Drama between Budapest and Vienna*, this applied only to numbers, not quality: "The fighting during the fateful year of 1943, which brought the turning point of the war, had brought such high casualties that they could not be made up rapidly enough with trained replacements suitable for frontline duty. As a result, combat power decreased rapidly." The majority of the new arrivals were conscripts, and this was true for the *Waffen-SS* divisions as well. Thus in the course of the month, in the SS panzer divisions that had combat experience, the tankers worked feverishly to prepare the new men. However, according to the opinion of Maier, "when speaking of the SS divisions of 1945, it is necessary to keep in mind that these were not at all those divisions of three or even two years before, with a different combat spirit and a different combat capability." Nonetheless, despite such assertions by the former German officer, the SS panzer divisions even in 1945 remained a serious adversary and were more powerful than their counterparts in the *Wehrmacht* formations.

It should be said that the secrecy surrounding the movement of the Sixth SS Panzer Army didn't help much – despite the fact that Soviet intelligence failed to detect the headquarters of this army itself right up to the start of the March offensive, the intelligence organs of the Red Army uncovered a major German panzer grouping in front of the 3rd Ukrainian Front. This allowed preparations to repel the enemy offensive in March 1945.

The planning for the offensive in the Lake Velence – Lake Balaton – Drava River – Danube River area, which received the code name *"Frühlingserwachen"* [Spring Awakening], was initiated by the German command in the latter half of February 1945. In addition to the Sixth SS Panzer Army, units of Army Groups South and E were to take part in the operation.

The first option for the offensive plan, which later received the designation "Course of Action C1", was worked out by *General der Panzertruppen* Balck and presented to the OKH on 20 February 1945. According to Balck's draft plan, the Sixth SS Panzer Army was to attack west of the Sárviz Canal with two panzer corps, after which its right flank would pivot and attack to the south. One day later, *Armeegruppe Balck* would attack east of the Sárviz Canal, and then advance in the direction of Adony, in order to seal the gap between Lake Velence and the Danube. In the operation's third phase, two panzer divisions of the III Panzer Corps would make a deep penetration between the Danube and Lake Velence to the area of Szekszárd.

Having been reworked by Lieutenant General von Grolman, this draft plan received the designation "Course of Action C2". According to it, the offensive *Schwerpunkt* would push to the east of the Sárviz Canal with the intention to drive to the Danube River crossings at Dunaföldvár and Paks, while the Red Army units located northeast of Lake Velence were to be encircled by the enveloping attacks of five divisions. Simultaneously, the Second Panzer Army would launch attacks, as well as Army Group E in the direction of Pécs.

The headquarters of the Sixth SS Panzer Army presented its own plan for the offensive, which was later called "Course of Action A". It proposed to wait until the Red Army went on the offensive toward Vienna (which was anticipated to set in motion at the beginning of March), and then to launch an attack with the SS panzer divisions to the northeast along Lake Velence, in order to link up with an infantry group that would attack to the southeast out of the area north of Zámoly. It would then regroup and launch an attack to the south and east to link up with the Second Panzer Army.

On 25 February 1945, the various draft plans for Operation *Frühlingserwachen* were reviewed by Hitler at the *Führer* Brief in the Reich Chancellery. In the course of the discussion, "Course of Action C2" was adopted. The plan included units of the Sixth SS Panzer Army, *Armeegruppe Balck*, the Second Panzer Army (71st Infantry, 1st *Volks-Gebirg* Infantry and 118th *Jäger* Divisions, and the 16th SS Panzer Grenadier Division *Reichsführer-SS*), as well as the LXXXXI Army Corps from Army Group E in order to implement it.

An abandoned Wespe self-propelled howitzer. The tracks have been removed, most likely as a matter of convenience for towing.

German armored vehicles seized by Soviet troops: A Hummel self-propelled howitzer and a Pz. IV tank. Note the arcs welded onto the Hummel's fighting compartment to provide for a tarpaulin covering.

A StuG 40 self-propelled gun, which has become the booty of Soviet troops. A shield for a machine gun is visible on the roof.

A deeply mired Panther, abandoned by its crew. Spare track sections have been mounted on the tank's turret as supplementary protection.

Commander of Sixth SS Panzer Army, *Oberstgruppenführer und Generaloberst der Waffen-SS* Josef "Sepp" Dietrich (left). (Bundesarchiv, Bild 183-J28625, photo: Roeder)

9

German Panzer Forces

The main shock grouping for Operation *Frühlingserwachen* was the Sixth SS Panzer Army. The panzer armies were Germany's operational groups of panzer troops in the Second World War. However, in distinction from the Soviet tank armies, which had a fixed combat roster, in the German panzer armies only the headquarters were a constant; the subordinate formations and units could change. If you will, however, the Sixth SS Panzer Army was something of an exception. It began forming up on 6 September 1944 on the basis of the LXXXX Army Corps headquarters. At the end of the month, the army became subordinated to Army Group B on the Western Front, and in December 1944 it took part in Operation *Wacht am Rhein* – the German offensive in the Ardennes.

The core of the Sixth SS Panzer Army consisted of the I SS Panzer Corps (the 1st SS Panzer Division *Leibstandarte Adolf Hitler* and 12th SS Panzer Division *Hitlerjügend*) and the II SS Panzer Corps (2nd SS Panzer Division *Das Reich* and 9th SS Panzer Division *Hohenstaufen*). These two panzer corps remained as part of the Sixth SS Panzer Army right up to the end of the war. However, at various times, they were joined by other divisions and various *kampfgruppen*.

At the start of Operation *Frühlingserwachen*, the Sixth SS Panzer Army consisted of the I and II SS Panzer Corps, the I Cavalry Corps (the 3rd and 4th Cavalry Divisions, which were reformed in February 1945 on the basis of the 3rd and 4th Cavalry Brigades), as well as the 23rd Panzer and the 44th *Volksgrenadier* Division. In addition, *Armeegruppe Balck*, which was operating on the left flank of the Sixth SS Panzer Army, included the 1st and 3rd Panzer Divisions and the 356th Infantry Division.

The SS panzer divisions that took part in Operation *Frühlingserwachen* were organized according to the TO&E adopted in 1944. According to it, the division consisted of a headquarters, one panzer regiment, two panzer grenadier regiments, an artillery regiment, plus a Panzerjäger battalion, a Flak battalion, a signals battalion, as well as reconnaissance, engineer, motor transport, commissary, sanitary and reserve battalions and a repair depot.

The panzer regiment consisted of a headquarters, a headquarters company (3 Panthers, 5 Pz IV and a platoon of 37mm Flakpz. IV Mobelwagen anti-aircraft vehicles), two panzer battalions (one equipped with Pz. IV, the other with Panthers), and a repair company (4 Bergepanther recovery-repair tanks). Each panzer battalion included a headquarters with a headquarters company (8 tanks and 5 Sd.Kfz.251 armored halftracks, and a Flak platoon), and four line companies (each with 22 tanks). Thus, a fully-equipped and staffed panzer regiment numbered 208 tanks, 10 armored halftracks and 4 Bergepanthers).

The panzer grenadier regiments of the panzer division were of different structures. The first regiment consisted of a headquarters, a headquarters company, two motorized panzer grenadier battalions, a combat engineer company, and a battery of heavy self-propelled sIG 33 infantry support guns – 6 Sd.Kfz.138/1 Grille built on the chassis of the Pz. 38(t) tank. The second panzer grenadier regiment was significantly stronger and consisted of a headquarters, a headquarters company (9 Sd.Kfz.251 armored halftracks) and two panzer grenadier battalions, the first of which was mounted in armored halftracks (88 Sd.Kfz.251, of which 12 were Sd.Kfz.251/9 *Stummel* halftracks equipped with 75mm guns, and 21 were Sd.Kfz.251/17 halftracks equipped with 20mm guns), the other in trucks. However, the latter included an engineer company in armored halftracks (14 Sd.Kfz.251, one of which was equipped with 20mm Flak guns, and 6 Sd.Kfz.251/16 flamethrower halftracks), and a battery of sIG 33 heavy self-propelled infantry support guns – 6 armored vehicles. Altogether the two panzer grenadier regiments numbered 111 armored halftracks of various modifications, 44 mortars, 18 20mm Flak guns, 30 flamethrowers and 12 150mm self-propelled guns.

The panzer artillery regiment consisted of three battalions: one self-propelled (6 Hummel 150mm self-propelled howitzer vehicles, 12 Wespe 105mm self-propelled howitzer vehicles, 6 Sd.Kfz.251 armored halftracks, 6 Beobpz. III forward artillery observation vehicles constructed on the basis of the Pz. III tank, and 2 ammunition carriers converted from the Wespe self-propelled howitzer), and two towed battalions (12 105mm leFH 18 howitzers, 8 150mm sFH 18 howitzers and 4 105mm K.18 guns). In addition, the panzer artillery battalions had 20mm Flak platoons.

Each panzer division had a powerful reconnaissance battalion, which was capable of conducting many combat assignments independently. It included a headquarters with a headquarters company, four armored halftrack companies, and a logistics company – altogether 111 armored halftracks of various modifications (55 Sd.Kfz.250, 56 Sd.Kfz.251). It also had 16 Sd.Kfz.234 armored cars.

A Panzerjäger battalion had a composite structure: it included both towed anti-tank guns (12 75mm PaK 40 anti-tank guns) and assault guns (21 StuG III assault guns), 1 Sd.Kfz.251 armored halftrack, and 2 Bergepanther.III recovery tanks.

The Flak battalion included various weapons – 12 88mm Flak guns, 9 37mm Flak guns, and 12 20mm Flak guns. The engineer battalion was also equipped with armored halftracks – altogether 33 Sd.Kfz.251 (including several Sd.Kfz.251/7 assault engineer vehicles with fittings to carry assault bridge ramps on the sides), as was the signals battalion (16 Sd.Kfz.251, among which were the Sd.Kfz.251/3 communications Funkpanzerwagen, fitted with extra radio equipment for command use, and the Sd.Kfz.251/11 telephone line layer).

Altogether, a fully-equipped and staffed panzer division was to have more than 19,000 men and 571 armored vehicles (208 tanks, 49 assault and self-propelled guns, 6 artillery observation vehicles, 6 recovery/repair tanks, 2 armored ammunition carriers, 290 armored halftracks and 16 armored cars), as well as 156 guns and mortars and 848 machine guns. The *Wehrmacht* panzer divisions that took part in Operation *Frühlingserwachen* were formed according to an analogous TO&E.

According to its composition, one fully-equipped German panzer division was superior to both the Red Army's tank corps and mechanized corps. The presence of a large number of various armored vehicles (tanks, self-propelled guns, and armored halftracks and Flak self-propelled guns) in it enabled it to carry out the most varied combat missions. The Germans also made wide use of *kampfgruppen*, which normally consisted of a composite mixture of armor, panzer grenadiers, assault engineers and artillery, which enabled them to conduct more agile maneuvers on the battlefield in a changing situation.

For the sake of justice it should be said that in 1945, not a single panzer division (either *Wehrmacht* or SS) was fully equipped according to the TO&E. This was due to the heavy losses at the fronts and the diminishing output of armored vehicles from Reich factories. In order somehow to get around the situation that had arisen, back in the autumn of 1944 the decision was taken to substitute a company of Pz. IV/70 self-propelled guns in place of the authorized Pz. IV or Panther tanks, of which there was not enough. In addition, the possibility was foreseen of forming panzer battalions with a fewer number of tanks in the panzer company – each with 17, 14 or even just 10 tanks instead of the table number of 22. However, even these measures were not enough to offset the situation.

In addition to the panzer divisions, other tank units took part in Operation *Frühlingserwachen*. The most powerful of them (according both to their composition and number of tanks) were the heavy panzer battalions equipped with King Tigers. Both the SS 501st Heavy Panzer Battalion and the *Wehrmacht's* 509th Heavy Panzer Battalion took part in the fighting at Lake Balaton.

According to the TO&E that was adopted in November 1944, the Tiger battalion included a headquarters and a battalion headquarters company (3 tanks altogether), three line companies of 14 tanks each (three platoons of 4 tanks each, plus 2 tanks of the company headquarters), a Flak platoon (8 Flak Pz. IV Wirbelwind), a transportation column (16 trucks and 2-3 18-ton Sd.Kfz.9 halftrack prime movers), a maintenance company, and a supply company with 35 trucks. Altogether, the heavy panzer battalion numbered 45 Tiger tanks, 8 Flak Pz. IV, and 97 trucks and prime movers.

As of 6 March 1945, the 509th Heavy Panzer Battalion had 35 serviceable King Tigers, while the SS 501st Heavy Panzer Battalion had 31; another 23 tanks from both battalions were undergoing repair. In addition, in reserve was *Feldherrnhalle's* heavy panzer battalion with 33 serviceable King Tigers, as well as a company of 8 Tiger I heavy tanks in the SS Panzer Division *Totenkopf*. Altogether, not less than 65-70 Tigers and King Tigers took part in Operation *Frühlingserwachen*.

The battles near Lake Balaton became one of the few on the Eastern Front where the heavy Jagdpanther tank destroyers were used, which were based on the chassis of the Pz. V Panther tank. They equipped the 560th Heavy Panzerjäger Battalion, which was formed in the summer of 1944. True, by March 1945, this battalion had just 6 serviceable Jagdpanther and 12 Tiger tanks, of which 6 were undergoing repair.

In addition to the tank units, the German formations at Lake Balaton had a large quantity of tank destroyers lighter than the Jagdpanther, and assault guns. In the first place, in addition to those present in the panzer and panzer grenadier divisions, there were the assault gun brigades: *Armeegruppe Balck's* 303rd Assault Gun Brigade and the Second Panzer Army's 261st Assault Gun Brigade. According to TO&E, the assault gun brigade consisted of a headquarters, three batteries and a transportation company, amounting altogether to either 45 (33 StuG 40 and 12 StuH 42) or 31 (22 StuG 40 and 9 StuH 42) assault guns. At the start of Operation *Frühlingserwachen*, the 303rd Assault Gun Brigade numbered approximately 30 assault guns, while the 261st Assault Gun Brigade had approximately 25.

Panzerjäger elements, in addition to the battalions that were part of the panzer divisions, were also present as panzerjäger companies in the infantry, grenadier and *Volksgrenadier* divisions. According to the adopted TO&E, the panzerjäger company consisted of a headquarters, which had two tank destroyers, and three platoons of 4 tank destroyers each, totaling altogether 14 Hetzer light tank destroyers. By the start of March 1945, 81 such panzerjäger companies had been organized.

In addition to the aforementioned formations and units, *Armeegruppe Balck* had the 219th Assault Gun Battalion, which as of 6 March 1945 had no less than 20 Brummbär assault guns; these were 150mm guns set in a casemate-style armored superstructure mounted on the chassis of the Pz. IV tank, which were designed to provide direct infantry fire support. *Armeegruppe Balck* also had the 351st Flammpanzer Company, which numbered 7 flame throwing Pz. III Flammpanzers.

By the beginning of 1945, the primary tank that armed the German panzer units was the Pz. V Panther – during Operation *Frühlingserwachen*, more than half the tanks in the panzer regiments consisted of Panthers. In addition, there was also a rather large quantity of *Jagdpanzer* IV/70 and Hetzer tank destroyers, as well as assault guns. During the March fighting near Lake Balaton, these self-propelled guns comprised almost one-third of the German armored vehicles.

A separate subject that merits discussion is the use of infrared night vision optics in the Lake Balaton fighting. In Germany, work to develop such devices was being done by the AEG firm from the beginning of the 1930s. In 1939, the prototype of such a device for use by the German Army was created. It underwent testing on the 37mm PaK 35/36 anti-tank gun, but the results were disappointing to the military. They desired night optical sights with capabilities equivalent to firing at daytime.

A knocked-out Panzerjäger IV tank destroyer. Note the Zimmerit coating covering the armor.

A disabled Pz.IV Ausf.H. The camouflage is clearly visible, as are the spare track sections installed on the tank's frontal armor.

A Panther tank, prepared for the repair of its drive train and abandoned during a retreat.

A King Tiger from the 509th Heavy Panzer Battalion that has been destroyed by an internal explosion.

A knocked-out King Tiger of the 509th Heavy Panzer Battalion. The number "52" was applied by the Soviet inspection team.

An abandoned Bergepanther repair-recovery tank; Hungary, January 1945.

An abandoned Panther of the 23rd Panzer Division. The divisional insignia is visible on the front armor, as is the number applied by the Soviet inspection team – "62".

In the autumn of 1942, tests of a night optical sight for the 75mm PaK 40 gun were started, which concluded in the middle of the following year. Despite the fact that the results were not bad – firing was possible out to a range of 400 meters – the *Wehrmacht's* arms bureau delayed in giving its approval for the device. At the beginning of 1944, the AEG firm at its own initiative, without waiting for final approval, produced 1,000 night optical sights for the PaK 40 anti-tank gun.

The combat operations in Normandy in 1944 served as a stimulus for work on infrared optics. The Allied air forces ruled the skies over Normandy, and often the German troops could shift locations only under the cover of darkness. Thus, night optical equipment began to arrive in the *Wehrmacht* by the autumn of 1944.

The sight consisted of an infrared searchlight and an image converter. The infrared searchlight might be of various diameters (for example, 30 centimeters on the PaK 40 or Marder self-propelled guns), but they all received the designation Uhu (Owl). In accordance with their intended use, there were different versions of night vision devices – three types for nighttime gunnery, the Zielgerät ("aiming device") 1128, 1221 and 1222; an equal number for night driving, the Fahrgerät (FG) 1250, 1252 and 1253; and one for observation, the Beobachtungsgerät ("observation device") 1251. The main difference among these devices was the dimensions of the searchlight and image converter, and whether they could be mounted on tanks, self-propelled guns or vehicles.

In the autumn of 1944, a night vision device mounted on a Panther tank underwent testing. For this, the observation device Beobachtungsgerät 1251 was used, which was mounted on the commander's cupola. In addition, the tank was equipped with an auxiliary generator and batteries sufficient to ensure the device's operation for up to four hours. The given assembly received the designation *Sperber* (Sparrowhawk). Despite the fact that it provided the tank commander with night vision out to 300 meters, assisting both night driving and especially gunnery, the device required considerable expertise and a well-knit crew. The point was that only the tank commander could see both the road and the target at night, and he would have to direct the actions of both the driver and gunner.

In order to increase the night-time field of vision, the Uhu 600mm night vision device was created. It was mounted on the Sd.Kfz.251/20 halftrack, which received its own name, Falke (Falcon). The Uhu allowed night-time vision out to a range of 600 meters. The Sd.Kfz.251/21 Falke was to operate together with the Panthers, in order to detect targets and report on them over the radio to the Panther crews.

There is no precise data about how many tanks equipped with infra-red night vision optics took part in Operation *Frühlingserwachen*. There are mentions that several such vehicles were sent to the front, including one Sd.Kfz.251/21 Falke. There are also mentions in the Soviet literature on the battle about the German use of tanks equipped with night vision optics. In any case, the question about the combat use of vehicles with infra-red night vision devices in the fighting at Lake Balaton in March 1945 requires additional research.

A few words on the numerical strength of the German assault groupings. Naturally, the most powerful was the Sixth SS Panzer Army, which as of 5 March 1945 numbered more than 125,000 officers and soldiers. *Armeegruppe Balck* had 45,000 officers and soldiers. Thus, the German assault grouping that attacked between Lake Balaton and Lake Velence numbered more than 170,000 officers and soldiers. Units of the Second Panzer Army, which launched an attack south of Lake Balaton, had up to 50,000 men, while the units of Army Group E, which was to force a crossing of the Drava River, numbered approximately 40,000 men.

Regarding the number of armored vehicles that were involved in the German offensive, according to a report from the headquarters of Army Group South dated 5 March 1945 (see Table 5), the Sixth SS Panzer Army had 333 serviceable tanks and self-propelled guns (excluding the Wespe and Hummel self-propelled howitzers). *Armeegruppe Balck* added another 184 tanks and self-propelled guns (including the two Tiger battalions, but excluding the 303rd Assault Gun Brigade and the 219th Assault Gun Battalion). Thus, the Germans had assembled more than 500 tanks and self-propelled guns between Lake Balaton and Lake Velence by 6 March, and this doesn't include the reserve 6th Panzer Division or those armored vehicles that were under repair.

According to information for 13 March 1945 (see Table 6), the Sixth SS Panzer Army alone had 583 operational tanks and self-propelled guns (150 more than were reported as serviceable on 5 March), while nearly another 400 were undergoing repair. Despite a week of combat, the number of German combat-ready tanks and self-propelled guns increased by almost 50%. Such a discrepancy can be explained by only one thing – the superb performance by the repair services of the Sixth SS Panzer Army, which worked actively to return damaged or disabled tanks and self-propelled guns back to service. Thus, one can confidently state that no less than 750 German tanks and self-propelled guns took part in the German offensive between Lake Balaton and Lake Velence.

Table 5 The Number of Tanks and Self-propelled Guns in the Divisions of Army Group South as of the Evening of 5 March 1945

Division	Serviceable									Under Repair
	Pz. IV	Pz. V	Pz. VIB	Pz. IV Flak	Pz. IV/70, Jagdpanzer IV and Jagdpanzer 38 Hetzer	StuGs	Jagdpanther	Turan	Total tanks and self-propelled guns	
71st Infantry	–	–	–	–	7	20	–	–	27	?
1st Volks Gebirg	–	–	–	–	–	12	–	–	12	?
16th SS Panzer Grenadier	–	–	–	–	–	24	–	–	24	?
118th Jäger	–	–	–	–	–	7	–	–	7	?
3rd Cavalry	–	–	–	–	7	11	–	–	18	0/13
4th Cavalry	4	–	–	–	2	–	–	–	6	?
1st SS Panzer	14	26	–	6	–	15	–	–	61	?
12th SS Panzer	12	9	–	2	14	13	–	–	50	?
2nd SS Panzer	24	6	–	8	9	23	–	–	70	?
9th SS Panzer	19	24	–	5	10	16	–	–	74	?
23rd Panzer	15	14	–	–	11	11	–	–	51	41/22
44th Reichs Grenadier	–	–	–	–	3	–	–	–	3	0/5
1st Panzer	5	23	–	–	–	–	–	–	28	?
3rd Panzer	12	22	–	–	13	2	–	–	49	?
5th SS Panzer	3	9	–	–	6	–	–	–	18	39/49
3rd SS Panzer	5	16	6	–	–	12	–	–	39	58/10
s.Pz.Abt. 509	–	–	35	8	–	–	–	–	43	?
s.Pz.Abt. 501 (SS)	–	–	31	–	–	–	–	–	31	23/0
s.Pz.Jg.Abt. 560	–	–	6	–	–	–	6	–	12	6/0
I/24 Panzer Regiment	–	32	–	–	–	–	–	–	32	?
s.Pz.Abt. Feldherrnhalle	–	–	26	7	–	–	–	–	33	?
6th Panzer	22	68	–	–	12	–	–	–	102	?
2nd Panzer (Hungarian)	–	–	–	–	–	10	–	12	22	?
Total	135	249	104	36	94	176	6	12	812	167/99

Note: The number to the left of the slash in the figures below the column heading "Under repair" indicates the number of tanks under repair, while the number to the right gives the number of self-propelled guns under repair.

Table 6 Status of the Armor Complement of the Sixth SS Panzer Army's Divisions as of 13 March 1945

Divison	Serviceable			Short–term Repair			Long–term Repair			Written off		
	Tanks	SPGs	HTs	Tanks	SPGs	HTs	Tanks	SPGs	HTs	Tanks	SPGs	HTs
1st SS Panzer	86	22	198	26	10	28	32	–	18	12	1	–
12th SS Panzer	54	67	194	20	27	22	19	22	55	5	2	–
2nd SS Panzer	51	53	223	40	39	90	–	–	–	4	5	–
9th SS Panzer	56	57	224	33	30	36	–	–	37	4	–	–
23rd Panzer	53	29	98	16	9	19	25	13	13	6	3	1
44th Volks Gebirg	–	10	–	–	5	–	–	–	–	–	–	–
3rd Cavalry	–	22	8	–	13	6	–	–	–	–	–	–
4th Cavalry	4	16	12	2	15	4	–	–	–	–	–	–
Total	304	276	957	137	148	205	76	35	199	31	11	1

Abbreviations: SPGs – self-propelled guns; HTs – half tracks

10

Plans of the Soviet Command

Immediately after the fighting ended in Budapest on 17 February 1945, the *Stavka* of the Supreme High Command issued an order to the commanders of the 2nd and 3rd Ukrainian Fronts regarding the preparation of an offensive on the Vienna and the Bratislava – Brno axes. However, the situation soon changed – intelligence came in that a major German offensive in the sector of the 3rd Ukrainian Front was pending. In connection with this, it should be stated that unlike the January German offensives (the *Konrad* operations), when the German managed to achieve surprise, the preparations for Operation *Frühlingserwachen* were detected by Soviet intelligence.

For example, two panzer divisions of the Sixth SS Panzer Army (the 1st SS Panzer Division and the 12th SS Panzer Division) were detected on 17-18 February 1945 in the sector opposite the 2nd Ukrainian Front, during the fighting at the bridgehead on the Gran River, north of Esztergom. Subsequently, radio intelligence detected the movement of these two divisions to the south. According to agent reports, the movement of the 2nd SS Panzer Division *Das Reich* and the 9th SS Panzer Division *Hohenstaufen* through Munich to Székesfehérvár in February 1945 was revealed. In the period between 18 and 25 February, the work of four headquarters of enemy panzer divisions was revealed in the areas of Koprivnica, Đurđevac and Virovitica (all in present-day Croatia). From the testimonies of a number of prisoners, the preparations for a new German offensive and the movement of fresh panzer units into the area of Székesfehérvár became known. On the basis of this and other evidence, the Soviet command concluded that the Germans were preparing another offensive, the launching of which the 3rd Ukrainian Front expected in the period no later than 10 to 12 March 1945.

Based on the current situation and the objectives which the enemy had set for the January offensives, the 3rd Ukrainian Front believed the following courses of actions by the Germans were most likely:

1. If the enemy still shows itself compelled to weaken its forces in the south by shifting part of its formations to the north – an attack out of the area of Székesfehérvár between Lakes Balaton and Velence with the aim of wearing down our forces and making them incapable of resolving active assignments for a lengthy period of time. Thus, make yourself safe in the south, and create the possibility of transferring part of your force from the southern sector of the front.

2. If the enemy, regardless of his defeats in Pomerania, Brandenburg and Silesia, will nevertheless direct his primary active efforts against our troops in the staging area on the right bank of the Danube – by a concentric attack with major, primarily tank forces out of the areas of Székesfehérvár, Nagykaniža, and from the southern bank of the Drava River out of the Osijek – Donji Mijohlac area with the aim of defeating the forces of the 3rd Ukrainian Front, throwing them back beyond the Danube, and thereby guaranteeing the safety of the directions to Vienna and Graz for a long time. The attack might be launched either simultaneously from three directions or sequentially.

The Soviet command was thus anticipating three German alternatives. The first option was an attack first out of the Nagykaniža area to the east and out of the Osijek – Donji Mijohlac sector across the Drava River to the north along the Danube River, with the aim of diverting Soviet forces from the 3rd Ukrainian Front's right wing, and thereby ensuring the success of the subsequent main attack out of the Székesfehérvár area. The main attack would be launched to the east and southeast, only once a sufficient amount of strength had been diverted from the Front's right flank. In the main attack, the German troops were to advance to the banks of the Danube River, thereby splitting the 3rd Ukrainian Front in two. The main attack was anticipated to be delivered south of Lake Velence (although the possibility of an attack north of the lake as well wasn't excluded). Subsequently, a German attack south of the Danube was expected, with the objective to smash the right flank of the 3rd Ukrainian Front and the left flank of the 2nd Ukrainian Front.

The second German alternative, as seen by the Soviet command, was the launching of the enemy attack south of Lake Velence with the same objectives as in the first alternative, but with only pinning attacks against the Front's forces south of Lake Balaton and on the Drava River.

The third alternative from the Soviet view was a simultaneous attack by the enemy from all three directions. The main attack would come out of the Székesfehérvár area.

As of 4 March 1943, the 3rd Ukrainian Front command estimated that the opposing enemy grouping consisted of 10 panzer divisions (the 1st, 3rd, 6th and 23rd Panzer Divisions, the 1st, 2nd, 5th, 9th and 12th SS Panzer Divisions, and the Hungarian 2nd Armored Division), 19 infantry divisions (the 16th SS Panzer Grenadier Division *Reichsführer-SS*; the 11th, 13th, 22nd, 31st, 41st, 96th, 104th, 117th, 118th, 181st, 264th, 297th 356th and 711th Infantry Divisions; the 7th *Gebirgs* Division; and the Hungarian 20th, 23rd and 25th Infantry Divisions; two cavalry divisions (1st Cossack and Hungarian); and two German cavalry brigades (the 3rd and 4th Cavalry). Altogether in the estimation of the 3rd Ukrainian Front's headquarters, the enemy had more than 310,000 officers and soldiers, 5,630 guns and mortars, 1,430 tanks and assault guns (of which 877 were operational), 900 armored personnel carriers, and approximately 850 aircraft. The main portion of this grouping was concentrated on the axis of the main attack – between Lakes Velence and Balaton:

> From the roster of the [German] Sixth Army, the 356th Infantry Division, the III and IV Panzer Corps (six panzer divisions, an assault gun battalion, two battalions of heavy Tiger tanks, and two assault gun brigades) have been concentrated opposite the Front's right flank; altogether 258 operational tanks, 114 assault guns, and more than 400 armored personnel carriers.
>
> The Sixth SS Panzer Army consists of the I and II SS Panzer Corps (the 1st, 2nd, 9th and 12th SS Panzer Divisions), as well as of three infantry divisions (the German 44th, and the Hungarian 20th and 25th Infantry), one panzer (the 23rd) and two cavalry brigades (the 3rd and 4th), two heavy tank battalions, an assault gun battalion and a battalion of anti-tank guns. These formations and units have 303 serviceable tanks (of which 114 are heavy tanks), 132 assault guns and approximately 500 armored personnel carriers. The Sixth SS Panzer Army has been replenished once again with more combat-capable Nazi cadres and refitted with the most up-to-date combat equipment of the time. Its personnel have undergone special training for night operations.

Here it should be clear that the Soviet intelligence data naturally differed from the actual strength of the German shock grouping in personnel and equipment. However, for sake of justice it should be noted that the discrepancies were not so great, and were actually quite close to being accurate with respect to the German armor. True, most likely armored vehicles that were under repair were included in the number of combat-ready vehicles. As concerns the indicated strength of the troops (310,000 men, 5,630 guns and mortars, etc.), these data relate to the entire Army Group

South, and not just to the assault groupings that took part in Operation *Frühlingserwachen*. After the war, a number of Soviet scholars assigned these numbers to the German units that took part in the March 1945 offensive, thereby greatly increasing the size of the German offensive. Given this sleight of hand, naturally the correlation of forces looked completely differently and much less favorably to the Soviet side than was actually the case.

A scout commander reviewing an order. In the background is an M3 Scout Car, obtained through Lend-Lease. These armored cars equipped the reconnaissance units of the Soviet tank and mechanized corps.

A collecting station for disabled equipment which has been seized by attacking Soviet troops. In the foreground is a Panther Ausf.G; in the background a Tiger Ausf.E heavy tank and several more machines are visible.

11

Defensive Preparations

In accordance with the obtained intelligence information on the looming German offensive, by Order No. 0012 of 20 February from the headquarters of the 3rd Ukrainian Front, the troops were directed to be ready to repel an enemy attack, while continuing preparations for their own offensive toward Vienna. On 24 February, however, the Front commander warned the troops that they should expect a massed enemy armored attack, and demanded them to be ready to repulse it both in daytime and nighttime. On the following day, the document "Directions for organizing an anti-tank defense" was distributed, which stated:

1. The defense should be deep and anti-tank, calculated to repel a concentrated attack by enemy tanks and infantry supported by artillery and combat aircraft.
2. The all-arms commander, who is organizing the defense in the sector of his formation, is responsible for organizing the anti-tank defense, and is obliged to ensure the cooperation of all types of forces and the knitting together of anti-tank fire with engineered obstacles.
3. Battalion strongpoints and company areas of defense, situated on tank-vulnerable directions, must be set up as anti-tank. The company anti-tank area will consist of a rifle company, 3-5 guns, and a group of anti-tank rifles, mortars and machine guns. Do not permit any further parceling out of anti-tank means. Company anti-tank areas and battalion anti-tank strongpoints are to be equipped with anti-tank obstacles, the approaches to which must be securely covered by the area's system of fire.
4. Ensure the depth of the anti-tank defenses by means of creating strong anti-tank regions on the most important directions vulnerable to tanks. These anti-tank regions must include significant anti-tank artillery means (up to an artillery regiment or brigade), deployed in compact combat formations and having the assignment to destroy a large amount of enemy tanks that having broken through into the depth.

   Set up the anti-tank regions with the assistance of engineers and have mobile anti-tank means [mines]. The anti-tank regions must have reserves: of ammunition – not less than 1.5 combat loads; of fuel and lubricants – two to three refuelings.

   The anti-tank regions will include mortar, machine-gun and combat engineer elements with an extra supply of mines.

   Appoint the senior artillery chief (the commander of the artillery regiment or brigade) as commandant of the anti-tank region in the depth [of the defenses].

This document also called for lines with readied direct fire positions for all the howitzer and heavy cannon artillery on those directions where massed tank attacks were anticipated. Given the enemy's possession of heavy tanks, it was proposed to move up separate howitzers and heavy guns into the second echelon of the rifle troops' anti-tank defenses.

The maneuver scheme for the artillery planned to employ division, corps and army anti-tank reserves, as well as artillery shifted from less important directions. Despite the extremely limited amount of time – seven or eight days from the moment of this document's distribution until the start of fighting – the majority of the directives were carried out.

In the course of two weeks (starting from 20 February), the armies of the first echelon were able to create a deeply echeloned defense consisting of many belts, while paying particular attention to the organization of anti-tank defenses. In order to secure the necessary resilience of the defense, it was ordered to plan and thoroughly organize the broad maneuver of all types of reserves both along the front and from the depth, so that at the moment of any enemy attack, the next line in the depth of the defenses would already be manned and ready.

Despite its large size, the staging area occupied by the troops of the 3rd Ukrainian Front on the right bank of the Danube nevertheless restricted the maneuver of forces and complicated the work of the rear echelons to keep the troops supplied with everything necessary. Nevertheless, the terrain, cut as it was by a large number of canals and rivers, contributed to the creation of a strong defense with a number of defensive belts and lines. There was a large number of paved and dirt roads in the bridgehead, although the latter were almost impassable to wheeled vehicles due to the spring thaws. The first half of March 1945 featured dreary weather; there were frequent rains mixed with snow, and thick fogs in the mornings; the air temperature fluctuated between 4°C. and -7°C.

On many sectors of the front, there were areas suitable for the concealed deployment of troops. However, in the sector between Lakes Velence and Balaton, where the main German attack was expected, the local terrain in the area of the front lines of the 3rd Ukrainian Front was flat, which complicated the deployment and camouflaging of the guns that had been moved up in order to fire over open sights. In addition, the presence of a large number of rivers and streams, the swampy terrain, and the high water table hindered the digging of rifle pits for the infantry, gun pits for the guns or regulation observation posts. It was thus necessary to strengthen the bottom of trenches with planking, especially beneath the wheels of the guns, and to build dikes, earthworks, palisades and so forth in order to increase the depth of shelters.

The armies of the first echelon constructed three belts of defense. The first, main defensive belt, with a depth of 5 to 7 kilometers, consisted of three lines echeloned in depth with one to three trench lines in each, linked by communication trenches. The latter served simultaneously as switch lines or intermediate positions. The second belt of defenses consisted of two trench lines. Behind it was the rear, army belt. The distance between the first and second belts was 8 to 12 kilometers, and between the second belt and the rear belt was 6 to 10 kilometers. Defensive positions were also constructed in the interval between the belts. All major settlements within the defensive belts or between them were converted into defensive strongpoints.

Fortified lines, including intermediate and switch lines, were being prepared behind the armies' own defensive belts. On the whole, the depth of the Soviet defenses between Lakes Velence and Balaton stretched for 30 to 50 kilometers behind the front line.

Minefields were laid along the entire front, with an average density of mines in the sector of the 4th Guards, 26th and 57th Armies amounting to 730 anti-tank mines and 670 anti-infantry mines per kilometer of front; on the directions more vulnerable to tanks, the density of mines grew to 2,700 and 2,500 mines respectively.

It should be said that despite the rather extensive depth of the 3rd Ukrainian Front's defense, it was weaker than the one that had been created in the Kursk bulge (some authors try to make these operations comparable). The main defensive fortifications in the area of Lake Balaton consisted of entrenchments for the infantry, guns and tanks, as well as mine fields. There were practically no barbed wire barriers, anti-tank obstacles, pillboxes or other such fortifications. For example, on 27 February the 4th Guards Army's chief of staff confirmed a plan to use "knocked-out enemy tanks as immobile firing points". It was proposed set up 38 tanks in this fashion in the period between 28 February and 10 March, but it is unknown whether the idea was ever implemented.

By the beginning of March 1945, the 3rd Ukrainian Front had five all-arms armies (the 4th Guards, 26th, 27th, 57th, and Bulgarian First Army) as well as the Yugoslav Third Army's 12th

Army Corps, one air army (the 17th), and two tank, one mechanized and one cavalry corps, for a total of 407,357 men, 6,163 guns and mortars (not including rocket artillery), 407 tanks and self-propelled guns, and 965 aircraft.

The 4th Guards Army (commanded by Lieutenant General N. Zakhvataev), consisting of three rifle corps (the 20th, 21st and 31st Guards) and one fortified district, was occupying a defense along the line Gánt, Zámoly, eastern suburbs of Székesfehérvár, Seregélyes, which extended for 39 kilometers. By 1 March the numerical strength of its rifle divisions was as follows: up to 4,500 men – 1 division; up to 5,000 men – 1 division; up to 5,500 men – 5 divisions; and up to 6,000 men – 1 division.

The 4th Guards Army had the assignment to prevent a breakthrough of enemy tanks and infantry north and south of Székesfehérvár in the direction toward Budapest. It was also to cover the right flank of the 26th and 27th Armies from the north.

In its first echelon, the army had the 20th and 21st Guards Rifle Corps and the 1st Guards Fortified District, which were occupying the first and second defensive belts. The 31st Guards Rifle Corps was in reserve. On average, each division in the sector between Gánt and Lake Velence was occupying 3.3 kilometers.

The army's left flank, south of Lake Velence, was significantly weaker. Here the 1st Guards Fortified District (five separate machine-gun – artillery battalions with approximately 650 men in each) was defending a 10-kilometer front between Dinnyési and Seregélyes. The fortified district had three battalions in the first echelon, with two battalions in reserve. The total depth of the defenses here did not exceed 5 kilometers; the second belt of defenses was unoccupied. On its own (with no artillery attachments), the fortified district's density of strength was equivalent to half of a battalion, 19 machine guns, and 7 guns and mortars per kilometer of front.

Of the army's 32 reserve artillery regiments, nine were attached to divisions of the rifle corps of the first echelon, and five (of which three were destroyer anti-tank artillery regiments) were attached to the 1st Guards Fortified District. In addition, there was a powerful army-level artillery group, which numbered 113 guns of between 152mm and 203mm, as well as an army-level anti-tank artillery reserve of four regiments.

The 26th Army (commanded by Lieutenant General N. Gagen), consisting of three rifle corps (the 30th, 135th and 104th), was defending a 44-kilometer sector that stretched from Seregélyes to Lake Balaton. The strength of its rifle division on 1 March was as follows: up to 3,500 men – 1 division; up to 4,500 men – four divisions; up to 5,000 men – four divisions; and up to 5,500 men – one division.

At the start of the German offensive, the 26th Army had all three rifle corps in the first echelon. The army reserve consisted of only the 21st Rifle Division.

Its right-flank 30th Rifle Corps was defending on a sector of 20 kilometers, with all three of its divisions (the 155th Rifle, 36th Guards Rifle and 68th Guards Rifle) in the front line. The divisions defending on the main axis of the German attack held narrower sectors of defense (the 155th Rifle's sector was 6 kilometers, and the 36th Guard Rifle's sector ran for 4 kilometers). The 30th Rifle Corps' absence of a second echelon to a certain extent was compensated by the fact that the army reserve – the 21st Rifle Division – was positioned behind it.

In the 135th Rifle Corps, two divisions (the 74th and 233rd Rifle) were positioned in the first echelon and one, the 236th Rifle, in the second, while in the 104th Rifle Corps, the arrangement was the opposite – one division (the 93rd Rifle) was in the first echelon and two (the 66th Guards Rifle and the 151st Rifle) were in the second.

Thus, the main belt of the defenses of the 26th Army was defended by six divisions, while the second defensive belt was being held by four divisions. On average, each division was holding 4.4 kilometers of frontage.

A divisional M-30 Model 1938 122mm howitzer in action. By 1945, these guns made up the bulk of the artillery in the Red Army's rifle divisions.

Cavalrymen occupying a defensive position. The crew of a 45mm anti-tank gun is manhandling the gun into a firing position. Note the characteristic fur caps worn by Soviet cavalrymen.

Lieutenant G. Kuzmin's company attacks with the support of a 45mm anti-tank gun. By 1945, these guns were already virtually useless against the latest German tanks, but nevertheless were still in use in the Red Army.

The on-board ammunition within this Panther Ausf.G has clearly exploded. The tactical marking "AJ9" is visible on the turret. Presumably, this tank belonged to the 2nd SS Panzer Division *Das Reich*.

The army command was most of all concerned about covering its flanks, especially the right flank, where the 30th Rifle Corps was holding the line (incidentally, the subsequent fighting proved that these concerns were well-grounded). Thus of the army's 34 reserve artillery regiments, 15 were attached to this rifle corps, which provided for a density in its sector of 25.7 guns and mortars per kilometer of front(including the artillery of the rifle divisions).

In addition, in the sector of the defense being held by the 30th Rifle Corps, the army corps deployed more than half of the artillery belonging to the army – the army-level artillery group, the army-level anti-tank artillery reserve, and the majority of the anti-aircraft guns and rocket launchers. As a result, in the 30th Rifle Corps' sector, there were 34 guns and mortars per kilometer of front.

It should be said that in the distribution of the artillery within the 30th Rifle Corps, most of the guns were concentrated on its right flank. The 155th Rifle Division defending here received eight artillery regiments and one artillery battalion as reinforcements, while the other two divisions received a combined five artillery regiments and two artillery battalions. Such an arrangement of artillery means allowed the creation of a density of 67 guns and mortars per kilometer of front in the Seregélyes – Sárviz Canal sector on the anticipated axis of the main German attack. These measures enabled the creation of a powerful anti-tank defense, and in the course of the subsequent fighting, the Germans made almost no headway in this sector.

On the left flank of the 26th Army, in the sector of the 104th Rifle Corps, the density of artillery amounted to 35.4 guns and mortars per kilometer of front, but this was achieved not by the attachment of a great number of artillery units, but by narrowing the 104th Rifle Corps' sector of defense to 8 kilometers.

Naturally, this strengthening of the army's flanks didn't come without costs – the 135th Rifle Corps, which was defending in the center on a front of 16 kilometers, had just 306 guns and mortars, and 16 BM-13 rocket launchers. Thus, the density of artillery in its sector was one and a half to two times lower than in the other rifle corps.

Thus, if in the 26th Army's disposition of its divisions practically no attention was given to the concentration of the main forces on the anticipated axis of the enemy's main attack, with respect to the artillery this found a more concrete expression in the 30th Rifle Corps, which received the largest number of reinforcing artillery units.

The 57th Army (commanded by Lieutenant General M. Sharokhin), which was defending on a sector of 133 kilometers (including the bank of Lake Balaton), from the beginning to the end of the operation had in fact only two corps (the 6th Guards Rifle and 64th Rifle) with six subordinate divisions. The numerical strength of its rifle divisions was somewhat greater than in the other armies. On 1 March, it had five rifle divisions numbering up to 5,500 men each and one division numbering up to 6,000 men. The 133rd Rifle Corps, of which the 57th Army took operational control on 5 March, was sent on the following day to eliminate an enemy breakthrough in the sector of the Bulgarian First Army, where it remained until 21 March, while the 104th Rifle Division of this corps was pulled back into army reserve. The 6th Guards Rifle Corps was assigned a sector of defense that stretched for 34 kilometers, while the 64th Rifle Corps' sector ran for 26 kilometers. The sector of the defense that ran along the shore of Lake Balaton was covered by two motorcycle regiments and a battalion of amphibious vehicles.

The axis along the Nagybajom – Kaposvár highway south of Lake Balaton in the sector of the 64th Rifle Corps was considered the most critical. The 64th Rifle Corps was arranged in two echelons. In the first echelon were the 73rd Guards Rifle Division, which was defending an 11-kilometer sector, and the 299th Rifle Division, which was occupying a 15-kilometer sector. Behind the 73rd Guards Rifle Division, in the second belt of fortifications, was the corps' second echelon – the 113th Rifle Division.

The 57th Army, which was defending an axis considered secondary by the Front command, received just two artillery regiments and two mortar regiments as reinforcements. Together with the artillery directly under the command of the 57th Army headquarters, they were transferred to the operational control of the subordinate rifle corps.

To the left of the 57th Army, defending a front of 150 kilometers along the northern bank of the Drava River was the Bulgarian First Army, commanded by General Vladimir Stoychev. It consisted of the 3rd, 8th, 11th, 12th and 16th Infantry Divisions, two anti-tank battalions, and an engineering regiment and anti-aircraft artillery battalion that were directly subordinate to the First Army's headquarters. Despite the fact that the Bulgarian divisions numbered up to 12,000 to 13,000 men each, their combat experience and combat capabilities were regarded by the Soviet command as significantly lower than those of their Red Army counterparts, and this opinion was subsequently confirmed by events. True, an enemy offensive on this axis was considered relatively improbable, in part because the Bulgarian positions had the Drava River in front of them. To the left of the Bulgarians, on a 40-kilometer sector to the confluence of the Drava and Danube Rivers, units of the 12th Army Corps of General Nađ's Yugoslav Third Army were defending.

Units of the 27th Army (three rifle corps) were in the 3rd Ukrainian Front's second echelon. The divisions of this army, which had just joined the Front on 20 February 1945, were weaker with respect to men and equipment in comparison with the other Soviet divisions; as of 1 March, it had one division with 3,300 men, two divisions with up to 4,000 men, four divisions with up to 4,500 men, and two with up to 5,000 men.

Its 35th Guards Rifle Corps (the 3rd Guards Airborne Division and the 78th and 163rd Rifle Divisions) and 37th Guards Rifle Corps (the 108th, 316th and 320th Rifle Divisions) were positioned in the rear army-level defensive lines stretching from Lake Velence to the Danube River. The 27th Army's third corps, the 33rd Rifle Corps (the 202nd, 206th and 337th Rifle Divisions) was in reserve on the left bank of the Danube River. A substantial flaw that complicated the defense of the sector between Lake Velence and the Sárviz Canal was its shallow depth. For example, from the forward line of the rear defensive belt, which was occupied by units of the 27th Army, to the Danube River was just 8 to 15 kilometers. Thus, in the event that the enemy reached this line, the army's rear areas could be placed under artillery fire, which would complicate any regrouping of forces.

Mobile units were in the Front reserve. They included the 18th and 23rd Tank Corps, the 1st Guards Mechanized Corps, and the 5th Guards Cavalry Corps.

The 23rd Tank Corps was occupying a position behind the right flank of the 4th Guards Army, north of Lake Velence in the Lovasberény area. The 18th Tank Corps was positioned behind the boundary between the 4th Guards Army and the 26th Army in the Sárosd area. Its position had been selected so that it could reinforce the defense on any portion of the army-level intermediate line either in the sector of the 1st Guards Fortified District or in the sector of the 26th Army's 30th Rifle Corps. The 1st Guards Mechanized Corps was assembled behind the center of the 26th Army and could be used, depending on the situation, to strengthen the army-level intermediate line together with the 18th Tank Corps.

The 5th Guards Cavalry Corps (the 11th Guards, 12th Guards and 63rd Cavalry Divisions) was occupying a position on the Front-level defensive belt in the Alap area. Behind it was the Front reserve – the 84th Rifle Division. In case of extreme necessity, the Front's courses for junior lieutenants, as well as reserve rifle regiments (two from the 27th Army and one from the 4th Guards Army), an artillery regiment and a tank regiment could be committed in order to strengthen the defense. The overall numerical strength of these units was equivalent to two divisions (excepting artillery).

At the end of February and in the first few days of March 1945, select groups of officers assigned by Front headquarters conducted inspections of all the armies and Front units in order to determine their readiness to repel a German offensive. As a result of the inspections, reports were compiled and forwarded to Front headquarters. It is not without interest to cite an excerpt from the report, "On the conditions of the defenses and the defensive capabilities of the 26th Army", which was put together by staff officers of the Front headquarters on 1 March 1945, especially since it was this army that received the Sixth SS Panzer Army's main assault (the situation with the defenses was similar for the other armies):

1. Organization of the defense
    The 135th Rifle Corps: The depth of the combat formations does not exceed 5-7 kilometers. The forward edge of the defense runs along the line at which the troops halted during their own offensive. As a consequence of this, on separate sectors the forward edge doesn't conform to its [defensive] role (poor visibility and fields of fire, and limited possibilities for creating earthworks).

    Organization of the system of fire: The system of infantry fire has been organized without sufficient thought by the commanders of elements and units. As a rule, in units of the first echelon, all the machine guns and anti-tank rifles have been positioned in a single line along the forward edge, and no depth whatsoever has been created. The exceptions are the 36th and 68th Guards Rifle Divisions, where the battalions of the first echelon have heavy and light machine guns positioned behind the front line.

    The commanders and crews of the machine guns know their assignments. Plans of supporting artillery fire have been put together in all the formations and units. The preparation of initial gunnery data has been completed by all the artillery units and elements. The guns have been sighted in and targets registered. The accuracy of the registration fire is satisfactory.

    The system of anti-tank defense has been organized by means of creating anti-tank areas and by deploying guns for direct fire on the directions vulnerable to tanks. Anti-tank means have primarily been echeloned in depth, but there are cases where the anti-tank artillery has been positioned in a single line.

    The artillery in concealed firing positions hasn't been fully prepared for all-round defense and for repelling tank attacks by direct fire (9 batteries of the 65th Artillery Regiment of the 36th Guards Rifle Division).

    Heavy guns in indirect firing positions haven't been prepared for anti-tank defense (9 batteries of the 25th Cannon Artillery Brigade in the sector of the 36th Guards Rifle Division). Ammunition for all types of weapons in the trenches and positions consists of 1 to 1.5 standard combat loads. In the 36th Guards Rifle Division's 39th Destroyer Anti-tank Artillery Battalion, there are few armor-piercing shells in the gun positions for direct fire. This battalion's No. 1 gun of the 2nd Battery has just 17 armor-piercing shells.

2. Engineering support for the defenses
    Defensive fortifications among the troops haven't been completed and the work is progressing very slowly. Not a single division of the first echelon has a full profile, continuous trench along the forward edge. There are gaps of 100-300 meters between regimental sectors and even battalion areas of the defense. The plans and norms of constructing defensive positions aren't being carried out.

    The trenches along the forward edge have various depths – from 0.4 meters to 1.4 meters. There are no places for dispersing the troops in the trenches. It is very difficult to carry wounded along the trenches. In the sandy and sandy-loamy soil (36th Guards Rifle Division), trenches are collapsing and are not being rebuilt.

Machine-gun emplacements are poorly equipped, uncovered, and as a result a lot of the positions, especially where the soil is sandy and loamy, have fallen into disrepair. Trenches in the sense of combat and accommodations for the troops are poorly furnished or are completely unfitted. There are no bunkers below the parapet, and not more than 10 to 15% of the dugouts where the troops can rest have been built, and those have thin overhead protection.

In the 36th Guards Rifle Division, the majority of the personnel of the artillery units and second-echelon units are resting in huts. The digging of the second and third line of trenches has been completed.

Minefields in 2-4 belts have been laid in front of each division. A system of fire covers the minefields. No other engineered obstacles have been put in place. The artillery positions, including those of the anti-tank regions as well, are not protected by minefields. The mobile blocking detachments in the divisions (with 250 mines each) and in the regiments (with 50 mines each) are mounted in light vehicles and wagons.

Up to 70% of the troops in the field have been provided with an entrenching tool.

3. Security of the boundaries
    The boundaries have been secured according to the scheme that was proposed by army headquarters to the Front headquarters.

4. Organization of command and control
    All of the command posts of the regiments, divisions and corps are located in populated locations, in huts. All of the signal stations are in huts. There are no prepared bunkers for accommodating the command posts; only slit trenches are available. Local civilians are living in the vicinity of the command posts, including in the area of the army command post, while in the 36th Guards Rifle Division, local civilians are even present at the command post and the observation posts of the regiments and battalions.

    The observation posts in the majority of cases are primitive: a bunker with a thin cover, or else observation is done from buildings, haystacks, etc. Around the clock sentry duties have been organized at the observation posts. Communications with the command and the interaction of all the links have been organized.

5. Organization of battlefield reconnaissance
    Observation of the battlefield has been organized insufficiently clearly. Reconnaissance patrols for seizing "tongues" [prisoners willing to talk] are being conducted by non-essential individuals and in the majority of cases are having no success (155th, 36th Guards, and 233rd Rifle Divisions).

6. Vigilance and combat service
    Most of the unit personnel know their assignments. At nighttime, entire companies of the first echelon at the forward edge are on the alert, while in daylight hours 50 to 60% of the personnel are resting. Vigilance of the personnel is not on a sufficiently high level. Everyone knows the password, but as a rule it is not requested, and everyone trusts the word "of their own guys" both at the front line and in the depth of the combat formations.

    Discipline in certain combat units of the army is not on a sufficiently high level. The appearance of many officers and soldiers is slovenly (without epaulets, belts, unbuttoned, etc.)

7. The manning level of the rifle companies and the count of personnel:
    30th Rifle Corps – 155th Rifle Division's companies are at average strength: 286th Rifle Regiment – 20 men per company; 436th Rifle Regiment – 80-90 men per company; 659th Rifle Regiment – 75-80 men per company; 36th Guards Rifle Division – companies have about 80 men each; the 68th Guards Rifle Division – companies average 55-60 men each.

    135th Rifle Corps – 233rd Rifle Division: companies are at 30 to 35 men each; 74th Rifle Division: 55 to 60 men each; 236th Rifle Division: 40 to 50 men each.

8. Morale and living conditions of the officers and soldiers
    The morale of the personnel is fully healthy. Soldiers and officers in the overwhelming majority honorably and conscientiously carry out their assigned tasks.

    Nutritional sustenance has been organized fully satisfactorily. Officers and soldiers on the meal plan for the front receive two high-caloric, hot meals per day, which are in the majority of cases tasty. There was not a single complaint from the officers and soldiers about poor rations.

    The conditions of the uniforms is basically satisfactory, but of various types. Many soldiers and officers are wearing civilian attire, especially in those divisions that fought in Budapest.

CONCLUSIONS
1. Organization of the defense basically conforms to the established tasks, the demands of the Front's order, and the combat experience of the troops, with the exception of the aforementioned shortcomings.
2. Work on the defenses is being conducted according to plan, but is behind schedule, and the quality of the work is low. Control over the fulfillment of the work on the defenses has been organized with insufficient clarity.
3. Troops of the army are in a state of constant combat readiness.
    Results of the inspection have been passed along to the commanders of the units and formations. The uncovered shortcomings, time allowing, are being eliminated on location.
    The group of officers of the Front headquarters that conducted the inspection of the condition of the army's defense. … (signatures)

The defensive operation of the Soviet forces at Lake Balaton in March 1945 is interesting for the fact that the main role in repelling the German offensive and in the struggle against enemy tanks was played by artillery units. Therefore, let's take a closer look at them.

The 3rd Ukrainian Front on 6 March 1945 had 185 artillery and mortar regiments. All of these units, as well as the artillery elements of the rifle divisions, numbered a total of 2,556 82mm – 160mm mortars, 2,955 45mm – 203mm guns, 612 20mm-85mm anti-aircraft guns, and 293 *Katiusha* rocket launchers.

Many artillery units of the 3rd Ukrainian Front had prior experience of actions on the defensive, especially anti-tank defense, which they acquired during the January 1945 battles. However, their combat capability had been reduced by the significant deficit of guns, and of vehicles especially. For example, if the equipage of the artillery units of army and Front subordination with mortars, and 57mm and 76mm guns amounted to only 57 to 65% of table strength, and with towing means 70 to 85%, then with vehicles – only 28.3% of table strength. Only the 105th Large-caliber Howitzer Brigade and the 12th Destroyer Anti-tank Brigade (16 76mm ZIS-3 cannons and 20 57mm ZIS-2) were fully equipped according to their respective TO&E.

As concerns the rifle divisions, the equipage of their artillery units was even lower. For example, on 3 March 1945, in the divisions of the 4th Guards Army there were available only 6 regimental and 20 divisional 76mm guns each, and 9 122mm howitzers; in the 26th Army's divisions, there were 4-5 regimental and 12 divisional 76mm guns each, and 7 122mm howitzers; in the 27th Army, the respective numbers were 9, 22 and 10-11 guns each.

The majority of the artillery was distributed among the armies and corps. Front reserve had the 19th Breakthrough Artillery Division (seven artillery brigades), the 12th Destroyer Anti-tank Artillery, 170th Light Artillery and 208th Self-propelled Artillery Brigades, the 105th Large-caliber Howitzer Brigade, three "Katiusha" rocket launcher brigades, two artillery regiments, a heavy mortar brigade and a mortar regiment. In addition, the 19th Breakthrough Artillery Division had been set aside only for supporting the forthcoming offensive; its use on the defensive was banned by the *Stavka* of the Supreme High Command.

The artillery that had been distributed for supporting the rifle corps, divisions and regiments was merged into artillery groups of various sizes. Regimental artillery groups were created in all the divisions of the first echelon: for example, two divisions of the 4th Guards Army's 20th Guards Rifle Corps had five such artillery groups, consisting of two 76mm regiments, a howitzer regiment and a mortar regiment each, while six divisions of the 26th Army had 16 artillery groups (of 6 mortar and 6 artillery regiments each). As a rule, two to four battalions comprised an artillery or mortar regiment. In the 57th Army, which had less artillery than the others, 12 artillery groups of one to two battalions each had been created. The inherent artillery of the rifle regiments or rifle battalions was not included in the artillery groups.

In addition to the regimental artillery groups, the 5th Guards Airborne Division and the 155th and 36th Guards Rifle Divisions, which were defending especially important directions, had divisional artillery groups. The latter could bring concentrated artillery fire down across the division's entire defensive front.

Corps artillery groups were organized only in three rifle corps – the 135th, 6th Guards and 64th. In addition, the 4th Guards and 26th Armies created army artillery groups of two artillery brigades each. They were able to bring down concentrated artillery fire simultaneously on an area of up to 30 hectares, drop a moving artillery barrage on a front of 1,300 meters, or a fixed artillery barrage on a front of 3,000 meters.

Taking into account the deficit of artillery guns and vehicles, and in anticipation of the large scale of the forthcoming battle, the Front command developed several alternatives for maneuvering the artillery units, depending on the enemy's actions.

12

Anti-tank Defenses

As has already been mentioned, directives of the Front commander with respect to organizing anti-tank defenses went out to the troops on 25-26 February. In addition to the anti-tank artillery, the directives called for involving the guns of the rifle units, all the cannon batteries of the divisional and army artillery, as well as the reinforcing artillery, all of the anti-aircraft artillery of medium caliber, and tanks and self-propelled artillery vehicles in the struggle against the enemy tanks. This totaled more than 4,000 guns with a caliber ranging from 45mm to 152mm.

Particular attention was paid to organizing the anti-tank defenses on the sector between Lake Velence and Lake Balaton: At the order of the Front commander, seven of the eight destroyer anti-tank artillery brigades and two of the three light artillery brigades were subordinated to the 4th Guards Army and 26th Army, in the process giving the former 12 and the latter 16 destroyer anti-tank and light artillery regiments, or 2/3 of all the available artillery regiments.

In the defensive sectors of these two armies, a network of powerful anti-tank regions was developed, starting at a distance of 500-800 meters behind the front lines and extending back from the front lines to a depth of up to 30 to 35 kilometers. There were 32 such anti-tank regions in the sector of the 4th Guards Army, and 34 in the sector of the 26th Army.

Anti-tank regions were located on the most likely directions vulnerable to tanks. For example, in the sector between Lake Velence and the Sárviz Canal, the Soviet command determined three such directions: Dinnyés – Kis Velence, which ran along the southern shore of Lake Velence; Seregélyes – Adony; and Aba – Sárkeresztúr. On the first of these, there was a highway, but lying in front of the 1st Guards Fortified District that was defending here, there was a valley that in the first days of March was in flood from the melting snow. Thus there was only one anti-tank area on this axis. The town of Seregélyes, which was a major road hub, was located on the second axis vulnerable to tanks. In order to cover it, two large anti-tank areas with 20-25 anti-tank guns in each were positioned here, with another seven small anti-tank areas in the depth of the defenses. The Székesfehérvár – Cece highway and several smaller roads ran through the third axis that was vulnerable to tanks. In order to protect the given sector, three anti-tank areas with 15-20 anti-tank guns each were organized in the first line of defense, backed up by two anti-tank areas in the depth of the defenses. In addition, on all the possible sectors of German tank movement, lines for deploying the anti-tank reserves and the mobile blocking detachments were prepared.

The artillery units that were situated in indirect firing positions were also prepared for the struggle against tanks; some of the guns were deployed so that they could fire over open sights or lay long-range direct fire. In the depth of the defenses, additional anti-tank areas set up with self-propelled artillery regiments and brigades, as well as the artillery and tanks of the mechanized and tank corps.

In order to counter the enemy tanks more successfully, so-called "ambush" and "decoy" guns were widely used. The former as a rule were positioned perpendicular to the anticipated direction of advance of the enemy tanks and were to wait for the opportunity to open close-range flanking fire. The "decoy" guns, on the other hand, were used to attract the attention of the German tanks and self-propelled guns in order to lure them into the sights of other guns that hadn't yet opened fire.

The 3rd Ukrainian Front command, considering the experience of the January fighting, paid particular attention to preparations to repel enemy tank attacks at night. For this purpose, combat security was intensified at night, and special outposts were set up, which were to give early warning to the troops during enemy tank attacks and were to illuminate the surrounding terrain with flares or fires. Special exercises focusing on night-time gunnery and direct fire were conducted with the artillery units. When selecting positions to fire over open sights at tanks at night, particular attention was paid to ensure that there were no objects near the gun's position that could serve as orienting markers for the German tanks, or with a backdrop that would reveal the gun when it fired. Also, all easily flammable objects were removed from around the artillery positions. When training for the upcoming battle, the crews of the anti-tank guns practiced firing at targets at night that were either illuminated by flares or visible in the moonlight.

Table 7 Artillery and Mortars in the Units of the 3rd Ukrainian Front on 6 March 1945 (Excluding the Bulgarian First Army and the Yugoslav Corps)

	4th Guards Army	26th Army	27th Army	57th Army	Front-level units	Total
82mm mortars	409	285	280	451	192	1,617
107mm mortars	–	–	24	–	–	24
120mm mortars	229	226	117	191	120	883
160mm mortars	–	–	–	–	32	32
Mortars, Total	638	511	421	642	344	2,556
45mm anti-tank guns, M1937 and M1942	143	93	143	102	35	516
ZIS-2 57mm anti-tank guns	63	34	–	–	32	129
76mm regimental anti-tank guns, M1927 and M1943	48	44	46	65	29	232
76mm divisional guns, M1936, M1939 and ZIS-3	308	305	225	205	124	1,167
75mm PAK 40	–	16	–	–	–	16
88mm PAK 43	5	–	–	–	–	5
105mm FH18	–	3	–	–	–	3
122mm M1910/30 and M-30	172	144	94	87	101	598
122mm A-19	–	36	12	–	–	48
152mm ML-20	109	41	24	42	32	248
203mm B-4	4	4	–	–	22	30
Guns, Total	852	720	544	501	375	2,992
Total guns and mortars	1,490	1,231	965	1,143	719	5,548
37mm M1939 anti-aircraft	91	112	16	55	240	514*
85mm M1939 anti-aircraft	48	22	–	–	28	98
Anti-aircraft guns, Total	139	134	15	55	268	612
Total guns, mortars and anti-aircraft	1,629	1,365	981	1,198	987	6,160
BM-8, BM-13 and BM-31-12 rocket launchers	60	88	22	24	99**	293***

* Including the anti-aircraft artillery of the 17th Air Army; of the 514 anti-aircraft guns, 13 were of the caliber of 20- to 25mm.
** Of this number, 8 rocket launchers belonged to the Bulgarian First Army.
*** Of which, 28 were BM-8 rocket launchers, 198 were BM-13 rocket launchers, 42 were BM-31-12 rocket launchers, and 25 were M-30 rocket launching frames.

Particular attention was also paid to the potential maneuvering of the anti-tank reserves. This foresaw moving up artillery units to various areas and lines of defense, depending on the directions of the enemy attack and the unfolding situation. In order to ensure the most rapid shifting of anti-tank reserves to threatened sectors, anticipated movement routes were reconnoitered in advance. The most preferable routes were not necessarily the shortest, but those that were most suitable for the movement of artillery.

In addition to the artillery, orders called upon the widespread use on the defense of mobile blocking detachments – combat engineer elements with an extra supply of anti-tank and anti-personnel mines. Altogether by 5 March, there were 68 such detachments, which were equipped with 73 motor vehicles, 164 horse-drawn wagons, 30,000 anti-tank mines, 9,000 anti-personnel mines, and 9 metric tons of explosives. Directly subordinate to the Front command were three motorized blocking detachments, which were composed of a motorized engineer battalion and two combat engineer companies, and each of which were armed with 4,500 anti-tank mines. The 4th Guards Army formed two such motorized detachments on the basis of its engineer-sapper battalion, and each had 3,200 anti-tank mines and 1,000 anti-personnel mines. In the 26th Army and 57th Army there was one such detachment (a company of combat engineers with four vehicles and 1,000 anti-tank mines). The corps blocking detachments, as a rule, consisted of companies or platoons of sappers with an extra supply of 300-500 anti-tank mines. Divisions had 10 to 25 sappers each, with one vehicle and 200-250 mines, while regiments had 5 to 7 combat engineers with 100 anti-tank mines in horse-drawn wagons.

Each blocking detachment had its own plan of movement to one or another direction, depending on the situation. Their actions were linked with the anti-tank artillery and rifle units.

On the basis of obtained intelligence information, the 3rd Ukrainian Front command came to the conclusion that the German units might launch an offensive at any moment. Thus on the evening of 5 March, Front headquarters notified the troops of a possible start of an enemy offensive the next morning. The army and corps headquarters issued an order to bring the formations and units up to full combat-readiness. For example, the artillery headquarters of the 26th Army's issued the following combat order:

> The intensified movement toward the front line of enemy motorized transport and personnel in the course of the day has been established through observation. There is evidence that the enemy will initiate active operations. For the timely forewarning of active enemy operations, the commander of the corps artillery has ordered:
>
> 1.   On the night of 5-6 March 1945, all the officer staff will be at their posts; battery commanders up to the commanders of the artillery are to be at their observation posts and are to check the readiness of all the artillery to conduct massed fire according to the plan of counter preparatory fire. The artillery positioned to lay direct fire is to be at full readiness to repel enemy tank attacks.
> 2.   Personnel are to be at their guns or the observation posts (50% on duty, 50% resting).
> 3.   Ready the ammunition for conducting fire at enemy tanks and troops.
> 4.   Check communications and the direction of fire, from the commander of the division's artillery down to the battery commander of both inherent artillery and attached artillery. In case of an interruption in cable communications, immediately switch to radio sets.
> 5.   Confirm the receipt and report on the execution of this order.

An SU-76 self-propelled gun in combat in a village. These self-propelled guns were second in prevalence only to the T-34 tank in the Red Army.

Soviet artillery caught in a traffic jam on one of the roads at the front. Studebaker trucks acquired from the United States were used to tow the 76mm divisional cannons.

A Soviet anti-tank artillery regiment, equipped with 57mm ZiS-2 anti-tank guns, on the march.

A Soviet anti-tank regiment, equipped with captured 75mm PAK-40 guns, on the march. A
Studebaker truck obtained through Lend-Lease is being used as a tow vehicle.

Soviet soldiers training to use a captured PAK-40 75mm anti-tank gun.

A disabled and burned-out King Tiger of the 509th Heavy Panzer Battalion, vicinity of Lake Balaton, March 1945.

13

The Armored Units of the 3rd Ukrainian Front

By the start of March 1945, the 3rd Ukrainian Front had the 6th Tank Army (which didn't take part in the defensive fighting and thus won't be examined in the present chapter), two tank corps (the 18th and 23rd) and one mechanized corps (the 1st Guards), the 32nd Separate Guards Mechanized and 208th Self-propelled Artillery Brigades, four tank and six self-propelled artillery regiments (not including the regiments of the tank and mechanized corps), two motorcycle regiments, and eight self-propelled artillery battalions. At the beginning of the defensive fighting, two more self-propelled artillery brigades – the 207th and 209th – were transferred to the control of the 3rd Ukrainian Front.

The majority of the units had suffered heavy losses in the January and February 1945 fighting, and was significantly below table strength in equipment. This especially applied to the tank and mechanized corps, although the self-propelled artillery regiments and brigades were in better shape.

At the beginning of 1945, the TO&E for a Red Army tank corps included three tank brigades and one mechanized brigade; three self-propelled artillery regiments (light, medium and heavy); mortar and anti-aircraft regiments; motorcycle, engineer and medical-sanitary battalions; a signals battalion; a battalion of Guards mortars (Katiusha rocket launchers); a chemical defense company; a fuel and lubricant train; two mobile repair depots (wheeled and tracked vehicles); equipment and artillery repair shops; and a number of other subordinate elements. Altogether, a tank corps numbered 12,010 men, 207 T-34 tanks, 63 self-propelled guns (21 SU-76, 21 SU-85 and 21 ISU-152), 80 guns (36 76mm, 16 57mm, 12 45mm and 16 37mm), 102 mortars and rocket launchers (42 120mm, 52 82mm and 8 BM-13), 149 anti-tank rifles and 1,456 trucks and cars.

The 18th "Znamenskii" Red Banner Tank Corps (the 110th, 170th and 181st Tank Brigades, the 32 Mechanized Brigade, and the 1438th and 363rd Guards Heavy Self-propelled Artillery Regiments) as of 6 March 1945 had serviceable just 42 T-34 tanks and 5 ISU-152, 16 ISU-122 and 17 SU-76 self-propelled guns; by the number of combat vehicles, it was equivalent to just a reinforced tank brigade.

The 23rd Red Banner Tank Corps (the 3rd, 39th and 135th Tank Brigades, the 56th Mechanized Brigade, and the 1443rd and 1891st Self-propelled Artillery Regiments) was in no better shape. As of 6 March 1945, it had 20 T-34/85, 7 ISU-122 and 1 IS-2 operational.

At the beginning of 1945, the TO&E of a Red Army mechanized corps included three mechanized brigades and a tank brigade; three self-propelled artillery regiments (light, medium and heavy); mortar and anti-aircraft regiments; a motorcycle, anti-aircraft and medical-sanitary battalions; a signals battalion; a battalion of Guards mortars (Katiusha rocket launchers); a chemical defense company; a fuel and lubricant train; two mobile repair depots; equipment and artillery repair shops; and a number of other subordinate elements. Altogether, by its TO&E, a full-strength mechanized corps numbered 16,422 men, 133 tanks, 63 self-propelled guns (21 SU-76, 21 SU-85 and 21 ISU-152), 96 guns (36 76mm, 8 57mm, 36 45mm and 16 37mm), 162 mortars and rocket launchers (54 120mm, 100 82mm and 8 BM-13), 287 anti-tank rifles and 1,849 trucks and cars.

The Red Army mechanized corps, even at the end of the war, was often equipped with American tanks, as a rule Sherman tanks, which had been received through Lend-Lease. The 1st Guards Order of Lenin Mechanized Corps (the 1st, 2nd and 3rd Guards Mechanized Brigades, the 9th Guards Tank Brigade, and the 382nd and 1821st Self-propelled Artillery Regiments) was no exception. It was equipped with M4A2 Sherman tanks. By the beginning of March 1945, this mechanized corps had suffered heavy losses, and had only 47 M4A2 Sherman tanks, 15 SU-100 and 3 T-34 still operational on its roster.

Thus, by 6 March 1945 the tank and mechanized corps of the 3rd Ukrainian Front had a large deficit of armor. This circumstance determined their use – their brigades were positioned on the defense, and the tanks were reinforcing their motorized rifle battalions. In addition, in order to strengthen the corps, they received self-propelled artillery regiments and brigades as attachments.

The Red Army's separate tank regiments by 1945 had converted to either the TO&E No. 010/463 (T-34/76 tanks) or the TO&E No. 010/464 (T-34/85 tanks). They consisted of a head-quarters with a command platoon (1 T-34 tank); two tank companies (10 T-34 each); reconnaissance, repair and motorized transport platoons; an administrative squad and a medical aid station. Altogether by TO&E a separate tank regiment numbered a total of 225 men (234 if equipped with T-34/85 tanks) and 21 T-34 tanks. One separate tank regiment, the 249th, which was equipped with T-34/76 tanks, took part in the fighting at Lake Balaton.

In addition, each division of the 5th Guards Cavalry Corps had one tank regiment, respectively the 54th, 60th and 71st Tank Regiments. They had suffered large losses in the preceding fighting and by now numbered between 1 and 7 armor vehicles, two of them being American light M3A1 Stuart tanks. These regiments had all been reformed according to the TO&E No. 010/414, which meant they each had four tank companies, one of which was a light tank company.

A Red Army separate motorcycle regiment according to its TO&E No. 010/433 consisted of a headquarters, a motorcycle battalion, a destroyer anti-tank artillery battalion, and four companies – a tank, a mortar, a machine-gun and a vehicle and supply company, for a total of 1,188 men, 10 T-34 tanks, 18 M3A1 armored halftracks, and 3 BA-64 armored cars. Two motorcycle regiments – the 3rd Guards and the 53rd – took part in the fighting at Lake Balaton; both were subordinate to the 57th Army.

From the point of view of the use of the tank units and formations, the main burden of the fighting at Lake Balaton in March 1945 lay upon the self-propelled artillery. Its elements consisted of light, medium and heavy self-propelled artillery regiments.

The light self-propelled gun regiments, which were equipped with SU-76 self-propelled guns and were formed according to TO&E No. 010/484, included a headquarters with a command platoon (1 SU-76), four batteries of 5 SU-76 each, and rear services (combat supply, repair and transport platoons, a medical station, and an administrative squad), for a total of 225 men and 21 SU-76. The 3rd Ukrainian Front had four such regiments – the 1896th, 1891st, 1202nd and 864th. In addition to the light self-propelled artillery regiments, the separate self-propelled artillery battalions of the rifle divisions were also equipped with the SU-76. They began forming up back at the beginning of 1944. These battalions were included on the unit roster of the rifle divisions in place of the separate destroyer anti-tank artillery battalions, but kept the same numerical designations of the anti-tank artillery battalions that they replaced.

According to TO&E No. 04/568, a self-propelled battalion consisted of a headquarters with a command platoon (1 SU-76), three batteries of 5 self-propelled guns each, and a combat supply platoon, for a total of 152 men and 16 SU-76. The 3rd Ukrainian Front had eight such battalions in March 1945 – six subordinate to the 4th Guards Army (the 8th, 13th, 75th, 88th, 122nd and 44th Guards), one in the 26th Army (the 72nd) and one in the 27th Army (the 432nd).

Medium self-propelled artillery regiments according to TO&E No. 010/462 included a head-quarters with a command platoon (1 self-propelled gun), four batteries of 5 self-propelled guns each, and rear services (the same as is in the case of the light self-propelled artillery regiments), but also a submachine gun company and a combat engineer platoon, for a total of 318 men and 21 self-propelled guns. Initially these regiments were equipped with SU-85 self-propelled guns, but from November 1944 they began to be re-equipped with the new SU-100 self-propelled gun. In the March battles, three such regiments took part – the 382nd and 1821st Medium Self-propelled Gun Regiments of the 1st Guards Mechanized Corps, which on 6 March had a total of 15 SU-100 self-propelled guns and the 1201st Medium Self-propelled Gun Regiment subordinate to the 57th Army. In place of self-propelled guns, however, the last named regiment was equipped with 14 T-34 tanks.

The defensive operation of the 3rd Ukrainian Front marked the debut of the medium self-propelled artillery brigades of the Supreme High Command. They began forming up in December 1945 according to TO&E No. 010/500. According to the latter, the brigade consisted of a head-quarters with a command company (2 SU-100); a reconnaissance company (3 SU-76), an anti-aircraft – machine-gun company and an anti-tank company; three self-propelled artillery regiments organized according to TO&E No. 010/462 (21 SU-100 in each), and a technical service company, for a total of 1,492 men, 65 SU-100 and 3 SU-76.

The SU-100 self-propelled artillery brigades formed on the basis of tank brigades, the 1st "Leningrad" Tank Brigade, the 118th "Dvinsk" Tank Brigade, and the 209th Tank Brigade, and received the numerical designations 207th, 208th and 209th respectively. At the beginning of February 1945, all of the SU-100 brigades were sent into the Acting Army – the 207th and 209th to the 2nd Ukrainian Front, and the 208th to the 3rd Ukrainian Front. After the start of the German offensive, the 207th and 209th Self-propelled Artillery Brigades passed to the control of the 3rd Ukrainian Front. The combat operations at Lake Balaton in March 1945 saw the heaviest use of the SU-100 tank destroyer – here on a relatively narrow sector, more than 200 of these self-propelled guns operated.

The Guards heavy self-propelled artillery regiments (they had received the honorific Guards title upon forming up) according to TO&E No. 010/461 consisted of a headquarters with a command platoon (1 ISU-122 or ISU-152), four batteries of five self-propelled guns each, a submachine gun company, and combat engineer and administrative platoons, for a total of 420 men and 21 ISU. Not including the heavy self-propelled artillery regiments in the tank and mechanized corps, only one such regiment – the 366th Guards – took part in the fighting at Lake Balaton.

As of 6 March 1945, the tank formations and units of the 3rd Ukrainian Front had 398 armored vehicles – 193 tanks and 205 self-propelled guns, of which 95 (46%) were light SU-76. The latter moreover comprised more than a quarter of the Front's total tank park. With the arrival of the two SU-100 brigades after the start of the German offensive, the number of self-propelled guns comprised more than 60% of the Front's armor vehicles. Thus, self-propelled guns played the primary role in the defensive operation of the 3rd Ukrainian Front in March 1945.

Table 8 Available Armor in the Armored Forces of the 3rd Ukrainian Front as of 24.00 5 March 1945

	T-34	M4A2	IS-2	T-70	M3A1	ISU-152	ISU-122	SU-100	SU-76	Total
Units under Front command:										
18th Tank Corps	42	–	–	–	–	5/1	16	–	12	75/1
23rd Tank Corps	20/1	–	1	–	–	–	7/1	–	–	28/2
1st Guards Mech. Corps	3	47/1	–	–	–	–	–	15/2	–	65/3
208th SPA Bde	2	–	–	–	–	–	–	63	3	68
366th Guards Hvy SPA Regt.	–	–	3	–	–	4	–	–	–	7
71st Tank Regt., 5th Guards Cavalry Corps	7	–	–	–	–	–	–	–	–	7
60th Tank Regt., 5th Guards Cavalry Corps	–	–	–	–	2	–	–	–	–	2
54th Tank Regt., 5th Guards Cavalry Corps	–	–	–	–	1	–	–	–	–	1
1896th SPA Regt., 5th Guards Cavalry Corps	–	–	–	–	–	–	–	–	8	8
Total under Front command:	74/1	47/1	4	–	3	9/1	23/1	78/2	23	261/6
4th Guards Army:	74/1	47/1	4	–	3	9/1	23/1	78/2	23	261/6
1891st SPA Regt.	–	–	–	–	–	–	–	–	2	2
Separate SPA battalions of the rifle divisions	–	–	–	–	–	–	–	–	26	26
Total, 4th Guards Army									28	28
27th Army:										
432nd Separate SPA Btn.	–	–	–	1	–	–	–	–	7	8
26th Army:										
1202nd SPA Regt.	–	–	–	–	–	–	–	–	14	14
72nd Separate SPA Btn.	–	–	–	–	–	–	–	–	2	2
Total, 26th Army	–	–	–	–	–	–	–	–	16	16
57th Army:										
32nd Guards Mech. Bde	19/2	–	–	–	–	–	–	–	–	19/2
249th Separate Tank Regt.	10/1	–	–	–	–	–	–	–	–	10/1
1201st SPA Regt.	14	–	–	–	–	–	–	–	–	14
864th SPA Regt.	1	–	–	–	–	–	–	–	21	22
3rd Guards Motorcycle Regt.	10	–	–	–	–	–	–	–	–	10
53rd Guards Motorcycle Regt.	10	–	–	–	–	–	–	–	–	10
Total, 57th Army	64/3	–	–	–	–	–	–	–	21	85/3
Total, 3rd Ukrainian Front	157/4	47/1	4	1	3	9/1	23/1	78/2	95	417/9

Note: numbers to right of a slash are non-serviceable vehicles

An SU-85 on the move. These self-propelled guns were used as tank destroyers, but with the widespread introduction of the T-34/85 tank they lost their significance, since they were no longer better armed than the T-34 and lacked turrets.

A T-34/85 tank, camouflaged with branches, waits in ambush.

ISU-122 self-propelled guns. Despite its slow rate of fire, the 122mm cannons of these self-propelled guns were used with success in combat with German panzers.

14

Operation *Frühlingserwachen*

As was in fact expected by the Soviet command, the German offensive got underway on 6 March 1945 with virtually simultaneous attacks on three directions. The enemy's first attack came in the sector of the Bulgarian First Army, which was defending along the Drava River. At 1.00, units of the LXXXXI Army Corps quickly forced a crossing of the river in five locations in the Osijek, Valpovo, Donji Miholjac area, drove back the defending elements of the Bulgarian and Yugoslav armies, and by the end of the day established two small bridgeheads on the opposite bank of the Drava. At 6.00, the Second Panzer Army of Army Group South went on the offensive against the 57th Army after an artillery preparation.

However, the main attack came at 8.47, when the Sixth SS Panzer Army and *Armeegruppe Balck* jumped off between Lakes Velence and Balaton. The attack was preceded by a powerful 30-minute opening artillery barrage. Most of this artillery fire was intended to suppress our troops, which were occupying the primary belt of defenses. As the preparatory artillery fire wound down, it was joined by German tanks and self-propelled guns, which placed rather effective direct fire on targets along the Soviet front line from a range of 800 to 1,000 meters. However, the German indirect artillery fire was less effective: the shells often exploded some distance off-target, and the majority of the Soviet artillery batteries were unaffected by the German barrage. *Luftwaffe* activity during the preparatory artillery phase and in support of the attack was badly hampered by the low layer of clouds, snowfall and the poor conditions of the German airfields.

With the start of the German artillery preparation, the artillery of the Soviet rifle divisions and of the army artillery groups of the 4th Guards and 26th Armies responded. The Soviet artillery fire targeted previously detected aggregations of German infantry and tanks.

On the boundary between the 4th Guards Army and the 26th Army, the enemy launched an attack with units of *Armeegruppe Balck's* 1st Panzer Division and the 356th Infantry Division on both sides of Seregélyes. Simultaneously, up to two regiments of infantry and 30 tanks attacked the positions of the 1st Guards Fortified District and the right flank of the 155th Rifle Division. Soviet artillery fire managed to separate the German infantry from their tanks, while the tanks, lunging ahead, came under fire from the guns of the battalion anti-tank strongpoints of the 155th Rifle Division. Thanks to the tenaciousness of the Soviet defenders and the well-organized system of artillery fire, the German attack here was broken up. In the process, in the sector of the 155th Rifle Division's 436th Rifle Regiment alone, the Germans left behind 15 tanks and 5 armored personnel carriers that were knocked-out during the failed attack.

However, the situation in the 1st Guards Fortified District's sector of defenses deteriorated in the very first minutes of the battle. This was connected with the fact that the Fortified District's command didn't pay sufficient attention to the organization of artillery fire and observation of the enemy. As a result, during the pause between the end of the German preparatory barrage and the start of the attack, the commanders of the 10th Machine-gun – Artillery Battalion and the 1963rd Destroyer Anti-tank Artillery Regiment decided that the enemy wasn't going to attack their positions, and gave the order to their troops to stand down. Meanwhile, German infantry with the support of tanks, exploiting the snowfall that had started, unexpectedly attacked one rifle battalion's positions, and the Soviet infantry fled in disorder through the combat positions of Guards

Lieutenant Colonel Polubinsky's 1963rd Destroyer Anti-tank Artillery Regiment. Left without infantry protection, the artillerymen hastily re-manned their guns and opened fire. They managed to knock out 10 German tanks, but lost almost all of their guns in the fighting. That evening the regiment was withdrawn for refitting.

At 10.15, the Germans managed to break into the northern outskirts of Seregélyes, as a result of which the threat of a breakthrough of the main belt of defenses on the boundary between the 4th Guards Army and the 26th Army emerged. The commander of the 155th Rifle Division hastily pulled his 786th Rifle Regiment back to the area south of Seregélyes, where it took up a defense with its front facing the north along with the 407th Light Artillery Regiment and the 320th Separate Destroyer Anti-tank Artillery Battalion.

The commandant of the 1st Guards Fortified District also threw his reserves into the fighting – a submachine gun company and two batteries of anti-tank guns. In addition, at the order of the commander of the 4th Guards Army, two mortar batteries and two anti-tank gun batteries deployed to the north of Seregélyes, while the 1670th and 338th Destroyer Anti-tank Artillery Regiments took up positions east of the town. In the process, the latter anti-tank regiment immediately joined battle.

Simultaneously with these initial responses, the command of the 4th Guards Army and of the 26th Army took a number of other measures to strengthen their boundary – artillery and mortar units, as well as rocket launchers, were moved up closer to the front line. The army artillery groups, as well as the artillery of the 21st Guards Rifle Corps that was positioned north of Lake Velence, were also called upon to bring fire down upon the attacking Germans.

As a result of the maneuver of these artillery units, the firepower of the units of the 155th Rifle Division and the 1st Guards Fortified District was significantly enhanced. Meanwhile, the regimental artillery groups and the anti-tank artillery units were rendering substantial assistance to the rifle units in repelling the intensifying German attacks.

The attacking units of *Armeegruppe Balck* were unable to realize any initial success as a result of the adopted measures, despite the ferocity of their attacks. By the end of day 6 March, the Germans here managed only to make a shallow penetration of 3 to 4 kilometers in a narrow sector of the Soviet front, no wider than 3.5 kilometers. The *Armeegruppe* headquarters noted that this was insufficient in order to make full use of the 3rd Panzer Division. The latter didn't take part in the attack on 6 March, because it was unable to move into its jumping-off area in time.

The combat on 6 March did expose the vulnerability of the boundary between the 4th Guards Army's 1st Guards Fortified District and the 26th Army's 30th Rifle Corps. Despite the fact that a significant portion of the 26th Army's artillery had been concentrated in the sector of the 30th Rifle Corps' 155th and 36th Guards Rifle Divisions, it had proven incapable of helping its neighbor on the right. In addition, the artillery units that were supporting the 1st Guards Fortified District with indirect fire were ineffective because of weak command and control and poorly organized cooperation.

In conjunction with the attack at the boundary between the 4th Guards Army and 26th Army, units of the Sixth SS Panzer Army – its I Cavalry Corps and I SS Panzer Corps (the 3rd and 4th Cavalry Divisions, the 1st SS Panzer Division *Leibstandarte Adolf Hitler* and the 12th SS Panzer Division *Hitlerjugend*) assaulted Soviet positions between Lake Velence and the Sárviz Canal. The main attack, which was launched to the south along the Székesfehérvár – Cece highway, struck the positions of the 30th Rifle Corps' 68th Guards Rifle Division. Here the Germans threw up to four infantry regiments and 60-80 tanks and assault guns into the attack. The tanks advanced in the first echelon, followed by infantry on foot, and behind them came assault guns and infantry mounted in halftracks.

As a result of the fighting, the left-flank 68th Guards Rifle Division wound up isolated from the corps' remaining units, and had direct contact only with its neighbor on the left – the 135th Rifle

Corps' 233rd Rifle Division. However, thanks to the well-organized system of artillery fire, the German infantry became separated from the leading tanks and the latter wound up in the zone of fire from the anti-tank guns of the battalion anti-tank strong points. During the battle, the guns of the 202nd Guards Rifle Regiment alone accounted for 11 knocked-out enemy tanks.

The German attack in the sector of the 233rd Rifle Division was met with indirect artillery fire on pre-registered areas. However, because of the low light and fog, it was difficult to determine the effectiveness of this fire, so the commander of the 135th Rifle Corps ordered the artillery to switch to placing barrier fire. In addition, the infantry opened fire with rifles, machine guns, and guns that had been deployed to fire over open sights. The first German attack was driven back. Subsequently, having detected the boundaries between the defending regiments, the Germans began to attack these more vulnerable locations.

After 9.00, the ground in the Soponya – Káloz area became blanketed with fog, and visibility didn't extend beyond 200 meters. Because of this, the effectiveness of the indirect Soviet artillery fire sharply dropped. Taking advantage of this, the German infantry with the support of tanks managed to approach quite close to the Soviet front line, before launching another assault on the positions of the 68th Guards Rifle Division and 233rd Rifle Division. This time the enemy managed to push back the left-flank battalion of the 68th Guards Rifle Division and seized a commanding height in the area.

That afternoon, after a powerful artillery preparation, units of the I SS Panzer Corps – up to a regiment of infantry with the support of several dozen tanks and assault guns – again went on the attack, trying to break through to Káloz, on the road toward Cece. The commander of the 68th Guards Rifle Division committed all of his available reserves and all of his artillery into the fighting, including the attached 1966th Destroyer Anti-tank Artillery Regiment, but was unable to stop the German attack. Suffering heavy losses, the division began to fall back, and the bridgehead on the western bank of the Sárviz Canal that it had been holding rapidly shrank in width and depth. In order to strengthen the defense, the commander of the 26th Army transferred his anti-tank artillery reserve to the 68th Guards Rifle Division – the 1965th Destroyer Anti-tank Artillery Regiment, which had crossed to the western bank of the Sárviz Canal, moved into positions west of Káloz. With the onset of darkness, the German attacks didn't cease – in the twilight, up to 20 tanks attacked the sector of the 198th Guards Rifle Regiment. In the course of the fighting, a company of enemy infantry and six German tanks reached the position of one of the batteries of the 1966th Destroyer Anti-tank Artillery Regiment. At the order of the battery commander, scouts illuminated the terrain with flares, and simultaneously one gun platoon opened fire at the tanks with armor-piercing shells, while the other opened fire with canister and hurled fragmentation grenades at the infantry. The very first shots managed to disable one tank, and the remaining tanks stopped and with fire from fixed positions began to support the attack of their infantry. After more than an hour of fighting, the German attack in this sector faltered and was driven back. Altogether on 6 March 1945, the artillerymen of the 1966th Destroyer Anti-tank Artillery Regiment disabled or destroyed 11 enemy tanks, without losing a single gun in return.

The attack of the 3rd and 4th Cavalry Divisions against the left flank of the 26th Army ended in failure – units of the 74th and 151st Rifle Divisions threw the enemy back with a counterattack. Documents of the Sixth SS Panzer Army noted, "The cavalry corps was pushed back on both sides of the Siófok – Lepsény road to a point 300 meters in front of the friendly main line of resistance. The enemy had also launched counterattacks out of Enying."

As concerns the II SS Panzer Corps, because of delays in deploying, it didn't go on the attack on the Aba – Sárkeresztúr axis until 18.30. Even then, it could only attack with insignificant forces, as a result of which it made practically no headway on 6 March.

Having assessed the situation after the first day of combat, the 3rd Ukrainian Front command took a number of measures to strengthen the defenses on the revealed directions of enemy attacks.

For example, two brigades of the 18th Tank Corps (the 110th and 170th Tank Brigades) and the 35th Guards Rifle Corps' 3rd Guards Airborne Division were moved up into the second belt of defenses east and southeast of Seregélyes. A tank regiment of the 1st Guards Mechanized Corps was sent to a previously prepared line in the Sárkeresztúr area, and south of it the 21st Rifle Division deployed, having been transferred to control of the 30th Rifle Corps from the 26th Army reserve. The 27th Army's 33rd Rifle Corps received an order to move out to the Dunaföldvár area, and to be ready, depending on the situation, to enter the fighting either east or west of the Sárviz Canal.

In addition, a regrouping of artillery units was conducted – from the left bank of the Danube, two howitzer brigades and a mortar brigade crossed the river and moved into the area of the 30th Rifle Corps' defense, as well as an artillery regiment, an anti-tank regiment, a mortar regiment and a rocket launcher regiment. One artillery brigade from the Front reserve moved up into the Káloz – Sárkeresztúr area, to the boundary between the 36th and 68th Guards Rifle Divisions.

The German command also didn't rate the successes of the first day of Operation *Frühlingserwachen* very highly. For example, the commander of Army Group South General Wöhler reported the following to the General Inspector of Panzer Troops Guderian shortly after midnight on 7 March:

> The armored forces could barely be used at all, as ground conditions did not permit cross-country movement, and the roads were either bad or blocked by minefields and anti-tank obstacles. For these reasons, the attack had to be mainly carried out by infantry.
>
> That would continue to be the case. One could not expect a rapid breakthrough; instead, it was to be a tough infantry fight, and this would also consume more ammunition than we had previously intended.
>
> In general, the enemy was expecting a friendly attack. However, his outposts were surprised by the choice of the time and place ….

On the morning of 7 March, after an artillery preparation and air strikes, the units of *Armeegruppe Balck* and of the I and II SS Panzer Corps again went on the attack in the direction of Seregélyes, Sárosd and Sárkeresztúr. On 7 March, in the sector of the 26th Army alone, the enemy attacked with up to nine infantry regiments and more than 170 tanks, assault guns and self-propelled artillery. Particularly stubborn fighting developed in the sector of the 155th Rifle Division, where the Germans launched five attacks, one after another. As on the first day of the fighting, the battalion anti-tank strongpoints and anti-tank areas, supported by indirect artillery fire, played the main role in repelling these attacks. Because of the rapidly fluctuating situation, the artillerymen often had to pivot their guns by 90 to 100 degrees in order to fire at attacking tanks.

Only after both the defense's field works had been demolished by hostile enemy artillery fire and air strikes and the Soviet anti-tank artillery had suffered heavy losses did the enemy succeed in taking a few strongpoints south of Seregélyes. In the sector of the 1st Guards Fortified District (which for command convenience was made subordinate to the 27th Army on 7 March, because Lake Velence separated it from the rest of the 4th Guards Army), the Germans also expanded their breakthrough sector in the direction of Lake Velence, but thanks to the timely arrival of Soviet reserves, the Germans were unable to advance further. The enemy advance south of Seregélyes was stopped by the two tank brigades of the 18th Tank Corps that had been thrown into the fighting.

However, the bitterest fighting went on west of the Sárviz Canal, in the Soponya – Káloz sector. At 6.00 on 7 March, units of the I SS Panzer Corps – up to 40 tanks and armored personnel carriers with infantry – attacked the positions of the 1965th Destroyer Anti-tank Artillery Regiment. The tanks went into the attack at high speeds, covered by assault guns that were firing from sheltered positions. The Soviet artillerymen wound up in an extremely difficult situation, since because of the thick fog, visibility was less than 400 meters. The anti-tank batteries had to deal with both enemy tanks and infantry simultaneously. As a result of savage fighting, the 6th Battery knocked out six tanks, but lost all of its guns in the process due to fire from enemy assault guns. The 3rd Battery knocked out another three German armored vehicles, before its guns were overrun by German tanks that were breaking through to the rear. However, a subsequent attempt by the German armor to penetrate across the bridge that spanned the Sárviz Canal was unsuccessful – by the fire of two batteries of 85mm guns of the 974th Anti-aircraft Artillery Regiment that was positioned here, four German tanks were knocked out and the rest were forced to retreat.

However, the Germans didn't cease their attacks toward Káloz before the day's end. Batteries of the 1965th Destroyer Anti-tank Artillery Regiment that had remained intact after the morning action fought until they had expended their last shell, and even after their guns were destroyed, the artillerymen continued to fight as infantry. Despite the heroic resistance of the defending Soviet units, however, by the evening of 7 March, the I SS Panzer Corps took possession of Káloz.

North of this village, in the course of the entire day, four batteries of the 1966th Destroyer Anti-tank Artillery Regiment fought on in semi-encirclement. They managed to repel three German attacks, but having lost all their guns, the artillerymen were forced to retreat.

By the evening of 7 March, the situation on this axis had become so threatening that the commander of the 68th Guards Rifle Division had deployed almost all of the division's artillery to fire over open sights; with difficulty they were holding back the offensive of the SS tanks and infantry against the bridgehead across the Sárviz Canal, which shrank further to a width of 3-4 kilometers and a depth of just 1.5-2 kilometers. With the onset of darkness, the combat subsided, and the division's units abandoned the bridgehead and began to retreat across the Sárviz Canal to its eastern bank. Because of the losses it had suffered, on the following day the 68th Guards Rifle Division was pulled back into the 26th Army reserve.

Over two days of fighting, the 1965th and 1966th Anti-tank Artillery Regiments reported the disabling or destruction of 54 enemy tanks, self-propelled guns and halftracks, 7 vehicles, 3 guns and 12 machine guns. Their own losses were placed at 30 guns, 3 vehicles, and 12 men killed, 46 wounded and 23 missing in action. With the six remaining guns, the regiments were withdrawn into the Front reserve for rest and refitting.

Units of the 233rd Rifle Division and the neighboring 74th Rifle Division of the 135th Rifle Corps, under the pressure of units of the I SS Panzer Corps, by the evening of 7 March had fallen back to a new position south of Káloz. By this time the 233rd Rifle Division had 62 guns for a defensive front of 7 kilometers, while the 74th Rifle Division had just 35 guns for a defensive front of 14 kilometers. Despite this, the men of these divisions put up ferocious resistance to the Germans; frequently, the German attacks resulted in hand to hand fighting, after which the Soviet elements would pull back to the next line.

On 8 March, units of the 2nd SS Panzer Division *Das Reich* managed to breach the Soviet defenses between the villages of Sárosd and Aba, having cut the road between them in the vicinity of Hill 159.0. Striving to exploit this success, the Germans launched nine successive attacks. However, having been met by heavy indirect artillery fire, the fire of anti-tank guns, and especially of the heavy self-propelled artillery firing from ambush positions, they fell back, leaving 24 burned out or disabled tanks and self-propelled guns behind on the battlefield.

West of the Sárviz Canal, the I SS Panzer Corps, attacking on a broad front, forced the units of the 233rd and 74th Rifle Divisions to fall back to the second belt of defenses by the evening of 8 March. The 3rd and 4th Cavalry Divisions also managed to make some headway against the Soviet units at Lake Balaton.

On the night of 8-9 March, the 3rd Ukrainian Front command continued to bring up reserves to the sector between Lake Velence and the Sárviz Canal. By the morning of 9 March, additional artillery, howitzer and mortar brigades, four artillery and mortar regiments, a *Katiusha* battalion and the 1438th, 1453rd, 1821st and 382nd Guards Self-propelled Artillery Regiments had been

A column of T-34/85 tanks. This scene was typical for the Red Army – infantry
riding on the tank's hull, with cases of ammunition mounted on the sides.

An abandoned StuG 40 self-propelled gun in the area of Lake Balaton, February 1945.

A Jagdpanzer IV/70(A) tank destroyer, knocked out in the area of Lake Balaton. The machine has Drahtgeflecht [wire mesh] Schürzen side skirts and is wearing the remnants of winter camouflage.

A Wespe self-propelled howitzer destroyed by artillery fire; Lake Balaton area, February 1945.

Yet another knocked-out Wespe self-propelled howitzer. These self-propelled guns, possessing armor protection against shell fragments and firing from covered positions, were a hard nut to crack, and only a direct hit could knock them out.

A PzKpfw. VI Ausf.B King Tiger of the 509th Heavy Panzer Battalion. Its tactical designation "213" is visible on the turret.

A completely burned-out Pz.IV Ausf.J in the area of Lake Balaton, March 1945.

A Jagdpanther tank destroyer left burned-out on a street of a Hungarian village in the area of Lake Balaton, March 1945.

A Marder III self-propelled gun, abandoned by its crew. The abandoned tank destroyer is being used as a road sign; it bears a marker indicating the direction of Glatz.

An abandoned Jagdpanther on a road. The machine has no visible damage, so it may have broken down or run out of fuel. Vicinity of Lake Balaton, March 1945.

A broken-down Panther Ausf.G, abandoned by its crew. Lake Balaton area, March 1945.

deployed to the north, east and south of the sector that had been breached by the enemy. As a result of this, the density of the Soviet artillery surrounding the German breakthrough amounted to 65 guns and mortars per kilometer.

German units continued persistent attacks the entire day of 9 March on the 26th Army's entire sector of defense and in the sector between Lake Velence and Seregélyes. In the sector held by the 1st Guards Fortified District, *Armeegruppe Balck* succeeded in advancing along the southern shore of Lake Velence as far as Gárdony before it was finally halted. In the fighting on this axis, Colonel Vlasenko's 24th Destroyer Anti-tank Artillery Brigade, which was occupying a number of anti-tank areas in the sector of the 1st Guards Fortified District on a front of approximately 10 kilometers, played the largest role. In the course of fighting between 6 and 9 March, Vlasenko's brigade knocked out or destroyed 39 tanks, self-propelled guns and halftracks, while losing 16 of its guns in return.

The II SS Panzer Corps continued its attack toward the southeast. Units of the 9th SS Panzer Division *Hohenstaufen* launched a concentrated attack in a sector 1.5-kilometers-wide against elements of the 36th Guards Rifle Division, striving to make a breakthrough in the direction of Aba and Sárkeresztúr. However, with the support of massed artillery fire, the Guards division repulsed all the German attacks on this direction. The SS troops also failed to achieve any substantial results in the sector of the 155th Rifle Division, which in the course of the day repelled nine German tank attacks.

In the sector of the 26th Army's 135th Rifle Corps, units of the I SS Panzer Corps launched an attack on the night of 8-9 March. The main blow struck the positions of the 233rd Rifle Division in the vicinity of Aranyos. The division's limited amount of artillery was unable to render the needed support to the infantry. The 135th Rifle Corps' artillery was also not in the condition to conduct effective massed fire on the breakthrough sector at night. As a result, under the cover of the nighttime darkness, the German tanks managed to penetrate the second defensive belt. True, the situation was somewhat eased by the circumstance that the Germans also acted with uncertainty in the nighttime conditions and thus couldn't take full advantage of the success of their initial attack. Exploiting this, the units of the 233rd and 236th Rifle Divisions began an organized withdrawal to the south.

The command of the 26th Army back on 8 March had decided to reinforce the 135th Rifle Corps, and gave it the 208th Self-propelled Artillery Brigade out of the Front reserve. Such a powerful and mobile formation (63 SU-100 tank destroyers) was able to make a significant impact on the course of combat operations. However, the Soviet command was plainly late with introducing it into the fighting. The brigade received the order to move two of its regiments into ambush positions on the line Nagyherceg – Dég, and in cooperation with the units of the 233rd and 236th Rifle Divisions supported by the 1008th and 1245th Destroyer Anti-tank Artillery Regiments to prevent a breakthrough by enemy tanks and infantry along the western bank of the Sárviz Canal. Meanwhile, the third tank destroyer regiment of the 208th Self-propelled Artillery Brigade remained in the 26th Army reserve in the Szár area.

The brigade's regiments were slow to move out; the brigade's commander had no communications with the rifle divisions operating in front of him, and the reconnoitering of the approach route was poor. As a result, the 1068th Self-propelled Artillery Regiment, moving in column along the Cece – Székesfehérvár highway was unexpectedly attacked by the German tanks that had broken through; having rapidly lost 14 of its 21 SU-100 tank destroyers, the regiment hastily fell back to the Sáregres area.

The enemy's 23rd Panzer Division that was advancing along the highway was stopped north of Sáregres by units of the 11th Guards Cavalry Division. The attempt by hostile tanks to break though the army-level defensive belt and to seize crossings over the Kapos Canal from the march failed.

A powerful anti-tank region, which had been set up in the Cece – Simontornya area on the morning of 9 March played a major role in repulsing the enemy's attack in the direction of Cece with the aim of seizing crossings over the Sárviz Canal. Colonel Shpek, the commander of the 49th Destroyer Anti-tank Artillery Brigade, was appointed as the anti-tank region's commandant. In addition to two of his brigade's regiments, the 1008th and 1249th, the region included a battalion of the 407th Light Artillery Regiment, the 1089th Anti-aircraft Artillery Regiment, the 227th Separate Anti-aircraft Artillery Battalion, the 117th Destroyer Anti-tank Artillery Regiment, the 1953rd Self-propelled Artillery Regiment of the 209th Self-propelled Artillery Brigade, the "Avenger" Battalion (which had been formed between 6 and 10 January 1945 as part of the 4th Anti-aircraft Division at the order of the artillery commander of the 3rd Ukrainian Front in order to combat enemy tanks, and was armed with captured German 88mm anti-aircraft guns), and the 268th Guards Anti-aircraft Regiment. Altogether, this anti-tank region possessed more than 100 guns and self-propelled guns. With the assistance of units of the 11th Guards Cavalry Division, which had been hastily shifted to this sector, this anti-tank region in the course of 9 and 10 March repulsed all of the German attempts to seize crossings over the Sárviz and Kapos Canals in the Cece and Simontornya area.

However, in spite of this, by the evening of 9 March the situation of the 3rd Ukrainian Front had become precarious. East of the Sárviz Canal, units of the I SS Panzer Corps and the I Cavalry Corps had fully breached the primary defensive belt. Units of the 26th Army's 35th Guards Rifle Corps were with great difficulty holding back the enemy in an intermediate position. In the sector of defense of the 135th Rifle Corps, the Germans had penetrated to the army-level belt of defenses, thereby creating a real threat to break through it. The troops of the 26th Army by this time had suffered significant losses and were exhausted by the heavy fighting, while the defensive front they were trying to hold had stretched to 90 kilometers.

By this time, too, the Front's main reserves had already been committed. In particular, by the evening of 9 March 1945, the entire 18th Tank, 1st Guards Mechanized, and 5th Guards Cavalry

Corps had already entered the fighting, as well as all the units and formations of the Front's artillery reserve, including its anti-tank artillery reserve.

The Front commander Marshal of the Soviet Union Tolbukhin appealed to the *Stavka* of the Supreme High Command with a request to authorize the use of the 9th Guards Army, which was located in the Front's reserve, in the defensive fighting. However, the *Stavka* reaffirmed its prior decision – the 9th Guards Army would not be drawn into the defensive fighting, and the Front no later than 15-16 March would go over to the offensive. As a result, the 3rd Ukrainian Front command had to seek out so-called "internal resources" in order to liquidate the threat of the enemy breakthrough to the Danube, and initiated a force reshuffling.

To take the pressure off of the 26th Army, Tolbukhin decided to insert the 4th Guards Army's second-echelon 31st Guards Rifle Corps into the sector between Lake Velence and the Danube along a previously prepared line. He then assigned responsibility for the defense of the Front's sector between Lake Velence and the Sárviz Canal, and further along the eastern bank of that canal to Cece, to the 27th Army. The 1st Guards Fortified District and the 30th Rifle Corps with all their attached assets, as well as the 1st Guards Mechanized Corps and the 18th Tank Corps, which had been committed into the fighting from the Front's reserve, thereby passed to the control of the 27th Army.

Meanwhile, the 26th Army assumed responsibility for a shorter sector between Cece and Lake Balaton and took command of the 33rd Rifle Corps and the 208th and 209th Self-propelled Artillery Brigade. The 23rd Tank Corps together with the 207th Self-propelled Artillery Brigade and the 5th Guards Cavalry Corps were pulled back into Front reserve. In the process, the 33rd Rifle Corps, reinforced with the two self-propelled artillery brigades, replaced the units of the 5th Guards Cavalry Corps and moved into the defenses on the line Sáregres, Simontornya, Ozora.

In order to reinforce the 27th Army, which was now defending the critical sector, the 4th Guards Army transferred to it a destroyer anti-tank artillery brigade, a mortar brigade and an artillery brigade, as well as four artillery regiments. In addition, the 26th Army turned over to the 27th Army a breakthrough artillery division, an anti-aircraft artillery division, a destroyer anti-tank artillery brigade, five artillery and mortar regiments, as well as a breakthrough artillery division out of the Front's reserve.

On 10 March, fighting flared up with new intensity along the entire front. The Germans committed the 3rd Panzer Division into the area north of Seregélyes. Taking advantage of the heavy snow, the enemy tanks and infantry, attacking to the northeast out of the area north of Seregélyes, at dawn on 10 March managed to close on the Soviet positions unnoticed, and with a sudden attack began to drive back the elements of the 1st Guards Fortified District and the 3rd Guards Airborne Division. On other sectors, the Germans also stubbornly attempted to breach the defenses, and made advances in spite of their losses.

The 3rd Ukrainian Front command was compelled to throw its last reserve into the fighting in this sector – units of the 23rd Tank Corps and the 207th Self-propelled Artillery Brigade. The artillery and tanks of these formations, which deployed on the line Agárd – Csirib, substantially strengthened the 27th Army's defense.

Despite this, by the evening of 10 March, German tanks reached the second defensive belt, which was occupied by a division of the second-echelon 35th Guards Rifle Corps. The 3rd Guards Airborne Division of this rifle corps took up a cutoff position with its front facing to the north.

In the fighting for the intermediate position on 10 March, once again the main burden of the struggle against the enemy tanks lay upon the units of the destroyer anti-tank artillery, the self-propelled artillery and the anti-aircraft artillery. For example, the artillery regiments and battalions that were operating in the sector of the 30th Rifle Corps threw back 16-18 German attacks each day.

Combat operations didn't cease once the sun set. Thus, in the sector of the 155th Rifle Division, savage fighting for possession of the commanding height Hill 159.0, where the command posts of the corps and the division were located, went on without pause in the course of 9-10 March. On 9 March, the enemy attacked the hill five times, but all of these attacks were successfully repulsed by defending units of the Red Army, which were supported by massed artillery fire.

Having no success with frontal assaults, the Germans attempted to outflank the hill. A group of German tanks managed to penetrate into our defenses in the Aba area, but it was ambushed and destroyed by tanks of the 110th Tank Brigade.

With the onset of darkness, the attacks on the hill didn't cease. Slowly advancing, enemy tanks enveloped the hill in a semi-circle, and then opened machine-gun fire with incendiary-tracer bullets at the group of homes and outbuildings on top of the hill. The buildings began to burn, and some of the Soviet guns and tanks that were positioned near them were caught in a difficult situation: their crews were blinded by the flames, but they themselves became clearly visible to the Germans. The German tanks opened a heavy fire and began to approach. In their turn, the guns of the 155th Rifle Division fired at the muzzle flashes of the German tanks, but the fire of the enemy tanks (which had among them vehicles with infrared optics) proved to be more accurate.

At a critical moment of the battle, the commander of the 1964th Destroyer Anti-tank Artillery Regiment ordered one battery to move out onto the flank of the attacking tanks. Having quickly deployed, the guns opened fire at the moment when the lead enemy tank had approached to within 50 meters of the position. Aiming down the barrel alone, the artillerymen managed to knock out three tanks, which slowed the attack somewhat and gave the defending Soviet elements the opportunity to make an organized retreat from the hill to new positions.

Meanwhile, the 27th Army command committed its reserve 363rd Heavy Self-propelled Artillery Regiment (6 ISU-152 and 11 ISU-122) into the fighting. It moved into a line 1 to 1.5 kilometers east and southeast of Hill 159.0 and by its fire halted the advance of the German tanks. Taking advantage of this, the commander of the 1964th Destroyer Anti-tank Artillery Regiment withdrew his batteries from the hill. In this night action, batteries of the regiment knocked out up to 10 tanks and halftracks, while losing 8 guns in the process.

Simultaneously with the night attack on Hill 159.0, up to two battalions of German infantry with tanks launched an attack in the direction of Sárosd and seized the Csillag strongpoint between Sárosd and Aba. The 27th Army command committed the 68th Guards Rifle Division on this axis. At 4.00, this division's 200th Rifle Regiment (which had a two-battalion table of organization) drove the Germans out of Csillag with a surprise counterattack. All of the division's artillery was used to support this counterattack. Curiously, the 2nd Battalion of the 320th Howitzer Artillery Regiment throughout the battle fired illumination rounds, which constantly lit up a sector of 5 kilometers of the front and up to 3 kilometers into its depth. Over two hours, this battalion expended approximately 1,000 illumination rounds.

On the morning of 11 March, units of *Armeegruppe Balck* and of the II SS Panzer Corps again went on the attack, this time with broad *Luftwaffe* support for the ground units. As a result of repeated attacks, the Germans managed to shove back units of the 27th Army by 2 to 4 kilometers, and reached the line Kis Velence – Sándor.

The tenacious resistance of the units of the 3rd Ukrainian Front forced the enemy frequently to alter both the tactics and the direction of his attacks, undertaking them after a heavy artillery barrage or air strikes, or unexpectedly, with no preliminary preparation. For example, on 12 March the Germans attacked to the northeast toward Kis Velence, but on 13 March, they changed the direction of their attack – toward Pusztaszabolc and Adony, which is to say, toward the southwest. Up to four regiments of infantry and up to 100 tanks and self-propelled guns were concentrated on a narrow sector of the front in the attacks toward Pusztaszabolc and Adony. The tanks were advancing in packed combat formations, and coming under the massed fire of Soviet artillery they suffered large losses. In the end, the Germans managed nevertheless to make a shallow penetration into the defenses, but their further advance was stopped by units of the 23rd Tank Corps, supported by three artillery regiments.

On the evening of 13 March, approximately 90 German tanks and self-propelled guns with the support of infantry attacked out of the area of Tükres, but running into a powerful anti-tank defense here, the attack had no success. Thus, by the end of 13 March, *Armeegruppe Balck* only managed to push back units of the 163rd Rifle Division and to cut the Kis Velence – Adony road.

Considering the looming threat of a breakthrough by the German panzer divisions to the Danube River, the command of the 3rd Ukrainian Front and the 27th Army took all possible measures to halt the enemy's advance. In addition to the 23rd Tank Corps, between 10 and 12 March the 207th Self-propelled Artillery Brigade and three artillery and mortar regiments the were shifted to the 35th Guards Rifle Corps' sector of defense. Altogether over the course of three days, the Soviet command committed 14 artillery and mortar regiments and more than 150 tanks and self-propelled guns into the fighting in the sectors of the 78th Guards Rifle and 163rd Rifle Divisions, which significantly augmented the defense.

Simultaneously with the attacks by *Armeegruppe Balck*, the Germans undertook an offensive with the forces of the II SS Panzer Corps against units of the 30th Rifle Corps, having concentrated their main assault forces in the sector of the 68th Guards Rifle Division. After stubborn fighting, which continued through the entire day, the enemy managed to seize the Heinrich Estate.

That night, muffling the sound of the tank engines with artillery salvoes, 20 German tanks stealthily approached the left-flank elements of the 36th Guards Rifle Division and launched an attack. The German tanks advanced slowly, firing incendiary shells intensively, in order to set fire to any of the buildings they met on their path. Simultaneously, a specially assigned group of soldiers of the 36th Infantry Division illuminated the area with flares, but batteries of the 1249th Destroyer Anti-tank and 1821st Self-propelled Artillery Regiments that were positioned here instantly opened fire and knocked out three tanks. Meanwhile, Soviet artillery, having opened fire with incendiary shells, set fire to two structures on the path of advance of the German tanks, and two howitzer batteries opened fire with illumination rounds. This enabled the placement of concentrated artillery fire on the attacking German elements, and the attack faltered. Later that night, the Germans attempted three more attacks on this axis, but each ended in failure.

Considering that the enemy, having seized Heinrich, might encircle units of the 36th Guards Rifle Division, the Front commander ordered it to withdraw from the Aba area. At the same time, the commander of the 1st Guards Mechanized Corps received an order: "By the morning of 12 March, assemble [your] main forces on the line Sárosd – Sárkeresztúr, where in cooperation with the rifle divisions, organize a firm defense and don't permit an enemy breakthrough to the southeast."

All this time, artillery units had been moving up to the area of the Heinrich Estate. They were all grouped together under the direction of the commander of the 170th Light Artillery Brigade, which had arrived from the Front reserve. The commander of this brigade was ordered to take command of all the anti-tank artillery units in the 68th Guards Rifle Division's sector and to create a strong anti-tank area there.

As a result, by the morning of 12 March, a powerful artillery grouping, which numbered more than 400 guns and mortars, was ready to meet the German units that had broken through at Heinrich. In the fighting on 12 and 13 March, this grouping, exploiting its advantageous position for conducting flanking fire, inflicted heavy losses to the units of the II SS Panzer Corps, as a result of which all the attempts to penetrate the defenses on this axis had no success.

On 14 and 15 March, the command of *Armeegruppe Balck* made one more attempt to breach our defenses in the Sándor area. For this purpose, the 6th Panzer Division was thrown into the attack on a narrow sector of 2 kilometers after a preparatory artillery barrage and air strikes. However, units of the 3rd Guards Airborne Division and the 18th Tank Corps managed to repulse three German attacks in succession. Once again, the main role in this success belonged to the artillery units that had been shifted to this sector. As a result of the adopted measures, in the sector of the 3rd Guards Airborne Division, the density of anti-tank artillery guns alone on 14 March amounted to 35 guns per kilometer.

On the morning of 15 March, the Germans made their final attempt to attack the positions of the 35th Guards Rifle Corps with major panzer forces. However, this attack brought no success, and by the evening, the enemy attacks on the entire front of the 27th Army were halted.

In the sector of the 26th Army in the period of fighting between 11 and 15 March, the main events unfolded in the triangular area between Sáregres, Simontornya and Cece, where units of the 11th Guards Cavalry Division were holding a small bridgehead across the confluence of the Sárviz and Kapos Canals. Striving to seize crossings in this area, the I SS Panzer Corps relentlessly attacked both day and night. In the course of 48 hours alone – 10 and 11 March – the Germans undertook up to 20 attacks with the involvement of major tank and infantry forces.

The situation of the units of the 26th Army from the very beginning was complicated by the fact that the enemy had launched its attack against the bridgehead on the night of 10 March at a time when units of the 202nd Rifle Division were in the process of replacing the units of the 11th Guards Cavalry Division in the bridgehead. With a sudden attack, the Germans broke into the northern outskirts of Simontornya, and with the coming of dawn, after a strong artillery preparation attempted to break through to a bridge across the Kapos Canal. In the repulse of this attack, Guards Major Mrukalo's 227th Separate Anti-aircraft Artillery Battalion, which was equipped with 85mm anti-aircraft guns, played the decisive role. Engaging the attacking enemy tanks and infantry, it knocked out 10 armored vehicles.

Considering the situation that had emerged the 26th Army command decided to leave the units of the 11th Guards Cavalry Division within the bridgehead. In fighting on 11 March, these units restored the situation in northern portion of Simontornya; the group of German infantry from the 1st SS Panzer Division's 2nd Panzer Grenadier Regiment that had broken into the town was encircled, and the Germans were either killed or taken prisoner. The M-13 rocket launchers of the 45th Guards Mortar Regiment played a large role in this. Their fire blanketed the bulk of the enemy's tanks and infantry that had broken through.

The SU-100 tank destroyers operating in this sector were particularly effective. Concealed in ambush positions, they inflicted large losses on the German tanks with their surprise fire. For example, in combat on 11 March, the 2nd Battery of the 1953rd Self-propelled Artillery Regiment, which had taken up firing positions in a densely wooded area southeast of Sáregres, repelled an attack by 14 German tanks, of which three were knocked out by six shots from a range of 1,500 meters.

In order to illuminate the battlefield during night actions, anti-aircraft searchlights that were deployed on the eastern bank of the Sárviz Canal in the Cece area were successfully used. Acting in concert with the searchlights, the artillery of the 26th Army successfully repulsed four German night attacks with the participation of tanks in the Sáregres area. In one of these attacks, three tanks that were caught in the beam of a searchlight were destroyed by several artillery rounds. Flares, as well as fires lit from flammable materials, were used to illuminate the ground when repelling German night attacks in the Simontornya area.

With the onset of darkness on 12 March, units of the I SS Panzer Corps again drove out the Soviet elements that were defending the northern portion of Simontornya, and that night they forced a crossing of the Kapos Canal and passed up to two companies of infantry over to the southern bank. That same night, up to two battalions of German infantry with 14 tanks outflanked the anti-tank area from the south and penetrated into the southwestern section of Simontornya.

The 2nd Battalion of the 407th Light Artillery Regiment, which had taken position on the northern outskirts of Simontornya on 9 March, fought heroically on these days. On the night of 10 March, the battalion had fought for the northern portion of the town, and in the daytime had taken part in repelling three German tank attacks. By the evening of 12 March, the battalion had 10 knocked out or destroyed tanks to its credit.

In the evening twilight on 12 March, a group of German submachine gunners numbering up to 100 men infiltrated along a balka and closed upon the positions of the 2nd Battalion's 5th and 6th Batteries. That night, fighting without infantry protection, the battalion knocked out 7 tanks, but lost all of its materiel in return. The battalion's survivors swam across to the southern bank, because the bridge had already been blown up.

On 12 March, the 11th Guards Cavalry Division was withdrawn from the bridgehead. The artillery that had been attached to it, which was in defensive positions on the line Sáregres – Simontornya, was subordinated to the commander of the 202nd Rifle Division.

Simultaneously with the attacks in the Sáregres – Simontornya sector, the enemy also launched attacks against the bridgeheads at Ozora and Mezőkomárom on the right flank of the salient they had created in the Soviet defenses, in the sector of the 104th Rifle Division. Units of the 104th Rifle Division in the course of 11 March alone repelled 17 German attacks, but were nevertheless compelled to fall back to the southern bank of the Sió Canal. On the morning of 12 March under the cover of a smokescreen, and the suppressing fire of tanks and artillery as well, the enemy forced a crossing of the Sió Canal in the sector of the 74th Rifle Division and crossed up to a battalion of infantry to the southern bank, where it dug in. The struggle for the bridgeheads on both sides of the canal became savage.

In the fighting on 13 March, the main forces of the I SS Panzer Corps concentrated on liquidating the Soviet bridgehead on the northern bank of the Kapos Canal and on expanding its own bridgehead on its southern bank. The combat was extremely fierce; on the Soviet side, every artillery unit, including the anti-aircraft artillery, was drawn into the struggle against the German tanks and infantry. Thus, the 227th Separate Anti-aircraft Battalion of 85mm guns alone on 12 and 13 March repelled six tank attacks, destroying 14 tanks and self-propelled guns in the process. By the end of 13 March, only three guns remained in the battalion.

On the afternoon of 13 March, after 20 aircraft twice bombed the positions of the 26th Army's 202nd Rifle Division up to two regiments of German infantry with 25 tanks attacked elements of the rifle division on the Sáregres axis from the west and north. The struggle for this village continued until nightfall and didn't cease even then. In order to facilitate the conducting of fire at the German tanks, Soviet aircraft every 20-30 minutes dropped illuminating flares, while the infantry and artillery set fire to previously prepared piles of flammable materials and structures. However, the dense fog that developed that night strongly reduced the effect of the attempts to illuminate the area, and hindered the artillery fire. In the end, the Germans managed to fight their way into Sáregres, after which the units of the 202nd Rifle Division at the order from command withdrew to the Cece area, having first blown up the bridge across the Sárviz Canal.

On 14-15 March, units of the 1st SS Panzer Division *Leibstandarte Adolf Hitler* made a last attempt to expand the division's bridgehead on the southern bank of the Kapos Canal at Simontornya. They managed to make some progress, but this was the only achievement by the I SS Panzer Corps. By the evening of 15 March, the German offensive on the front of the 26th Army was halted.

15

Combat Operations in the Sector of the 57th Army

The offensive of Army Group South's Second Panzer Army against the forces of the 3rd Ukrainian Front's 57th Army began on 6 March 1945 at 6.00 after a 45-minute artillery preparation. The German units attacked north and south of Nagybajom with three divisions of the LXVIII Army Corps on one side, and one division of the XXII *Gebirgs* Corps on the other. It should be said that in distinction from the other sectors of the 3rd Ukrainian Front, in the sector of the 57th Army a preemptive artillery barrage was conducted in 3-kilometer-wide sector with 145 Soviet guns and mortars. Due to it, German units even before the start of the attack suffered losses, and the offensive jumped off 15 minutes late.

Initially, the attack in the sector of the 73rd Guards Rifle Division met with success: units of the 118th *Jäger* Division, supported by 20 assault guns, managed by 9.30 to drive one of the regiments of the 73rd Guards Rifle back 1.5 kilometers, and seized the first and second line of trenches. However, 30 minutes later, following a softening-up artillery barrage, a Soviet counterattack threw the enemy back.

The German command directed the main attack to strike south of Nagybajom following a powerful artillery preparation, which began at 6.45. Here, the 57th Army command was unable to conduct a preemptive barrage, because the bulk of the army's artillery was already firing on the enemy north of Nagybajom.

At 7.30, German units in strength of up to five infantry regiments supported by 30 tanks and assault guns struck the boundary between two defending regiments of the 299th Rifle Division on the Jákó axis. Advancing along communication trenches into the depth of the defenses, German infantry infiltrated into the rear and attacked the artillery's firing positions. For example, the 1st Battery of the 299th Rifle Division's 843rd Artillery Regiment was simultaneously attacked from the front, the flank and the rear, and after several hours of fighting in encirclement, it was virtually wiped out in hand to hand combat. Several German self-propelled guns even succeeded in breaking through to the Nagybajom – Kaposvár road, but here they ran into fire from one of the Soviet anti-tank regions and were destroyed.

At 10.00 the enemy succeeded in taking Kutas, and then Jákó as well. By the middle of the day, the real threat of a German breakthrough of the main belt of defenses on the boundary between the 73rd Guards Rifle and 299th Rifle Divisions emerged. Soviet aerial reconnaissance reported the movement of major enemy motorized columns toward the breakthrough sector from the area of Beleg.

With the authorization of the 57th Army command, the commander of the 64th Rifle Corps threw his second echelon into the fighting – the 113th Rifle Division. It moved up under the covering fire of the 1201st and 864th Self-propelled Artillery Regiments. The counterattack was preceded by a strike delivered by Soviet bombers and a 15-minute barrage delivered by more than 250 guns and mortars, which targeted aggregations of enemy personnel and equipment. With the coordinated attacks of infantry, artillery and aviation, the Germans were stopped, and then even forced to yield some of the ground they had gained. After a succession of attacks and counterattacks, after the day of combat on 6 March the enemy only managed to make a 2- to 4-kilometer advance.

By evening, the German attacks ceased, which allowed the 57th Army command to reshuffle its forces in order to strengthen the defense. Several artillery and mortar battalions were hastily moved up to the breakthrough sector. In the conditions of the poorly developed road network in the area and the spring thaw, the artillery formations were only able to move at an average speed of 25-30 kilometers per hour during the daytime, and 15-20 kilometers per hour at night.

The 3rd Ukrainian Front command, which was attentively following the course of the combat here, decided to transfer the 184th Destroyer Anti-tank Artillery Regiment and the 12th Destroyer Anti-tank Artillery Brigade to the control of the 57th Army. In their ensuing move to the new sector, the 184th Regiment in the muddy conditions of the spring thaw traveled 85 kilometers in six hours, while the 12th Brigade covered 190 kilometers in ten hours.

Simultaneously with the redeployment of the artillery units, measures were undertaken to mine the area. For this purpose, soon after the German offensive against the 57th Army began on 6 March, mobile blocking detachments of the 64th Rifle Corps and the 57th Army moved out to the Balázska area and got to work. Over the first few days of the offensive, these detachments emplaced more than 6,600 anti-tank mines and 1,300 anti-personnel mines. By the morning of 7 March, the entire sector of the enemy's penetration was saturated with minefields, and the density of mines in the depth of the main belt of defenses in the sector of the 113th Rifle Division reached 1,000 anti-tank mines per kilometer of front.

On the following days, the Germans didn't cease their attempts to breach the defenses of the 64th Rifle Corps, and on 7 March they introduced the 16th SS Panzer Grenadier Division *Reichsführer-SS* into the fighting. Units of the 57th Army put up stubborn resistance – the 113th Rifle Division alone on 7 March repulsed 15 German attacks. The fighting continued both day and night. Both the nighttime and daytime German attacks were faltering under concentrated artillery fire.

At 15.00 8 March, the Germans hurled all of the available serviceable tanks and self-propelled guns of the Second Panzer Army into the fighting, trying to break through in the direction of Balázska. However, the attack was repulsed with heavy casualties for the enemy. In this battle, the 4th Battery of the 113th Rifle Division's 872nd Artillery Regiment (the battery's commander was Lieutenant Selishchev), which was positioned northeast of Jákó, fought heroically. The artillerymen together with the infantry repelled an attack by two German battalions and 10 tanks and self-propelled guns, knocking out several armored vehicles in the process. Guns of the 872nd Artillery Regiment that were concealed in ambush positions were also effective.

Here is one example: At the foot of a nameless height, on a road that was the most likely path of advance of the German tanks, dummy minefields and dummy firing positions had been created. Only a narrow sector running alongside a swampy stream, fringed with sparse bushes, was left to the German tanks in order to bypass the dummy strongpoint. Two guns had been deployed in ambush behind a bush on the opposite bank of the stream. If the enemy tanks had managed to get around them, they would have wound up opposite an anti-tank region positioned on the height's reverse slopes. Atop the hill, one gun had been positioned, which gave credence to the dummy positions, in order to induce the German tanks to go around them.

After artillery preparation, up to a battalion of German infantry, with the support of several armored vehicles, moved off into the attack. Four self-propelled guns and two tanks were taking the lead. Indirect Soviet artillery fire managed to separate the German infantry from the armor. The enemy armor, approaching the dummy positions as they fired on the height, turned to the right and moved to bypass the false node of resistance. There they were met by the guns concealed in ambush, which with flanking fire from a range of 250-400 meters knocked out three self-propelled guns and one tank with 18 shots. Only the two armor vehicles bringing up the rear managed to escape.

In the sector of the 20th Guards Rifle Division, guns concealed in ambush were used in conjunction with decoy guns. The latter would open fire and force the German tanks to alter their direction of advance, which would place them under the flanking fire of the concealed guns.

For example, on 10 March in the area of Szenna, 10 enemy tanks were advancing along a road. Guards Sergeant Iakushev's decoy 76mm ZIS-3 anti-tank gun opened fire at them from a range of 500 meters. It caught the Germans' attention, and the German tanks moved to attack it, thereby exposing their flanks to a gun concealed in ambush, which from a range of 200 meters knocked out one tank. While the armored vehicles were pivoting to escape the ambush, the gun crew managed to torch another enemy tank, and the remainder fled.

Having met frustration in their attack against the center of the 64th Rifle Corps' defensive belt, on the night of 9-10 March, the enemy shifted the 16th SS Panzer Grenadier Division and the 1st *Volks-Gebirg* Division from the Jákó area to the Ötvöskónyi – Beleg area, opposite the boundary between the 64th Rifle Corps and the Bulgarian First Army. On the afternoon of 10 March, after a 40-minute artillery preparation and accompanying air strikes, with the forces of up to five infantry regiments and the support of 50 tanks and self-propelled guns, the Germans launched an attack that targeted the boundary between the 64th Rifle Corps' 299th Rifle Division and the Bulgarian 10th Infantry Division.

At this moment, the 299th Rifle Division was defending a sector that extended for 15 kilometers, which lacked an adequate depth of defense and reinforcing artillery. Taking advantage of this, already with the first rush the Germans seized the first line of trenches, and by 17.00 they had reached the northern outskirts of Kisbajom, having made a 3.5-kilometer advance.

The Soviet command hastily shifted the 184th Destroyer Anti-tank Regiment to this area in order to liquidate the enemy's penetration. But since prior to this, the regiment had already been involved in fighting and was occupying a position that was under enemy observation and fire, the regiment commander called for the placement of a smokescreen to facilitate the removal of the guns from their positions and to minimize losses. Under the smokescreen's cover, he pulled his unit out of its positions, and then made a 20-kilometer march, all in no more than an hour. At 16.00 it moved into a position on the northern outskirts of Szabás, where at 17.15 it joined battle with attacking enemy infantry and tanks. In the course of three hours, fighting without any infantry protection, the regiment knocked out two assault guns and two halftracks, and gave an initial check to the German attack. This pause allowed the Soviet command to bring up additional reserves to the Kisbajom – Szabás sector and to bring a halt to the German advance.

On 10 – 12 March, German units launched several attacks in the direction of Szabás and Nagykorpád, but they achieved no significant success, and by the evening of 12 March, they began to dig in on the line they had reached.

The command of the German Second Panzer Army, having regrouped its forces between 11 and 13 March, at 11.10 on 14 March launched an attack in the sector of the 6th Guards Rifle Corps, aiming toward Nikla and Osztopán. Units of the 61st Guards Rifle and 10th Guards Airborne Divisions that were defending here were engaged in bitter fighting with German units for the entire day, having deployed all of the divisional and regimental artillery to fire over open sights. In the course of 15 and 16 March, the 57th Army command shifted the 20th Guards Rifle Division to this sector, where together with the 32nd Guards Mechanized Brigade and the artillery units they brought the German offensive to a halt in the Tótszentpál area.

Having encountered stubborn resistance, the units of the Second Panzer Army on 17 March again altered the axis of their attacks, this time striking to the south out of the Szenyér – Marcali area. The enemy managed to batter its way forward for 1.5 kilometers, after which the attack in this sector ground to a halt. With this failure, the German attempts to break through the defenses of the 57th Army came to an end.

ISU-152 self-propelled guns on the march. The ISU-152 was equipped with the powerful 152mm gun and was an irreplaceable means of struggle against enemy fortifications and stone buildings in 1945.

A German Panther Ausf.G with the number "134", given to it by the Soviet inspection team. The tank has no visible damage. Probably it was abandoned by the crew after experiencing mechanical problems.

A Panther Ausf.G tank, stuck in the mud and disabled.

A German Pz.IV Ausf.H tank, knocked out by Soviet artillery. It offers a good look at its
camouflage.

16

Fighting on the Drava River

On the southern sector of the front, near the town of Osijek, the troops of *Generaloberst* Alexander Löhr's Army Group E on 6 March 1945 launched a two-prong attack against the position of the Soviet allies and forced a crossing of the Drava River. The first attack out of the Donji Miholjac area struck units of the General Vladimir Stoychev's Bulgarian First Army, while the second attack out of the Valpovo area hit elements of the Yugoslav Third Army. The Germans managed to seize several bridgeheads across the Drava River, and later expanded them each to an area 8 kilometers wide and 5 kilometers deep.

The Bulgarian 3rd and 11th Infantry Divisions had fallen apart in panic, and their commanders and the command of the 4th Army Corps, to which they were subordinate, made no effort to rally them. Only the intercession by the headquarters of the 3rd Ukrainian Front was able to restore the situation. In Directive No. 00/0P from the Front headquarters, Tolbukhin ordered: "Take measures to prepare the troops for night operations, having with the harshest measures prevented manifestations of panic in all of the [Bulgarian] army's units. Promptly begin investigating instances of panic in the 3rd and 11th Infantry Divisions and turn over the guilty senior commanders to a tribunal."

Not taking any more chances with the allies, the Soviet command on 7 March transferred units of the 133rd Rifle Corps and artillery to the areas of the German bridgeheads on the Drava River, and also committed aircraft. For the sake of justice, it should be said that units of the Yugoslav Third Army – the 16th and 51st Infantry Divisions – put up bitter resistance to the Germans, and with counterattacks managed to throw the enemy back across the river. The Yugoslav divisions had Soviet arms and equipment (in particular artillery), but had been formed on the basis of partisan detachments and were still not part of the regular army.

In subsequent days, the Germans were unsuccessful in their efforts to expand the Drava bridgeheads that they occupied. Powerful artillery fire and strikes by ground attack aircraft of the 17th Air Army prevented the attackers from transferring a sufficient number of troops to the northern bank. All of the German efforts to advance further on this sector of the front met with failure, although isolated attempts were noted right up to and including 16 March.

Thus, during Operation *Frühlingserwachen*, the German troops were unable to reach their assigned objectives. As a result of 10 days of stubborn fighting, at the cost of enormous losses, they were able to make a 30-kilometer advance west of the Sárviz Canal, but south of Lake Velence the advance didn't exceed 12 kilometers, and it was fewer still south of Lake Balaton, in the 57th Army's sector.

A SU-100 self-propelled gun. These self-propelled guns became the Red Army's serious counter to the German "beasts" – the Tiger and Panther tanks – at Lake Balaton.

A knocked-out Panther; most likely, this tank became the victim of anti-tank fire from both flanks – the gun is pivoted to the left, and a shell hole is plainly visible in the right side of the hull.

The same machine as in the previous photograph, seen from a different angle. It is clearly visible that the tank is lacking a Zimmerit coating.

A Panther Ausf.A, left abandoned by its crew.

17

The Use of the Front's Tank Forces

The use of the 3rd Ukrainian Front's tank forces during the March battles is of interest. It had been planned beforehand to use the tanks and self-propelled guns in order to strengthen the defense on prepared lines, and with the start of the German offensive, the tank formations were moved up to these lines.

The tactics of strict defense were adopted by the tank and self-propelled guns – the armored vehicles were dug into the ground among the infantry's combat positions, or else kept concealed in ambush. In order to facilitate a more responsive command arrangement over the tank formations, they transferred from subordination to the Front to the control of the army commanders.

The tank's combat formations on the defensive depended on the situation and the assignment. For example, the 18th Tank Corps, having taken position among the combat positions of the infantry south of Seregélyes, assigned each tank brigade its own sector of defense, while the motorized rifle brigade was distributed by battalion among the tank brigades. The defense was organized around individual strongpoints, each of which had 2-5 tanks, a platoon of motorized infantry, and 2-3 guns.

The 18th Tank Corps was reinforced with the 207th Self-propelled Artillery Brigade of SU-100 tank destroyers, which took up positions by battery in the second echelon of defense. At the same time, the tank destroyers had prepared firing positions in the first echelon, to which they moved up during enemy tank attacks. All of this allowed the creation of a dense wall of anti-tank and anti-personnel fire in front of the 18th Tank Corps' positions, and in the course of 10 days of savage fighting, the enemy was in fact unable to break through the defense in this sector.

Thus, on 7 and 8 March alone, units of the 18th Tank Corps knocked out or destroyed 33 German tanks and self-propelled guns. In return, their own losses amounted to a total of 16 tanks or assault guns, including 2 T-34, 2 ISU-122 and 3 SU-76 knocked out, and 6 T-34 and 3 ISU-122 burned out.

Part of the 1st Guards Mechanized Corps occupied positions in the Heinrich Estate, Sárkeresztúr, Cece, Sárbogárd area. Here the defense was organized around company-sized strongpoints, each of which contained 5 to 8 tanks or self-propelled guns. The strongpoints had standard trenches, machine-gun nests, dug-in combat vehicles, and anti-tank gun positions. The anti-tank guns moved up into their positions only in order to conduct fire, but spent the rest of their time in shelters. The SU-100 tank destroyer batteries were positioned in the second echelon, and with sudden counterattacks they would destroy the enemy's tanks and halftracks.

Tank ambushes were widely and successfully employed. For these, groups of tanks and self-propelled guns would take concealment on the flanks of the anticipated axis of advance of enemy tanks, calculating to take shots at their side or rear facing. Artillery guns were usually positioned in order to protect the tanks that were waiting in ambush. Combat experience demonstrated that when organizing tank ambushes, it was useful to use decoy tanks, which by their actions were supposed to lure the enemy armor into the flanking fire of the tanks concealed in ambush.

The 18th Tank Regiment of the 1st Guards Mechanized Corps, which was defending in the Sárkeresztúr area, adopted a rather curious tactic. When the regiment's positions were attacked by up to a battalion of infantry, in order not to reveal the locations of the tank ambushes, the regiment commander Lieutenant Colonel Lysenko decided to counterattack the enemy with T-34 recovery tanks and armored halftracks. In this fashion, the tankers repelled two attacks by German infantry and took 35 Germans prisoner.

The SU-100 self-propelled artillery guns showed themselves to be quite effective in the March battles. In addition to the SU-100s of the 208th Self-propelled Artillery Brigade and of the two regiments in the 1st Guards Mechanized Corps, with which the 3rd Ukrainian Front started the battle, on 9 March the 207th (62 SU-100, 2 T-34, 3 SU-57) and 209th (56 SU-100, 2 T-34, 3 SU-57) Self-propelled Artillery Brigades arrived to join the Front. Upon their arrival, the 207th Brigade was sent to the 27th Army, and the 209th Brigade went to the 26th Army. Thus, by 10 March 1945, the total number of SU-100 tank destroyers in the area of Lake Balaton (after deducting the combat losses) amounted to 188.

These self-propelled guns were actively used on the defense in cooperation with the infantry in order to repel enemy tank attacks, as well as to cover the bridges across the Sárviz and Sió Canals. They proved quite effective in these tasks. For example, the 208th Self-propelled Artillery Brigade over the course of 8 March and 9 March knocked out 14 German tanks and self-propelled guns, as well as 33 enemy halftracks, while losing 8 SU-100 destroyed and 4 disabled.

In order to combat enemy tanks, the SU-100s primarily operated out of ambush positions. SU-100 batteries were deployed in covered positions, camouflaged in woods, or on the reverse slopes of hills and ridges. In front of them, at a distance of 100-200 meters, firing positions with good visibility and good fields of fire were prepared, and as a rule, they offered 360° of fire. In the positions or next to them, observation posts were set up, in which there would be an officer who had a communications link with the battery. Whenever German tanks appeared at a distance of 1,000 to 1,500 meters, the tank destroyers would move up into their firing positions, fire several rounds, and then use reverse drive to pull back into cover. Such a tactic justified itself when repelling enemy attacks in the areas of Sáregres and Simontornya. For example, on 11 March, a battery of the 209th Self-propelled Artillery Brigade's 1953rd Self-propelled Artillery Regiment, having taken up an ambush position in a dense patch of woods west of Simontornya's train station, repelled an attack of 14 German tanks, three of which were set on fire at a range of 1,500 meters.

The normal range for firing from the SU-100 at heavy German tanks was 1,000 to 1,300 meters, but out to 1,500 meters, and sometimes even longer, when firing at medium tanks and self-propelled guns. The SU-100s as a rule fired from fixed positions, but sometimes from short halts. From the indicated ranges, the SU-100 could inflict damage to all types of German armor, and as a rule, with the very first on-target shell.

Cooperation between the self-propelled guns and other units was implemented in the following fashion. The commander of the self-propelled regiment and the rifle regiment commander as a rule were located in the same observation post or had telephone contact with each other. The commanders of the rifle battalion and of a self-propelled gun battery would personally work out all questions of cooperation on the spot, and in case of need, also had telephone communications. The commander of the SU-100 brigade maintained constant radio contact with the commander of the rifle division to which his brigade was attached. This allowed the transmission of information regularly in the course of fighting and the reaching of necessary decisions.

Nevertheless, during the battle, a number of genuine miscalculations in the organization of cooperation with the SU-100s were revealed. For example, fire cover provided by the field artillery for the self-propelled guns was poorly organized, the infantry didn't render assistance to the crews when attempting to pass through swampy areas of terrain, and several of the all-arms commanders tried to use the SU-100 in the role of infantry support tanks. For example, the commander of the

36th Guards Rifle Division ordered a battery of tank destroyers to lead an infantry attack. Because of the absence of infantry and artillery cover, the SU-100s came under the fire of German anti-tank guns, as a result of which three of the tank destroyers were left burning.

A substantial shortcoming of the SU-100, which was revealed in the course of fighting, was its absence of a machine gun. Because of this, the vehicle had no close range defense against infantry and proved defenseless against assaulting German infantry. As a temporary measure, it was proposed to give each crew a light machine gun, and to give 8-10 light machine guns to the company of submachine gunners in the SU-100 self-propelled artillery regiments.

In the first days of the German offensive, even training units were used to reinforce the Front's tank units. For example, on 8 March, the 22nd Tank Regiment, which was formed from a training regiment with the same numerical designation, arrived in the 26th Army. In a report it was noted that "in view of the fact that the tanks were from the table of equipment of a training tank battalion and were located on a training ground and in a tank park, and as well of the fact that it was 115 kilometers to its assigned place of assembly, the regiment was 11 hours late in arriving." Altogether, the 22nd Tank Regiment had 11 T-34, 3 SU-76, 1 SU-85 and 1 KV-1s. This unit conducted combat operations right up to 16 March.

As concerns the replenishment of materiel, over the period between 6 and 16 March, the 3rd Ukrainian Front received only one batch of replacement tanks and self-propelled guns – on 10 March, 75 SU-76, 20 Sherman tanks and 20 T-34 arrived from the rear. The self-propelled guns were used to replenish the 1896th, 1891st and 1202 Self-propelled Regiments, the 18th Tank Corps, and the self-propelled gun battalions of the 4th Guards Army, while the Shermans went to the 1st Guards Mechanized Corps and the T-34s went to the 23rd Tank Corps. In addition, a certain number of tanks were put back into service by the Front's 3rd Mobile Tank Repair Shop. For example, on 6 March the 18th Tank Corps received 20 repaired T-34s from it.

A bogged-down and abandoned Panther Ausf.G. Judging from the attached tow cable, the Germans had unsuccessfully attempted to free the tank from the mud.

An ISU-152 on the move. In the background, Hungary's characteristic hilly terrain is visible.

A Flakpanzer IV Wirbelwind self-propelled anti-aircraft vehicle, destroyed by the direct hit of a large caliber shell. The gaping hole in the side of the hull is clearly visible.

Soviet officers examining a Pz.IV tank, abandoned on a street of a Hungarian town. Note the tank's Schürzen armored skirting, designed to protect the tank against anti-tank rifle rounds and hollow-charge shells.

18

Conclusions

The final German offensive of the Second World War was planned on a grand scale. However, even at this time – spring 1945 was already around the corner – many German calculations were based on an underestimation of the enemy's possibilities.

In a tactical respect, the German panzer divisions proved to be much weaker than they had been in preceding operations, for example, in the January 1945 *Konrad* operations. Soviet documents on this subject stated:

> If in the preceding operation the enemy had employed broad maneuvers with his mechanized troops, then in the given operation, the maneuvering from one sector to another was insignificant. The enemy fought on one axis using only separate groups of tanks shifted from one sector to another within the boundaries of the formation's operations.

The defensive battles at Lake Balaton in March 1945 are interesting by the fact that the main burden of the struggle with enemy tanks lay upon the artillery. Soviet tank units played a secondary role in the fighting.

Tactically, the Soviet anti-tank, divisional and self-propelled artillery stood out in the most favorable light. The techniques for conducting fire from close range at the most vulnerable locations on the German tanks and self-propelled guns – the flank and rear – were firmly confirmed. In the process, the most combat capable German panzer army at that time – the Sixth SS Panzer Army – suffered heavy losses:

> In the period of the offensive, the German command undertook the commitment of tank groups consisting of 40 to 80 armored vehicles each simultaneously on several directions, with the aim of dispersing and breaking up our means of anti-tank defense. With such actions, the adversary obtained no success, and such a tactic led him to lose 80% of his tanks and self-propelled guns, which were destroyed by our anti-tank artillery, tanks, self-propelled guns and aircraft.

As concerns the losses in equipment, according to data of the 3rd Ukrainian Front, over the 10 days of fighting, 324 German tanks and self-propelled guns, as well as 120 armored halftracks, were left burned out on the battlefield; another 332 tanks and self-propelled guns, and 97 halftracks were knocked out (See Table 9).

According to German data, however, as of 13 March the irrecoverable losses of the Sixth SS Panzer Army amounted to 42 tanks and 1 halftrack (!). True, another 396 tanks and self-propelled guns and 228 halftracks were in the repair shop for short-term or long-term repairs. If you consider, though, that according to German documents a short-term repair could last for a month (and sometimes even longer), while no deadline at all was given for the completion of long-term repairs, then it will be clear that the German count of its armor losses is quite far from the truth. In addition, it should be considered that long-term repair was related to those vehicles that had to be evacuated from the battlefield. In addition, the German armor vehicles could switch from one

Table 9 German Armor Losses as Reported by the 3rd Ukrainian Front's Armies over 6-15 March 1945

	Burned-out tanks and Self-propelled Guns	Burned-out Half Tracks	Knocked-out Tanks and Self-propelled Guns	Knocked-out Half Tracks
4th Guards Army:				
6 March	–	–	5	–
7 March	–	–	2	–
Total:	–	–	7	–
26th Army:				
6 March	27	4	23	4
7 March	12	–	22	12
8 March	22	6	23	9
9 March	37	21	14	10
10 March	26	32	22	5
11 March	19	–	7	1
12 March	12	6	–	–
13 March	16	–	22	2
14 March	12	5	3	–
15 March	3	1	–	–
Total:	186	75	136	43
27th Army				
7-8 March	–	–	3	–
9 March	–	–	3	–
10 March	28	–	24	6
11 March	8	16	19	8
12 March	26	12	44	16
13 March	23	8	21	12
14 March	13	5	13	4
15 March	6	–	11	8
Total:	104	41	162	54
57th Army				
6 March	5	–	–	–
7 March	16	1	–	–
8 March	–	3	14	–
9 March	3	–	3	–
10 March	2	–	2	–
11 March	4	–	5	–
14 March	2	–	1	–
15 March	2	–	2	–
Total:	34	4	27	–
Grand Total:	324	120	332	97

category to another: initially short-term repair, then long-term, and then it might be written off as an irrecoverable loss. There you have it.

In sum, if we take the number of burned-out armor vehicles claimed by the 3rd Ukrainian Front, we won't be far from the truth. The photos of the knocked-out or abandoned German armor in the Lake Balaton region, which were taken in the second half of March 1945 and are reproduced in this book, serve as confirmation for this. The author possesses photographs of 279 German tanks and self-propelled guns, which were marked with numbers by the Soviet trophy team, of which there are 70 Panthers, 40 Pz IV, 28 King Tigers, 3 Tiger I, 44 tank destroyers (Pz IV/70 and Hetzers), 22 assault guns, 17 Hungarian tanks and self-propelled guns, and a number of other vehicles. At the same time, the highest identification number that is visible in the photographs of the knocked out armor is 355. Considering that the photos depict 279 armor vehicles and just one halftrack, it can be assumed that the missing numbers all relate to German halftracks. Thus, one can confidently state that the irrecoverable German losses of tanks and self-propelled guns in the course of Operation *Frühlingserwachen* amount to no less than 250. As concerns Soviet losses, then over the 10 days of fighting they amounted to 165 tanks and self-propelled guns, of which T-34s comprised the largest number (84), followed by SU-100s (48).

On 16 March 1945, the units of the 3rd Ukrainian Front went on the offensive according to plans for the Vienna operation. The Sixth SS Panzer Army, after the heavy losses it had suffered in Operation *Frühlingserwachen*, was unable to offer serious resistance, and it was driven out of Hungary and into Austria literally within two weeks. Its remnants later surrendered in part to the Soviets, in part to the Americans, near Vienna in May 1945.

This bogged down StuG 40 assault gun is fitted with a Saukopf gun mantlet and has a Zimmerit coating.

A Marder III self-propelled gun, destroyed by Soviet artillery fire.

In a literal sense, the German spring offensive became mired in mud: A Pz.IV Ausf.J tank, bogged down in a cornfield. Two more Pz.IV tanks are visible in the distance.

Notes

Introduction

1. Raigorodetsky, E.Ia., *K Al'pam* [*To the Alps*] (Moscow: Voenizdat, 1969), p. 123.

Chapter 1

1. Maier, Georg, *Drama between Budapest and Vienna: The Final Battles of the 6 Panzer-Armee in the East* (J.J. Fedorowicz Publishing, Inc., 2004), p. 15.

Chapter 2

1. TsAMO RF, f.320, op.4522, d.279, l.14

Chapter 3

1. Russianov, I.N., *Rozhdennaia v boiakh* [*Born in battle*] (Moscow: Voenizdat, 1982), p. 194.
2. Ibid.

Chapter 4

1. As cited by Malakhov, M.M., *Osvobozhdenie Vengrii i vostochnoi Avstrii (oktiabr' 1944 g. – aprel' 1945 g.)* [*Liberation of Hungary and eastern Austria (October 1944 – April 1945)*] (Moscow: Voenizdat, 1965), p. 123.
2. TsAMO RF, f.500, op.12462, d.243, l.31.
3. TsAMO RF, f.500, op.12462, d.243, l.45.
4. Raigorodetsky, E.Ia., *K Al'pam* [*To the Alps*] (Moscow: Voenizdat, 1969), p. 116.
5. TsAMO RF, f.17BA, op.6518, d.437, l.222.

Chapter 5

1. TsAMO RF, f.243, op.2900, d.2011, l.311.
2. TsAMO RF, f.243, op.2900, d.2011, l.313.

Chapter 6

1. TsAMO RF, f.500, op.12462, d.243, l.114.
2. TsAMO RF, f.240, op.2795, d.308, l.162.
3. TsAMO RF, f.240, op.2799, d.366, l.111.

Chapter 7

1. TsAMO RF, f.320, op.4522, d.279, l.175.
2. TsAMO RF, f.500, op.12462, d.243, l.255.
3. TsAMO RF, f.500, op.12462, d.243, l.35.
4. TsAMO RF, f.243, op.2928, d.147, l.11.

Literature and Sources

The Central Archive of the Russian Federation's Ministry of Defense. The following files were consulted: the Operational Branch of the Commander of the 3rd Ukrainian Front; Headquarters of the Armored and Mechanized Forces of the 3rd Ukrainian Front; Headquarters of the 3rd Ukrainian Front's Artillery Commander; Headquarters of the 4th Guards Army; Headquarters of the 26th Army; the Headquarters of the 27th Army; Headquarters of the 57th Army; Headquarters of the 18th Tank Corps; Headquarters of the 23rd Tank Corps; Headquarters of the 1st Guards Mechanized Corps.

Sandner, Leberecht, *Die Schlacht am Platensee. Erlebnisberichte zur Geschichte des Zweiten Weltkrieges. Der Landser* Band 1562 Orange.

Gosztonyi, Peter, *Der Kampf um Budapest 1944-45*. Studia Hungarica, 1964.

Jester, Werner, *Im Todessturm von Budapest 1945*. Rumerberg, Eigenverlag W. Jester, 1985.

Maier, Georg, *Drama between Budapest and Vienna: The Final Battles of the 6 panzer-Armee in the east, 1945*. J.J. Fedorowicz Publishing, Inc., 2004.

The photographs in the book come from the files of the Russian State Archive of Film and Photo Documents, the Central Museum of the Armed Forces, the archive of the Publishing House "Strategiia KM", as well as from the personal collection of I. Pereiaslavtsev.

Index

INDEX OF PEOPLE

Afonin, Major General Ivan Mikhailovich, 77, 88

Akhmanov, Major General A.O., 62-64, 66, 72-73, 92

Balck, *General der Panzertruppe* Hermann, 18-20, 40, 56, 60-61, 71, 93, 102

Breith, *General der Panzertruppe* Hermann, 35, 55, 58, 60

Filippovsky, Major General, 32

Gagen, Lieutenant General N.A., v, 65, 67, 121

Gille, *SS-Obergruppenführer* Herbert-Otto, iii–iv, 13, 16, 19–20, 22, 30, 33, 40–41, 43–45, 49–51, 55–58, 60, 62, 64, 66, 71, 91, 93

Gnedin, Major General P.V., 43

Gorshkov, Major General S.I., 30, 51, 58

von Grolman, Lieutenant General Helmuth, 102

Guderian, General Inspector of Panzer Troops Heinz, 19, 40–41, 101, 145

Himmler, Heinrich, 16, 41

Hitler, Adolf, 15–16, 24–25, 41, 101–103, 106, 143, 158

Jodl, Colonel General Alfred, 101

Kublanov, Lieutenant Colonel, 54

Lysenko, Lieutenant Colonel, 168

Maier, Georg, 58, 102

Malinovsky, Marshal R.Ia., v, 77–78, 88

Malyshev, Colonel M.F., 33

Managarov, Lieutenant General I.M. , 88

Nikitin, Major General S.I., 43, 45

Pfeffer-Wildenbruch, *SS-Obergruppenführer* Karl, 87, 89-90

Polubinsky, Guards Lieutenant Colonel, 142

Rotmistrov, Marshal P.A., 64

von Rundstedt, Field Marshal Gerd 20, 101

Russianov, General I.N., iv, 24, 26, 36, 40, 176

Schönfelder, *Obersturmbannführer*, 19

Sharokhin, Lieutenant General M., 124

Shlemin, Lieutenant General I.T., 24

Shpek, Colonel, 153

Skvirsky, Lieutenant General L.S., 65

Stoychev, General Vladimir, 125, 164

Sveshnikov, Colonel, 32

Tolbukhin, Marshal F.I., iv–v, 26, 30-32, 35-36, 40, 48, 50-51, 54, 57, 62, 63, 66, 78, 88, 91-92, 154, 164

Wenck, *General der Panzertruppe* Walther, 19, 40-41

Wöhler, *General der Infanterie* Otto, 19-20, 40-41, 58, 60, 145

Zakharov, Guards Lieutenant Colonel, 93

Zakharov, General G.F., iv, 23, 26, 30-32, 43, 51, 55, 61-62, 91, 93

Zakhvataev, Lieutenant General N., 121

Zatylkin, Colonel F.A., 65

Zheltov, Colonel General A.S., 64

INDEX OF PLACES

Aba, 51, 130, 144, 146, 152, 155–156
Adony, 65, 102, 130, 155–156
Agg. Szentpéter, 57
Agostyán, 24, 30–31
Aranyos, 152
Ardennes, the, 101, 106
Austria, 15, 174, 176

Bajna, 31, 33, 92
Balaton, Lake, vii–viii, 15, 23, 35, 43–44, 50, 54,
    62, 71, 73, 101–102, 108, 113, 117, 120–121,
    124, 128, 130, 135, 137–138, 146–148,
    150–152, 154, 164–165, 168, 172, 174
Balázska, 160
Baracska, 56, 58–59, 64, 66
Beleg, 159, 161
Bicske, 20, 30–33, 35, 58, 60
Borbály, 35
Börgönd, 72
Buda, 24, 60, 74–75, 77, 88–90
Budapest, iii–vi, 13, 15–16, 19–21, 23–25, 31–35,
    37, 40–43, 49–51, 56, 58–62, 65–66, 68, 71,
    73–77, 79–82, 84–91, 93–94, 96–98, 102, 116,
    121, 128, 176–177

Cece, 130, 143–144, 153–154, 157–158, 167
Croatia, 116
Csala, 40
Csillag, 155
Czechoslovakia, 88
Czertovaya Canal, 90

Danube River, 15–16, 20–24, 30–33, 35, 40–41,
    43–44, 50–51, 54, 56–57, 59–66, 71–74, 77,
    87–89, 102, 116–117, 120, 125, 145, 154, 156
Dinnyési, 121
Donji Miholjac, 142, 164
Dorog, 41
Drava River, iii, 50, 102, 113, 116–117, 125, 142,
    164
Dunaalmási, 24
Dunaföldvár, 102, 145
Dunapentele, 50, 65
Đurđevac, 116

East Prussia, 16, 25, 42
Enying, 144
Ercsi, 88–89
Esztergom, 25, 40, 116

Gran River, 25, 40, 116
Graz, 116
Györ, 43
Gyula, 40

Heinrich Estate 54, 156, 167
Herczegfalva, 54–55, 65
Hill 159.0, 146, 155
Hill 225, 35–36

Jákó, 159–161
Káloz, 144–146
Kapos, 21, 153, 157–158
Kapos Canal, 153, 157–158
Kis Velence, 130, 155–156
Kisbajom, 161
Komárno, 20, 42–43
Koprivnica, 116
Kursk, 22–23, 62, 64–65, 120
Kutas, 159

Lepsény, 48, 144
Lovasberény, 125
Málom, 21
Mány, 32–33
Margarethe Line, 15–16
Mezökomárom, 158
Mór, 20, 23, 30, 66

Nagybajom, 124, 159
Nagykaniža, 116–117
Nagykorpád, 161
Nikla, 161

Oder River, 101
Osijek, 116–117, 142, 164
Osztopán, 161
Ozora, 154, 158

Pátka, 40
Pázmánd, 59, 63
Pécs, 102
Pest, 74–77, 87–89
Pettend, 59, 63–64
Pilis Mountains, 40–41, 90
Poland, 16, 19, 25, 42
Prokhorovka, 62, 64, 92
Pusztaszabolc, 155

Rákos Canal, 74
Rákosszentmihály train station, 76

Sándor, 155–156
Sárbogárd, 167
Sáregres, 153–154, 157–158, 168
Sárkeresztúr, 42, 49, 130, 144–145, 152, 156,
   167–168
Sárosd, 54, 62, 125, 145–146, 155–156
Sárviz Canal, 21, 44, 48–50, 62, 102, 124–125,
   130, 143–146, 153–154, 157–158, 164
Seregélyes, 54, 63, 71–73, 93, 121, 124, 130,
   142–143, 145, 152, 154, 167
Silesia, 15, 116
Simontornya, 153–154, 157–158, 168
Sió Canal, 43, 48, 64, 158
Stuhlweissenburg, 56
Szabás, 161
Számbék, 33
Szár, 153
Székesfehérvár, 15–16, 21, 23, 32, 35, 43–44, 48,
   51, 55–58, 62, 64, 66, 70–73, 116–117, 121,
   130, 143, 153
Szekszárd, 102
Szenna, 161

Szomor, 41, 90

Tarján, 30–32
Tata, 20, 42
Tótszentpál, 161
Transdanubian Mountains, 20
Tükres, 156

Úrhida, 48

Vál, 59–60, 62–64
Vali River, 21, 57–58, 60, 64
Valpovo, 142, 164
Velence, Lake, 16, 41, 51, 54–60, 62–66, 71–73,
   91, 102, 113, 117, 120-121, 125, 130, 142-143,
   145–146, 152, 154, 164
Vereb, 59, 63–64
Vértes Hills, 20–21, 23–24, 35, 40, 64
Vienna, 50, 102, 116, 119, 174, 176–177
Virovitica, 116
Vistula River, 16, 61

Zámoly, 35–36, 40, 42, 55, 60, 62, 102, 121
Zaporozh'e, 24
Zsámbék, 33

INDEX OF GERMAN MILITARY UNITS

Army Groups (Heeresgruppen):
Army Group B, 106
Army Group Center, 19
Army Group E, 102–103, 113, 164
Army Group South, 19, 40, 58, 61, 89, 101, 113,
   117, 142, 145, 159

Army Groupings (Armeegruppe):
Armeegruppe Balck, iv, 18, 43, 50–51, 56, 58, 70,
   88, 91, 102–103, 106, 108, 113, 142–143, 145,
   152, 155–156

Armies:
Second Panzer Army, 50, 102–103, 108, 113, 142,
   159–161
Fifth Army, 101
Sixth SS Panzer Army, vii, xi, 19-20, 51, 56, 58,
   60, 62, 64, 93, 101–103, 105–106, 113, 115–117,
   126, 142–144, 172, 174 and *passim.*
Seventh Army, 101
Eighth Army, 19

Corps:
Korpsgruppe Breith, 35

I Cavalry Corps, 35, 106, 143, 153
I SS Panzer Corps, 106, 143–146, 152–153, 157–158
II SS Panzer Corps, 101, 106, 117, 144–145, 152,
   155–156
III Panzer Corps, 35, 58, 60, 65, 102, 117
IV SS Panzer Corps, iv, xi, 16, 19, 22, 24, 30–31,
   33, 35, 40–43, 48–51, 54, 56–61, 63–66,
   70–71, 73, 77, 88, 92–93, 117
IX SS *Gebirgs* Corps, 90–91
XXII *Gebirgs* Corps, 159
XXIV Panzer Corps, 16
LXVIII Army Corps, 159
LXXXX Army Corps, 106
LXXXXI Army Corps, 103, 142
403rd Volks Artillery Corps, 44, 58

Divisions:
1st Panzer Division, 43–44, 48, 55–56, 58, 65,
   71, 142
2nd SS Panzer Division *Das Reich,* vii, 102, 106,
   116, 123, 146
3rd Cavalry Division, 106, 143–144, 146
3rd Panzer Division, 43, 48, 50–51, 54-55, 65, 71,
   106, 154

3rd SS Panzer Division *Totenkopf,* iv, 22, 30-31, 33, 38, 42-45, 54, 57-58, 63–64, 70-71, 93, 102, 108

4th Cavalry Division, 106, 143–144, 146

5th SS Panzer Division *Wiking,* 16, 22, 30-33, 40–44, 51, 54, 57, 64, 66, 71–72

6th Panzer Division, 23, 29, 32-33, 40, 113, 156

7th *Gebirgs* Division, 117

8th Panzer Division, 23

8th SS Cavalry Division *Florian Geyer,* 74, 90

9th SS Panzer Division *Hohenstaufen,* 106, 116, 152

12th SS Panzer Division *Hitlerjügend,* 106, 116-117, 143

13th Panzer Division, v–vi, 74–75, 78, 87, 90

16th SS Panzer Grenadier Division *Reichsführer-SS,* 103, 117, 160

22nd SS Cavalry Division *Maria Theresia,* 74-75, 90

23rd Panzer Division, 23, 35, 43, 55, 65-66, 106, 112, 117, 153

24th Panzer Division, 43

71st Infantry Division, 103

96th Infantry Division, 22, 30

117th Infantry Division, 117

118th *Jäger* Division, 103, 159

181st Infantry Division, 117

264th Infantry Division, 117

271st Volksgrenadier Division, 23, 74

297th Infantry Division, 117

356th Infantry Division, 66, 70, 106, 117, 142

711th Infantry Division, 16, 22, 40, 117

Brigades:

4th Cavalry Brigade, 35

17th Volks Mortar Brigade, 44

261st Assault Gun Brigade, 108

303rd Assault Gun Brigade, 43, 57, 64, 108, 113

Regiments:

SS Regiment *Ney,* 55

2nd Panzer Grenadier Regiment, 157

6th SS Panzer Grenadier Regiment *Eicke,* 70

9th SS Panzer Grenadier Regiment *Germania,* 40

10th SS Panzer Grenadier Regiment *Westland,* 40–41

24th Panzer Regiment, 43, 55, 93, 114

871st Grenadier Regiment, 70

Battalions:

208th Panzer Battalion, 23

219th Assault Gun Battalion, 108, 113

501st SS Heavy Panzer Battalion, 108

509th Heavy Panzer Battalion, iv–v, vii–viii, 29, 43, 45, 48, 52, 57, 63, 71–73, 108, 110–111, 135, 149

560th Heavy *Panzerjäger* Battalion, 108

Miscellaneous / Other:

Gruppe Holst, 64, 66, 70

Kampfgruppe von Pape, 22, 30–33

Gruppe Phillip, 40–41

Luftflotte 4, 25

Luftlotte 6, 25

INDEX OF SOVIET MILITARY UNITS

Fronts:

2nd Ukrainian Front, v, 15, 23, 25, 50, 58, 61–62, 71, 75–78, 88, 91, 116–117, 138

3rd Ukrainian Front, iii–v, xi, 15, 23–26, 30–32, 35–36, 42, 44, 50–51, 56, 58, 61–62, 64–66, 77–78, 88, 91–93, 102, 116–117, 119–120, 125, 128, 130–132, 136–139, 144, 146, 153–156, 159–160, 164, 167–169, 172–174, 177

Armies:

4th Guards Army, iv, 23–24, 26, 30–33, 35, 42–45, 49–51, 54, 56, 59–63, 65–66, 72–73, 91, 120–121, 125, 129–132, 137, 139, 142–143, 145, 154, 169, 173, 177

5th Air Army, 25, 77

5th Guards Tank Army, 64

6th Tank Army, 136

7th Guards Army, 77, 91

9th Guards Army, 154

17th Air Army, 25, 41, 44–45, 49, 92–93, 131, 164

26th Army, v, 64–67, 72, 120-121, 124–126, 129–132, 137, 139, 142–146, 152–154, 157–158, 168–169, 173, 177

27th Army, 121, 125, 129, 131, 137, 139, 145, 154–157, 168, 173, 177

46th Army, 24–25, 31–32, 40–41, 56, 75, 88, 90

53rd Army, 88

57th Army, iii, 50, 64, 73, 120, 124–125, 129, 131–132, 137–139, 142, 159–161, 164, 173, 177

Corps:

1st Guards Mechanized Corps, iv, 24, 26–27, 32–33, 36, 40, 51, 55–56, 59, 66, 70–72, 93, 125, 137-138, 145, 154, 156, 167–169, 177

2nd Guards Mechanized Corps, 25, 31, 33, 41, 90

5th Guards Cavalry Corps, iv, 26, 30–31, 51, 56–59, 66, 90–92, 125, 137, 139, 153–154

5th Guards Tank Corps, 75, 88–89

6th Guards Rifle Corps, 124, 129, 161

7th Mechanized Corps, 23, 32, 35–36, 48, 55, 59

10th Ground Attack Aviation Corps, 59

18th Guards Rifle Corps, 75-77, 87, 91

18th Tank Corps, iv, 24, 30–33, 46, 48–51, 54, 60, 62, 64–65, 91–92, 125, 136, 139, 145, 154, 157, 167, 169, 177

20th Guards Rifle Corps, 23, 35–36, 66, 121, 129

21st Guards Rifle Corps, 23, 36, 55–56, 66, 121, 143

23rd Tank Corps, 61–66, 71–73, 75, 88–89, 91, 125, 136, 139, 154, 156, 169, 177

29th Tank Corps, 64

30th Rifle Corps, 50, 64–65, 75–77, 87–88, 121, 124–125, 128, 143, 145, 154, 156

31st Guards Rifle Corps, 23, 30, 121, 154

33rd Rifle Corps, 125, 145, 154

35th Guards Rifle Corps, 125, 145, 153–154, 156–157

37th Guards Rifle Corps, 88-89, 125

64th Rifle Corps, 124, 129, 159-161

68th Rifle Corps, 23

75th Guards Rifle Corps, 88, 137

104th Rifle Corps, 61-63, 65-66, 72, 121, 124

133rd Rifle Corps, 44, 50–51, 54, 64–65, 124, 164

135th Rifle Corps, 23, 36, 43, 45, 48–50, 55, 64-65, 75-77, 87-88, 121, 124-126, 128, 143–146, 152–154, 156

Divisions:

1st Guards Rifle Division, 24

3rd Guards Airborne Division, 61, 65, 125, 145, 154, 157

4th Anti-aircraft Division, 153

4th Guards Rifle Division, 24, 30

5th Guards Airborne Division, 35, 129

9th Artillery Breakthrough Division, 63

9th Cavalry Division, 75

11th Cavalry Division, 57–58

11th Guards Cavalry Division, 153, 157–158

12th Guards Cavalry Division, 32, 125, 153, 157–158

19th Breakthrough Artillery Division, 129

20th Guards Rifle Division,   23, 35–36, 42, 66, 117, 121, 129, 161

21st Rifle Division, 44, 54, 121, 145

34th Guards Rifle Division, 24

36th Guards Rifle Division, 72, 75, 121, 124, 126–129, 142-143, 145, 152, 155-156, 169

40th Rifle Division, 30, 33

41st Guards Rifle Division, 23, 30, 32-33

49th Guards Rifle Division, 25, 33

62nd Rifle Division, 30

63rd Cavalry Division, 57–59, 125, 153, 157–158

66th Rifle Division, 61, 72

68th Guards Rifle Division, 126, 128, 143–146, 155–156

69th Guards Rifle Division, 55

73rd Guards Rifle Division, 124, 159

74th Rifle Division, 128, 144, 146, 158

78th Rifle Division, 125

80th Guards Rifle Division, 24, 30, 33

84th Rifle Division, 125

86th Guards Rifle Division, 25, 31–32, 41

93rd Rifle Division, 30, 32, 48

99th Rifle Division, 41

100th Rifle Division, 24

104th Rifle Division, 4, 54, 121, 124, 158

108th Rifle Division, 88, 125

109th Rifle Division, 88

113th Rifle Division, 57, 88, 124, 159–160

122nd Rifle Division, 44, 54, 137

136th Ground Attack Aviation Division, 59

151st Rifle Division, 61, 63, 72, 75, 144

155th Guards Rifle Division, 129, 143

155th Rifle Division, 72, 75, 121, 124, 127-129, 142–143, 145, 152, 155

163rd Rifle Division, 125, 156

180th Rifle Division, 88, 90

202nd Rifle Division, 125, 144, 157–158

206th Rifle Division, 125, 144, 157-158

233rd Rifle Division, 64, 121, 127-128, 144, 146, 152-153

236th Rifle Division, 64, 128, 153

252nd Rifle Division, 43, 48–49, 57, 59

297th Rifle Division, 75, 90

299th Rifle Division, 124, 159, 161

316th Rifle Division, 88, 125

317th Rifle Division, 75

320th Rifle Division, 88, 125

337th Rifle Division, 88, 125, 144, 157-158

366th Guards Rifle Division, 138–139

Brigades:

1st Guards Mechanized Brigade, 36, 40, 51, 56

2nd Guards Mechanized Brigade, 56

3rd Tank Brigade, 63, 72-73, 75-77, 87

9th Guards Tank Brigade, 36, 40, 55, 72, 137

12th Assault Engineer-Sapper Brigade, 88

12th Destroyer Anti-tank Brigade, 128

14th Assault Engineer-Sapper Brigade, 75, 88

16th Mechanized Brigade, 32–33

17th Cannon Artillery Brigade, 75

18th Howitzer Artillery Brigade, 75

24th Destroyer Anti-tank Artillery Brigade, 152

25th Cannon Artillery Brigade, 126

27th Mortar Brigade, 75

32nd Guards Mechanized Brigade, 161

32nd Motorized Rifle Brigade, 54

37th Guards Mechanized Brigade, 41

39th Tank Brigade, 63, 72, 75, 77, 87

45th Guards Mortar Regiment, 157

49th Destroyer Anti-tank Brigade, 48

49th Guards Cannon Artillery Brigade, 75

56th Mechanized Brigade, 136

56th Motorized Rifle Brigade, 72

63rd Mechanized Brigade, 43

83rd Naval Infantry Brigade, 88, 90

95th Howitzer Artillery Brigade, 75

105th Large-caliber Howitzer Brigade, 128–129

110th Tank Brigade, 31, 33, 54, 136, 145, 155

118th Tank Brigade, 138

123rd Cannon Artillery Brigade, 35

135th Tank Brigade, 63, 72, 136

152nd Cannon Artillery Brigade, 75

170th Light Artillery Brigade, 156

170th Tank Brigade, 24, 30–31, 33, 54, 136, 145

181st Tank Brigade, 31, 33, 54, 136, 145, 155

207th Self-propelled Artillery Brigade, 138, 154, 156, 167-168

208th Self-propelled Artillery Brigade, 153-154, 168

209th Self-propelled Artillery Brigade, 138, 153–154, 168

209th Tank Brigade, 138

Regiments:

18th Tank Regiment, 168

22nd Tank Regiment, 169

48th Guards Mortar Regiment, 75

54th Tank Regiment, 137, 139

60th Tank Regiment, 137, 139

65th Artillery Regiment, 126

71st Tank Regiment, 137, 139

78th Guards Heavy Tank Regiment, 32

115th Destroyer Anti-tank Artillery Regiment, 75

117th Destroyer Anti-tank Artillery Regiment, 153

127th Cannon Artillery Regiment, 32

184th Destroyer Anti-tank Artillery Regiment, 160

188th Cannon Artillery Regiment, 35

198th Guards Rifle Regiment, 144

200th Mortar Regiment, 36

200th Rifle Regiment, 155

202nd Guards Rifle Regiment, 144

205th Mortar Regiment, 32

212th Howitzer Artillery Regiment, 36

221st Howitzer Artillery Regiment, 36

222nd Cannon Artillery Regiment, 32

230th Howitzer Artillery Regiment, 36

262nd Destroyer Anti-tank Regiment, 36

268th Guards Anti-aircraft Regiment, 153

286th Rifle Regiment, 128

320th Howitzer Artillery Regiment, 155

338th Destroyer Anti-tank Artillery Regiment, 143

363rd Guards Heavy Self-propelled Artillery Regiment, 136, 155

363rd Self-propelled Artillery Regiment, 31, 33

382nd Guards Heavy Self-propelled Artillery Regiment, 33, 65, 136, 146

382nd Medium Self-propelled Gun Regiment, 138

382nd Self-propelled Artillery Regiment, 137

407th Light Artillery Regiment, 143, 153, 158

436th Rifle Regiment, 128, 142

438th Destroyer Anti-tank Regiment, 36, 48

462nd Mortar Regiment, 88

581st Rifle Regiment, 72

659th Rifle Regiment, 128

786th Rifle Regiment, 143

843rd Artillery Regiment, 159

864th Self-propelled Artillery Regiment, 137, 139, 159, 169

872nd Artillery Regiment, 160

877th Howitzer Artillery Regiment, 59

928th Rifle Regiment, 48

932nd Rifle Regiment, 48

974th Anti-aircraft Artillery Regiment, 146

1008th Destroyer Anti-tank Artillery Regiment, 153

1068th Self-propelled Artillery Regiment, 153

1089th Anti-aircraft Artillery Regiment, 153

1201st Medium Self-propelled Gun Regiment, 138

1201st Self-propelled Artillery Regiment, 159

1202nd Self-propelled Artillery Regiment, 45, 65, 137, 139, 169

1232nd Cannon Artillery Regiment, 36

1245th Destroyer Anti-tank Artillery Regiment, 153

1249th Destroyer Anti-tank Regiment, 48

1289th Self-propelled Artillery Regiment, 32

1438th Guards Heavy Self-propelled Artillery
    Regiment, 65, 136, 146
1443rd Self-propelled Artillery Regiment, 72, 136
1453rd Guards Self-propelled Artillery Regiment,
    65, 136, 146
1670th Destroyer Anti-tank Artillery
    Regiment, 143
1821st Guards Self-propelled Artillery Regiment,
    65, 136-137, 146
1821st Medium Self-propelled Gun Regiment,
    138
1891st Self-propelled Artillery Regiment, 136-137,
    139, 169
1896th Self-propelled Regiment, 137, 139, 169
1953rd Self-propelled Artillery Regiment, 153, 157,
    168
1963rd Destroyer Anti-tank Artillery
    Regiment, 142–143

1964th Destroyer Anti-tank Artillery
    Regiment, 155
1965th Destroyer Anti-tank Artillery
    Regiment, 144–146
1966th Destroyer Anti-tank Artillery
    Regiment, 144, 146

Battalions:
39th Destroyer Anti-tank Artillery Battalion, 126
227th Separate Anti-aircraft Artillery
    Battalion, 153, 157
251st Destroyer Anti-tank Artillery Battalion, 35
320th Separate Destroyer Anti-tank Artillery
    Battalion, 143
Other:
Stavka, 24, 44, 88, 92, 116, 129, 154
1st Guards Fortified District, 43, 45, 48, 121, 125,
    130, 142–143, 145, 152, 154

INDEX OF BULGARIAN / HUNGARIAN / ROMANIAN / YUGOSLAV UNITS:

Bulgarian:
1st Army, xi, 50, 73, 120, 124–125, 131, 142, 161,
    164
4th Army Corps, 164
3rd Infantry Division, 164
10th Infantry Division, 161
11th Infantry Division, 164
16th Infantry Division, 125

Hungarian:
3rd Army, 55
VIII Corps, 58
1st Hussar Division, 74
2nd Armored Division, 117
8th Infantry Division, 42

10th Infantry Division, 74-75
12th Infantry Division, 74-75
12th Reserve Division, 74
20th Infantry Division, 42, 117
23rd Infantry Division, 42, 117
25th Infantry Division, 42, 117

Romanian:
7th Army Corps, 75, 77
19th Infantry Division, 75

Yugoslav:
Third Army, 120, 125, 164
12th Army Corps, 50, 120
51st Infantry Division, 164

INDEX OF MISCELLANEOUS TERMS

Course of Action A, 102
Course of Action C2, 102–103

Operation *Eisbrecher*, 50
Operation *Frühlingserwachen*, iii, 20, 102–103,
    106–108, 113, 116, 118, 142, 145, 164, 174
Operation *Konrad* I, iii, 22, 34–35, 43, 92–93
Operation *Konrad* II, iii, 35, 40–41, 43, 55, 59, 92

Operation *Konrad* III, iii, 42–43, 62, 66, 71, 88,
    92
Operation *Kräutergarten*, 43
Operation *Paula*, iii, 16, 19–20, 35, 42, 44
Operation *Wacht am Rhein*, 106

Vienna operation, 174
Vistula-Oder operation, 16, 42